To Bill Tafoya:

Friend, Mentor
& Role Model!

with Love,

Charles

Terrorism Within Comparative International Context

M.R. Haberfeld · Joseph F. King ·
Charles Andrew Lieberman

Terrorism Within Comparative International Context

The Counter-Terrorism Response and Preparedness

 Springer

M.R. Haberfeld
City University of New York
John Jay College of Criminal Justice
899 Tenth Ave.
New York NY 10019
USA
mhaberfeld@jjay.cuny.edu

Joseph F. King
City University of New York
John Jay College of Criminal Justice
899 Tenth Ave.
New York NY 10019
USA
jking@jjay.cuny.edu

Charles A. Lieberman
City University of New York
John Jay College of Criminal Justice
899 Tenth Ave.
New York NY 10019
USA
clieberman@jjay.cuny.edu

ISBN 978-0-387-88860-6   e-ISBN 978-0-387-88861-3
DOI 10.1007/978-0-387-88861-3
Springer New York Dordrecht Heidelberg London

Library of Congress Control Number: 2009932596

Printed on acid-free paper

Springer is part of Springer Science+Business Media (www.springer.com)

To my daughters, Nellie and Mia – you are the spirits behind my drive.

– Maria (Maki) Haberfeld

To my lovely wife Joyce – for her support and help.

– Joseph King

To my wife Lina and son Gabriel – for giving me the strength to achieve.

– Charles Lieberman

Acknowledgments

No matter how much work and endeavor goes into the completion of a book, it is always this final stage that brings the real sight of relief to the authors; one that is definitely a defining moment for those who would have not been able to implement the ideas that were conceptualized years ago, if not for the assistance and help of the following colleagues and associates.

We would like to start with thanking one of the original three researchers, Dr. Heath Grant, who, for personal reasons, needed to withdraw from this project. As always, Heath had a critical input into the thinking process and the ideas presented in this book, and we missed his input and contributions during the trips we took to complete this project that was first conceptualized almost 6 years ago.

To the National Institute of Justice and its International Center Directors, Jay Albanese and Cindy Smith and their staff, who in various stages of the research project monitored our progress and provided guidance, our gratitude is extended.

Once again, the acknowledgment needs to be made that all this would not have been possible without the amazing vision of Senior Editor Welmoed Spahr and her extraordinary Editorial Assistant Theresa Culver and the entire editorial and production team at Springer. Finally, we are thankful to all the external reviewers of our work. We are forever grateful for affording us the opportunity to see our research findings in a format that will allow us to spread them around the world.

The concluding words of the acknowledgment go to the ones who provided us with the funding resources for our frameworks of thinking and enabled us to translate our thoughts into tangible lessons that we learned and hope others will learn as well, so thank you Congressman Jerrold Nadler, New York's 8th Congressional District, and his staff.

Contents

About the Authors

M.R. Haberfeld is a professor of police science in the Department of Law, Police Science and Criminal Justice Administration at John Jay College of Criminal Justice in New York City. She was born in Poland and immigrated to Israel as a teenager. Prior to coming to John Jay, she served in Israeli Defense Forces, in a counter-terrorist unit and left the army at the rank of a sergeant; she then joined the Israel National Police, and left the force at the rank of Lieutenant. She also worked for the U.S. Drug Enforcement Administration, in the New York Field Office, as a special consultant. She holds two Bachelor of Art degrees, two master degrees, and a Ph.D. in criminal justice. Her main interests and expertise are in the area of police training and professional development, with particular emphasis on police ethics, integrity, leadership, counterterrorism and use of force in multicultural environments. Her recent publications include a book on police training titled *Critical Issues in Police Training* (2002), a co-edited book titled *Contours of Police Integrity* (2004) *Encyclopedia of Law Enforcement, the International Volume* (2005) *Police Leadership* (2005), a co-authored book titled *Enhancing Police Integrity* (Springer, 2006), co-edited book on *Comparative Policing: The Struggle for Democratization* (2007), co-edited book, *A New Understanding of Terrorism: Case Studies, Trajectories and Lessons Learned*, and a co-edited book, *Modern Piracy and Maritime Terrorism: The challenge of Piracy for the 21st Century*. She also recently co-authored two articles on counterterrorist response: "Proper Proactive Training to Terrorist Presence and Operations in Friendly Urban Environments" and "Police Activities to Counter Terrorism: What We Know and What We Need to Know" (forthcoming). For the past 8 years (2001–2009), she has been involved in developing, coordinating, and teaching in a special training program for the New York City Police Department, where she teaches courses in police ethics, leadership, and counterterrorism. For 3 years (2005–2008), she was also an academic coordinator of the Law Enforcement Executive Police Institute for the State of New York, where she oversaw the delivery of the training modules and taught leadership courses. She is involved in a major research study on Use of Force by the Police in 10 different countries, and a research project on police leadership training which also focuses on comparative studies of a number of countries around the world.

Joseph F. King received his Ph.D. from CUNY. His doctoral dissertation was on the police strikes of 1918–1919 in the United Kingdom and Boston, Massachusetts, and their lasting effects. He served for 33 years as the supervisory special agent in charge of the Terrorist and Middle East Division, US Customs in New York and 2 years as Chief, National Security Section, Department of Homeland Security, also in New York. He has extensive criminal investigative, undercover, and court testimonial experience in the European Union and the Middle East. He joined the faculty of John Jay College in September 2003. The works published by Dr. King include "Terrorism: Global Answer to Global Threat," in *Regulation of Migration Processes in the Russian Federation; Political, Legal and Law-Enforcement Aspects*; "Corruption Networks as a Sphere of Investment Activities in Modern Russia" in *Communist and Post-communist Studies*; and *The Development of Modern Police History in the United Kingdom and the United States*.

Charles Andrew Lieberman is an Assistant Professor in the Department of Criminal Justice at the University of New Haven and in the Department of Law, Police Science and Criminal Justice Administration at John Jay College of Criminal Justice. Prior to earning a Ph.D. in Criminal Justice at the CUNY Graduate Center, Charles retired as a detective from the New York City Police Department (NYPD) after 15 years of service. His main areas of interest and expertise are policing and terrorism, with a focus on community policing as a framework for proactive counterterrorism strategies. Charles has taught a variety of graduate and undergraduate courses, including a counterterrorism course in a special training program for the NYPD. In addition, he has instructed police supervisors through the Law Enforcement Executive Institute and the NYS Division of Criminal Justice Services. Charles has written numerous chapters for books on terrorism.

Chapter 1
Introduction

The introductory chapter of this book presents the concepts of the benefits inherent in the study of comparative approach for an effective counterterrorism response on the local law enforcement level and overviews the inception of the project.

Throughout the twentieth century and into the twenty-first century, especially after the events of September 11, 2001, the legitimacy of law enforcement practices has been cited as a major concern for international criminal justice. As policing practitioners and scholars throughout the world shifted focus from a traditional reactive, crime control stance to the need for accountability mechanisms to ensure the support of citizenry in combating crime and terrorism, the democratization of policing was seen as the best mechanism for achieving long-term gains in public order at the same time as protecting human rights.

While the need to maintain human rights remains an important issue, balancing these concerns with the important public safety interests of societies is paramount. In a climate of global change, in which traditional boundaries and the presence of a clearly defined enemy are no longer realities, law enforcement has also tried to evolve internationally. As policing moves away from its traditional responsibilities related to the control of local disorder, it will become increasingly less effective in meeting its objectives. Although local law enforcement has changed its practices, in response to viewing itself as the front lines and first responders in the "war on terror," the dangers of further building a military ethos for policing challenge the very legitimacy that makes it effective. Many law enforcement agencies struggle to find effective ways to mobilize diverse communities and generate their support and elicit information to assist the agency in international crime control and counterterrorism. In a quest to provide for some baseline understanding of the underlying queries, the researchers proposed to travel to a number of countries and conduct a series of interviews and focus groups to find answers to the following questions.

1.1 Research Questions

- What policies and practices have proven to be effective in combating terrorism in countries that have had many years of experience coping with the issue?

M.R. Haberfeld et al., *Terrorism Within Comparative International Context*,
DOI 10.1007/978-0-387-88861-3_1, © Springer Science+Business Media, LLC 2009

- What have been the positive and negative consequences of different strategies and approaches?
- Under what political and/or social contexts have specific strategies proven to be effective?
- How do training practices vary internationally related to counterterrorism, human rights, community mobilization, and other related areas?
- To what extent do law enforcement agencies mobilize the community and other sectors of society in crime control efforts generally, and homeland security specifically?

1.2 Research Methods

This study began in 2004 as a Fulbright-funded project between two John Jay College professors (Haberfeld and Grant) and the Institute for Security Sciences of the Turkish National Police. Recognizing the importance of this project, the researchers partnered with an additional John Jay College professor, Dr. Joseph King, who sought additional research funding to expand the partnering countries to include the United Kingdom, Ireland, Lebanon, and Spain, as well as one additional visit to Turkey. A four-part research model was proposed for the data collection in each participating country:

1. Prior to beginning on-site data collection, an extensive review is conducted on historical, cultural, and demographic information, including an in-depth review of the country's experience with terrorism and other public security issues. This analysis is used to tailor semi-structured interview guides that are used in all countries to the local contexts.
2. The researchers conduct stakeholder interviews with key members of the police force to document responses, challenges, as well as training approaches. Relevant official documents are requested for later review throughout the course of interviews.
3. Focus groups and interviews are held with the media, local politicians, businesses, and other community representatives to examine perceptions of the counterterrorism responses and their impact on legitimacy.
4. Training modules for law enforcement agencies are proposed based on the best practices documented in the researched countries covering all key findings. (This last part was later revised, as per the National Institute of Justice request, and replaced with a detailed, essay format, final report.)[1]

The proposed study sought to begin a formal process of information sharing between the United States and five countries that have battled issues of terrorism for

---

[1] NJ GRANT #: 49980-00 01

many years: Turkey, Ireland, United Kingdom, Spain, and Lebanon. As the study commenced, one of the primary investigators, Dr. Heath Grant, left John Jay College and some of the initial contacts and approvals secured by the researchers did not come through, and the increasingly volatile political situation in Lebanon became problematic for academic research. Dr. Haberfeld and King secured the approval of the National Institute of Justice to replace Lebanon, one of the original research sites, with two additional countries: the Netherlands and Sweden. The two countries were chosen due to their recent history of struggling with an emerging terrorist threat as well as the access to the relevant stakeholders within the community and the local law enforcement. However, due to numerous administrative hurdles, which included personnel change at the supervisory level at the National Institute of Justice, the research funds were frozen in 2006 and the researchers were denied the opportunity to complete their study in the Netherlands and Sweden. Dr. Lieberman and Mr. Konze joined the project at its later stage and contributed, respectively, the chapters on the United States and Germany.

Due to previously mentioned impediments, the book suffers from some data deficiency as the researchers were prevented from going back to the Netherlands and Sweden to conduct interviews and focus groups with the representatives of the local communities. Also, the German chapter presents only a partial picture of the interaction between the police and the public due to the nature of the local law enforcement and the way terrorism-related issues are policed in contemporary German. As such, this book represents a partial picture of what the researchers aimed to portray. Since the comparative approach to studying counterterrorist response is predicated in this study on the original concepts of Community-Oriented Policing (COP), the theoretical base for this study is presented in the overview of the concepts of COP and how the researchers found some of the basic tenets of this philosophy directly applicable to their research. Through the paradigms introduced over two decades ago to American policing, and subsequently to other democratic police forces around the world, the researchers present a customized approach to counter the phenomenon of terrorism in urban environment through mobilizing both the community and the local law enforcement around a concept of criminal activity that is more than just detrimental to the overall well-being of the society but rather poses an existential problem in its subversive nature.

The main focus of Chapter 2 is to introduce the reader to the tenets of Community-Oriented Policing philosophy that provided the theoretical framework for this study.

The section on COP modalities provides the reader with an overview of the contours and developments of various implementations and the research conducted on the feasibility of its implementation is interspersed with some comments from the authors of this study, as the researchers found certain approaches and explanations valid and relevant to their paradigms and utilized them in trying to elicit the answers from some of the focus groups and individual interviews. As this overview is supplemented with the most recent research published in this area, the original literature review provided the researchers with some templates for discussions and formulating the questions, which were sometimes provocative in nature, based on the findings of other researchers who probed and analyzed the intricacy of the complicated relations between the police and the public.

Despite various customized approaches around the world, 12 points of the Community-Oriented Policing and Problem Solving (COPPS) philosophy, illustrated in the Haberfeld (2002) book on police training, appear to resonate with many police forces around the world, and the researchers' approach to the data collection was primarily focused on the feasibility of implementation of the aforementioned points. The focus groups and individual interviews were very much informed by the researchers' curiosity with regard to how these points can be used to mobilize the desired response to the terrorism problem within a given community. The researchers aimed to find out if indeed the concepts of joint ownership of the problem, the responsibility, the accountability, the familiarity with resources, etc., would and could translate into the consciousness of the research subjects, both on the community and on the local law enforcement end. One of the goals of this study was to add yet another dimension to the list of critiques and recommendations about the successful implementation of the various modalities of the COPPS philosophy, which is also known as the Community-Oriented Policing (COP) philosophy.

Since the idea of COP was first introduced, it has been viewed as a positive development, in which politicians, citizens, police officials, and the media promote its function and use. However, many researchers and academics often question the effectiveness and ability of this policing strategy. Criticisms such as the disparity that exists on the meaning of community policing due to the lack of a universal definition, as well as the difficulty in testing the effectiveness and impact community policing has on communities, are frequently referenced. COP, by its very nature, must vary in its application in order to effectively respond to the needs and conditions specific to the individual community; therefore operationalization of community policing and empirical analyses of the effectiveness of its implementation across communities are problematic.

Although the effectiveness of applying COP to counterterrorism has not been empirically tested, there are two factors that may provide answers to its potential as a tool for local law enforcement. First, the way in which COP is defined may range among agencies, as well as the researcher or academic gathering the information and conducting the evaluations. It is important that the definition of COP is clearly operationalized in order to test whether its application is effective. Second, the expected results also require operationalization in order to consider the utilization COP as effective. If a decrease in terrorism indicates COP as an effective method for the prevention and regulation of terrorism, the extent of the decrease expected to occur should be determined. If effectiveness is viewed as obtaining information or intelligence that results in the apprehension of terrorists and the prevention of terrorist attacks from occurring, then the frequency of such occurrences should be defined.

Chapter 3 presents an overview of the research methodology of this study, concentrating on two primary modes of data collection and description: qualitative and quantitative. While the researchers chose to focus on the qualitative method the medium chosen for this data collection, focus groups and individual interviews are overviewed while emphasizing their strength and weaknesses. This chapter, which is essentially a literature review on the methodological hurdles, is interspersed with comments from the authors, pertaining to their field experiences in the various countries they visited.

Chapters 4, 5, 6, 7, 8, 9, and 10 overview the specific countries in which the field research took place, with emphasis on the research methodology used, from the generic pros and cons to the more specific examples based on the team's experiences, followed by the overview of the history of the visited country, its terrorism-related problems, the law enforcement response, and the impressions of the research team.

The researchers found a common theme as a result of the interviews and focus groups conducted among the various countries. In the United Kingdom, Northern Ireland, Ireland, Spain, and Turkey, the primary focus was on the domestic separatist or nationalist groups, primarily the IRA in the United Kingdom and Ireland, ETA in Spain, and the PKK in Turkey, with a limited focus on the "homegrown" extremist or fundamentalist groups. In the United States, the possibility of the existence of both the "homegrown" and the foreign groups was discussed. In all the countries examined, including the Netherlands, Germany, and Sweden, the growing Muslim populations, many of whom reside in communities that resist assimilation and acculturation, provide fertile grounds for fundamentalist ideologies. In recent years, most of the countries in which the researchers conducted studies have had rapid growth in the Muslim populations, excluding Turkey, which is predominantly Muslim to begin with, yet none of these countries' local law enforcement has provided sufficient resources or policies to engage these populations. Recent incidents in these countries, such as the transit bombings in Madrid in 2004 and London in 2005, the 2004 murder of Theo Van Gogh in Amsterdam, the November 2003 suicide bombings in Istanbul, and the 2008 arrests of three men suspected of financing and planning acts of terrorism in Stockholm, provide evidence that this threat must be addressed.

In democratic nations, the balance between security and civil rights is challenged by the phenomenon of terrorism, in that the government is required to respond, but an excessive response may lead to increased support among the passive supporters of groups and organizations that engage in extreme violence against civilian populations. The police agencies, both local and national, are required to respond, maintaining legitimacy by following governmental policies and the rule of law. There is always the fear that law enforcement will take it upon themselves to "fight fire with fire" violating the laws they seek to uphold, which will ultimately delegitimize the agency and provide the terrorists with fertile ground for recruitment and fundraising. It is only through an appropriate legitimate response by law enforcement that the agency will prevent the passive supporters, which tend to be significantly greater than the active supporters, from becoming active in the terrorist organization (see Chapter 7; re: the Turkish Police and the "velvet glove" approach).

The final two chapters of the book, Chapter 11, titled Best Practices – Lessons We Learned, and Chapter 12, titled Best Practices – Lessons to Be Learned, summarize the impressions and observations derived from the field research and identify a number of key issues that need to be addressed by law enforcement agencies in their attempts to respond to the phenomenon of homegrown and foreign terrorism. The chapters discuss the dire need to create the Intel File and customize the investigative techniques to the population under the investigation, as well as introduce a training module and the Power Points that were created based on the written materials, focus groups, and interviews in the countries where the research was conducted. There are additional Power Points and written materials that were presented to the researchers by the local law enforcement organizations in the United Kingdom and Holland; however, due to the confidentiality of the information included, they are not attached to this report but can be made available for the local law enforcement use and adaptation.

The primary goal of this research project was to create effective training modules to enable local law enforcement agencies, in the cross-comparative environment, to address terrorism-related incidents, to not just react but prevent and de-escalate resentment from community or support from community toward "homegrown" terrorist organizations and individuals. In the focus groups and interviews, the researchers attempted to operationalize "homegrown" terrorism as incidents and events that were, are, or will be perpetrated by various organizations, be it structured and well-known groups, or individuals associated with larger organization, or anybody who operates within the borders of a country, who resides there for a significant enough period of time to forge personal and professional relationships with the local populations.

The idea behind this operationalization was not to limit the concept of "homegrown" to people born in the country or naturalized citizens, but to include people who make a given country their home based on employment and social ties; even if they are peripheral to community, they would still identify themselves as stakeholder in a place where they have their primary residence, employment, place of operation, etc. In today's multicultural environment, "homegrown" cannot be defined by place of birth or even a citizenship in a given country. Even though terrorists and suspected terrorists may be foreign citizens, their prolonged presence in a given country (such as in the case of Theo van Gogh murder in Holland) would fall under the category of "homegrown" terrorism, as presented by the research team to the subjects of the interviews and focus groups.

The notion of "homegrown" terrorism is as problematic as the concept of Community-Oriented Policing (COP). It encompasses a multitude of factors and translates directly to the complexity of identification, minimization, and elimination by local law enforcement agencies, which, by default, are skewed toward orientation that is focused on legal, long-term residents, rather than transients or illegal aliens, about whom the local law enforcement has much less available intelligence to begin with and, furthermore, has much less possibility to interact with, under the COP model.

Historically and traditionally local law enforcement agencies tend to stay away and avoid intense interactions with minority groups for reasons that are partially political, operational, and xenophobic. The scarce interactions that existed in the past were more of a token like, symbolic in nature, bow toward the minorities than real, fully developed, interactions. This unfortunately appears to be the case nowadays as well, regardless of the country the researchers visited.

Looking at the local community of legal residents vis-à-vis local law enforcement, there is no doubt that the local legal residents are situated better to identify the potential threat that is either in its inception, or evolving, or ready to explode; they are simply in a much better logistical position than the local law enforcement. However, the biggest impediment to making use of this position is the lack of understanding on the part of the community of what is essentially evolving in front of their eyes, in terms of actually identifying the threat, in each of its various stages.

The local law enforcement, on the other hand, is much better positioned to identify the threat than any more sophisticated group within the community, and this is precisely at this junction that the researchers propose to identify some sort of bridging steps or missing links that can be filled based on the mutual cooperation between the community and local law enforcement. The local law enforcement can provide the community with the tools to be much more aware of their surroundings, which will enable the community to feed back information to the police.

How does this differ from the traditional COP approach, which emphasizes such cooperation? It differs in drastic manner, traditional COP approach focuses on traditional crimes, majority of which are recognizable and identifiable on the part of the community. Street crimes of various natures do not require explanation by local law enforcement to the community they police. Typical predatory crimes and vice crimes, like rape, robbery, assault, murder, burglary, prostitution, drug dealings, etc., are easily recognizable by most of the members of the community that is victimized by their occurrence. While community members can identify traditional crime, recognizing terrorist preparatory acts requires more education and information from the police to the community, with regard to the nature of terrorist activities, in their various developmental stages, and the specific intelligence law enforcement is looking for.

Terrorist-related preparatory and ancillary acts (see Smith, Damphousse, & Roberts, 2006) are much more subtle than the crimes we are accustomed to on a daily basis. There is, of course, the never-ending debate around the concept of terrorist versus freedom fighter, which exacerbates the problem of cooperation. In addition, the modus operandi of homegrown terrorists is much more subtle and invisible than the modus operandi of traditional criminals, the level of sophistication might not necessarily be much higher than in other traditional crimes, but the spherical behavior is different. The researchers examined patterns of behavior not well defined by local law enforcement in terms of indoctrination in the community.

By introducing some of the basic concepts from the existing literature to the law enforcement community (like Hacker's typologies of terrorists), the police can be placed in a much better position to identify the profiles of the local homegrown terrorists, and subsequently conveying these profiles for the consumption of the public or the local community. If the local police receive proper counterterrorist training (based on the outline of the modules identified by the researchers at the end of this chapter), they will have the requisite knowledge necessary to provide the information and education to the local community.

One cannot, of course, ignore the fact that by advocating for such a training that would be passed from the local police force to the public, during various community meetings, a dangerous possibility exists, one that might lead to mobilizing one neighbor against another. However, looking at the history of policing, and going back to England, prior to the Medieval times, the concept of avocational policing (occasional or obligatory, also referred to as frankpledge)[2] was the first concept of effective law enforcement for local communities that involved, among other things, community members identifying illegal or criminal behaviors of those who lived among them. Only when policing became increasingly political, which included primarily the collection of taxes for "the Crown," the move from avocational to vocational policing became the flavor of quite a few centuries continuing to the modern times.

Hence, going back to how policing originally developed or evolved, when small communities policed their own, through avocational mode and the Tything, what these researchers advocate appears to be a valid modality of policing of what emerges to be a local homegrown terrorism. The local community is therefore charged with identifying the threat, but also with proactive behavior, that can potentially reverse the original threat. An example of such target group would be found in our focus group in Spain. A local Muslim student, born and raised in Madrid and the third generation to live in Spain, complained, in an adamant manner, about feelings of alienation within the community his family has resided in for more than a century.

In a way, this community-oriented avocational type of policing of the homegrown threat is also a call to remove some of the burden placed on the shoulders of law enforcement over the past 15 centuries, to not just protect the community, but also try to minimize and eliminate the criminality within, which essentially is truly much more of a problem that needs to be tackled by the community itself and the larger government, and not primarily the local law enforcement.

Part of the perceptions and attitudes that shape or contribute to our biases is directly related to stated and written opinions expressed by our rulers, politicians, and religious leaders. Addressing individual perceptions and attitudes toward the "others" at a community level can be shaped and modified based on presentation of new information. The key to the effectiveness of this "re-education" lies in – or can be found in – the medium through which this new information is introduced. This is why the researchers paid a special attention to their interviews with the media people, be it journalists, television directors, or movie producers, as they have a tremendous impact on the way attitudes toward terrorism and terrorists are shaped. The role of the local law enforcement, albeit not an enviable one, would therefore be to try to counter the stereotypes introduced and reintroduced by the various media outlets, religious leaders, and some agenda-driven politicians. Since police organization is, by its very nature, a very political institution, this charge might be proven to be beyond difficult; however, with proper and non-threatening training, it can be achieved.

---

[2] Klockars (1985).

This research was an exploratory venture, attempting to identify the necessary components for the creation of effective law enforcement training that would be beneficial for the local police and at the same time fully accepted and supported by the community they serve. The recommendation for the creation of the useful and relevant training modules is based on the recognition that the current influence factors within the society that filer down the concepts about terrorism and terrorist are derived, beyond the governmental officials, from the religious leaders and the media to the community and should truly start with the community, and transferred through the local police forces to the government decision makers for the proper allocation of resources for the fight against the "enemy within."

References

Haberfeld, M. R. (2002). *Critical issues in police training*. Upper Saddle River, NJ: Prentice Hall.
Hacker, F. (1976). *Crusaders, Criminals, and Crazies: Terror and Terrorism in Our Time*. New York:
W. W. Norton.
Klockars, C. B. (1985). *The idea of police* (Vol. 3). Law and Criminal Justice Series. Beverly Hills, CA: Sage Publications.
Smith, B. L., Damphousse, K. R., & Roberts, P. (2006). Pre-incident indicators of terrorist incidents: The identification of geographic and temporal patterns of preparatory conduct. *US Department of Justice*. NIJ Award Number 2003-DT-CX-0003. Retrieved December 10, 2007 from http://www.ncjrs.gov/pdffiles1/nij/grants/214217.pdf.

Chapter 2
The Comparative Approach to Counterterrorism

2.1 Countering Terrorism with Community-Oriented Policing?

Community policing has become a common theme when discussing how a democratic society maintains law and order without jeopardizing the freedoms and rights of its citizens.[1] The definition of community policing varies among scholars and researchers, and an agreement of universal definition has yet to be established. Depending on the definition being utilized, confusion and difficulty may occur when attempting to determine whether or not community policing is actually being implemented within a police department.[2] However, the broad concept of community policing, which typically indicates problem solving and community involvement as key components for effective policing, seems to remain somewhat consistent among the majority of definitions.[3] Community policing may be defined as both a policing strategy and a philosophy that involves the partnership between police and the public in order to identify and solve community problems. As much controversy as the concept already created in the American literature on policing the international arena followed through with a myriad of customized interpretations based on the local needs and understanding.[4]

According to the Office of Community Oriented Policing Services (COPS), community policing employs proactive problem-solving techniques along with community partnership in order to control and reduce crime and social disorder.

> Community policing focuses on crime and social disorder through the delivery of police services that includes aspects of traditional law enforcement, as well as prevention, problem-solving, community engagement, and partnerships. The community policing model balances reactive responses to calls for service with proactive problem-solving centered on the causes of crime and disorder. Community policing requires police and citizens to join together as partners in the course of both identifying and effectively addressing these issues.[5]

---

[1] Ferreira (1996).

[2] Maguire and Mastrofski (2000).

[3] Skogan (2004).

[4] Haberfeld (1997, 2002) and Haberfeld, Walancik, and Uydess (2002).

[5] Office of Community Oriented Policing Services (COPS) (2008).

M.R. Haberfeld et al., *Terrorism Within Comparative International Context*,
DOI 10.1007/978-0-387-88861-3_2, © Springer Science+Business Media, LLC 2009

The 12 points of the Community Oriented Policing and Problem Solving (COPPS) philosophy are illustrated in the Haberfeld (2002) book on police training[6]:

1. Reassesses who is responsible for public safety and redefines the roles and relationships between the police and the community
2. Requires shared ownership, decision making, and accountability as well as sustained commitment from both the police and the community
3. Establishes new police expectations of and measurement standards for police effectiveness
4. Increases understanding and trust between police and community members
5. Supports community initiative by supplying community members with necessary information and skills, reinforcing their courage and strength, and ensuring them the influence to affect policies and share accountability for outcomes
6. Requires constant flexibility to respond to all emerging issues
7. Requires an ongoing commitment to develop long-term and proactive strategies and programs to address the underlying conditions that cause community problems
8. Requires knowledge of available community resources and how to access and mobilize them and the ability to develop new resources within the community
9. Requires buy-in of the top management of the police and other local government agencies as well as a sustained personal commitment from all levels of management and other key personnel
10. Decentralizes police services/operations/management, relaxes the traditional chain of command, and encourages innovation and creative problem solving
11. Shifts the focus of police work from responding to individual incidents to addressing problems identified by the community as well as by the police
12. Requires commitment to developing new skills through training

Despite various customized approaches around the world, these original 12 points appear to resonate with many police forces around the world, and the researchers' approach to the data collection was primarily focused on the feasibility of implementation of the aforementioned points.[7] The focus groups and individual interviews were very much informed by the researchers' curiosity with regard to how these points can be used to mobilize the desired response to the terrorism problem within a given community. The researchers aimed to find out if indeed the concepts of joint ownership of the problem, the responsibility, the accountability, the familiarity with resources, etc., would and could translate into the consciousness of our research subjects, both on the community and on the local law enforcement end.

Concepts and critiques of the professional model, as well as the findings and results from a series of police-focused experiments, compose the foundations of

---

[6] Haberfeld (2002, pp. 160–161).
[7] Haberfeld and Cerrah (2007).

community policing. The concept of community policing is often traced back to Sir Robert Peel, the chief architect of the 1829 Metropolitan Police Act[8] that provided Nine Principles of Policing[9] (see Appendix A), which included advocating for a strong relationship between the police and the public. The term community policing was not presented until more than a century and a half later. During the 1970s and early 1980s, community policing strategies were being developed and employed in an attempt to improve policing and establish a more effective and appropriate approach of policing.[10] As time progresses, new objectives and recommendations continued to occur, thus greatly contributing to the expansion and advancement of community policing and what it is today.[11] One of the goals of this study was to add yet another dimension to the list of critiques and recommendations about the successful implementation of the various modalities of this philosophy.

Kelling and Moore (1988) describe and distinguish three eras of policing, in which the third and present era is defined as the community problem-solving era. As policing evolved into the community policing/problem-solving era, a noticeable increase in the application of foot patrol began to occur throughout many law enforcement agencies. Increased foot patrol was first initiated by politicians, typically around election periods, as a campaign strategy to reduce and control crime in order to attain popularity and votes. Yet, its recognition and approval rapidly took hold among citizens, as well as police officials, and the utilization of foot patrol began to spread.

Research on the usage of foot patrol indicated that it aided in the reduction of fear, increased police satisfaction among the community, improved the relationship between police and citizens, as well as increased and enhanced police performance. One of the concepts the researchers intended to discuss with our focus groups centered on the perception of the foot patrol and its effectiveness in combating and/or preventing local terrorist activities. As the foot patrol was historically considered as the backbone of policing, our sense was that the need to retrain this particular unit would be an obvious realization, at least by the law enforcement officials, as preparedness to counter terrorist activities, on a foot patrol level, requires a new orientation and very specific training. To the team's dismay, as will be addressed later on, none of the forces visited implemented a special training for patrol officers to make them more effective in the fight against terrorist activities in urban environments.

Another concept that had derived during the progression into this present era of policing was the importance of information when it came to police managing issues pertaining to crime efficiently. Citizen cooperation, such as through providing information or intelligence, was thought to have significant impact on local law

---

[8] JSTOR: *1829 Metropolitan Police Act*. http://www.jstor.org/
[9] Reith (1948).
[10] Skogan (2004).
[11] Oliver (2000).

enforcement's ability to address crime and disorder. This communication between the police and citizens also allocated different problems and concerns of the community that police were unaware of beforehand. A shift toward a more proactive form of policing rather than the usual reactive technique also developed during the community policing era. Proactive policing encourages police discretion and decision making in order for police to manage and solve different problems that they as well as the community encounter.[12] The specific aspect of proactive approach based on intelligence and information provided by the community was yet another crucial aspect of the philosophy that the researchers decided to probe with regard to the terrorist phenomena. Would the local communities be more prone toward information sharing with the police when the "crime" is not on the list of the traditional ones like murder, rape, drug dealings, and theft but of a different nature and may be causality – like the act of terrorism?

Goldstein (1990) discussed the importance of analyzing problems police respond in order to develop operative tactics that could later be utilized in future similar situations.[13] The Problem-Oriented Policing (POP) approach encouraged police officers to search for patterns and commonality among the crimes they encounter, especially in cases where the crimes are habitual and frequent at a particular location or residency. The POP philosophy posits that understanding crimes and detecting solutions for their common causes will lead to a reduction in their occurrence. Goldstein (1990) further expanded upon these concepts to form the modern POP paradigm.[14]

Typically in police work, the different incidents that a police officer responds to or encounters during a given shift are viewed and handled as isolated occurrences, independent of one another. Most police officers mainly seek to solve the immediate problem, but once that is accomplished further investigation is rare. Attempting to establish connections among a series of crimes is atypical, unless by detecting a common crime pattern among similar crimes can help in identifying the perpetrator. POP, however, moves beyond this simple method of handling of incidents and provides a more profound and detailed perspective.

Police officers engaging in POP are required to identify and acknowledge relationships among crimes or disorder, as well as explore the factors that may contribute to their occurrence. Once a common cause among similar crimes is determined, an extensive amount of information gathering on this cause is essential in order to develop the most effective method for dealing with the issue.[15] POP promotes the use of research methods techniques in order to understand all aspects of the problem, in addition to the creation of a solution or method for controlling it. Furthermore, POP encourages police officers to assess their work and determine whether or not the solutions they established and employed were the most effective.[16]

---

[12] Kelling and Moore (1988).
[13] Skogan (2004).
[14] Goldstein (1990).
[15] Ibid.
[16] Skogan (2004).

In discussions of modern policing strategies, POP and community policing are often associated with one another. Both paradigms were developed early in the community problem-solving era and share similar characteristics, such as the use of problem solving and community involvement. However, these two policing strategies are not identical and can be distinguished between each other. POP focuses on problems, making them the center of which all police activity revolves around. Furthermore, POP works with the community as a means to address problems, while community policing incorporates the involvement of the community in order to improve public support and the relationship between community and police, as well as to help in identifying and solving community problems.[17] When these two methods of policing were first introduced, the debate on which was more effective was often questioned, in an attempt to determine which type of policing strategy to employ.[18]

Another theoretical crime prevention concept that emerged during the earlier stages of the community problem-solving era is known as Broken Windows theory, which is based on the idea that a broken window, when left unrepaired, will result in decay and disorder, which in turn leads to an increase in criminality. This theory posits that crime can be prevented through problem solving and effective community and police action. Broken Windows theory suggests that by regulating smaller concerns such as disorder and quality-of-life issues, larger and more serious problems will be prevented.[19]

Currently, community policing is considered a central method for police practices within the United States. Many police agencies at both the local and state levels proclaim to actively practice community policing.[20] One rationale for the rise in community policing popularity among law enforcement agencies occurred after the passage of the largest federal anticrime venture enactment in the history of the United States. In September 1994, President Bill Clinton passed the Violent Crime Control and Law Enforcement Act, which promoted community policing as an effort in the fight against crime. The 1994 Crime Act provided $8.8 billion to fund local law enforcement agencies to increase and improve their community policing capabilities. This act also resulted in the development of a new agency within the US Department of Justice, known as the Office of Community Oriented Policing Services (COPS), in order to direct and monitor grant programs that were being created.[21]

According to community policing advocates, such as Plummer (1999), the reasoning behind the massive movement toward this method of policing is not due to the pressures of politicians or legislative action; rather it is based on the fact that it works. The concept of creating a partnership between police and community in order to solve problems is an effective way for police to perform the tasks that

---

[17] Ibid.
[18] Capowich and Roehl (1994).
[19] Wilson and Kelling (1982).
[20] Oliver (2000).
[21] Zhao, Scheider, and Thurman (2002).

are associated with the occupation and expected from society, such as maintaining social order and protecting the public. This communication enables police to be aware of the community concerns as well as the problems that exist, providing them with the direction they need in order to target such issues.

Since the idea of community policing was first introduced, it has been viewed as a positive development, in which politicians, citizens, police officials, and the media promote its function and use.[22] However, many researchers and academics often question the effectiveness and ability of this policing strategy. Criticisms such as the disparity that exists on the meaning of community policing due to the lack of a universal definition, as well as the difficulty in testing the effectiveness and impact community policing has on communities, are frequently referenced.[23] Community policing, by its very nature, must vary in its application in order to effectively respond to the needs and conditions specific to the individual community; therefore operationalization of community policing and empirical analyses of the effectiveness of its implementation across communities are problematic.

According to Skogan (2004), the definitive test to determine whether community policing works is to examine crime levels subsequent to the implementation of policies that support community policing.[24] The correlation between community policing and the recent dramatic decreases in crime rates is often speculated. After the 1994 Crime Act was passed, an interest on the impact of community policing and its effects on the country's crime rate greatly increased. Due to the enormous funding provided to encourage police departments to utilize community policing, many interested stakeholders wanted to know whether or not the money was well spent. The findings of the Zhao et al. (2002) study, which employ multivariate analysis of violent and property crime rates in the United States from 1995 to 1999, "imply that COPS program funding to medium- and large-size cities has been an effective force in reducing both violent and property crime."[25] However, it appears that the empirical analysis of this influence is not very conclusive as it fails to fully take into consideration all the factors that influence crime rates in a given environment, and the debates about the role police play in crime reduction are a long and inconclusive one.

A recent study by Worrall and Kovandzic (2007) disputes the Zhao et al. findings, suggesting that COPS funding had little to no effect on crime rates, stating that "a strategy of throwing money at the crime problem, of simply *hiring* more police officers, does not seem to help reduce crime to a significant extent."[26] Federal government grants made directly to law enforcement agencies to hire additional officers and promote innovations may be an effective way to reduce crime on a national scale. These results support the claim that community policing can reduce crime

---

[22]Oliver (2000).

[23]Crank and Langworthy (1996).

[24]Skogan (2004).

[25]Zhao et al. (2002).

[26]Worrall and Kovandzic (2007, p. 185).

when it is utilized by law enforcement; however, determining whether or not such police departments really are practicing community policing may be more difficult to decipher.

The ideology of community policing greatly emphasizes the importance of police suiting the needs and expectations implied by the public. A key objective in policing is assuring the safety and well-being of citizens and make certain they feel secure within the community. When police make these goals a priority and their results are positive, an increase in police satisfaction within the community is likely to occur. The Xu, Fiedler, and Flaming (2005) study was conducted on the impact of community policing, which found that community policing reduces crime indirectly. Another focus of the study, which examined citizen perception, indicated that the individual's level of fear, judgment on the conditions of the community, and degree of life quality will greatly influence citizen satisfaction with the police. According to the study, when individuals experience fear of crime, they tend to feel as though the police lack either the motivation or the ability to handle community problems.[27]

The same philosophy can be applied when the conditions of community are poor and any motions for improvement are neglected. These factors emit the notion that the police have little concern for the welfare of the community they serve or the individuals residing in it. If citizens feel as though the police are performing inadequately and have little regard for the community, it is likely that police satisfaction among the community will greatly suffer.[28] In order for a positive relationship between police and community to persist, respect, trust, and communication must exist. If any of these elements starts to deteriorate, then the connection between the two groups will suffer.

Concepts of community policing are constantly being applied to different societal issues that affect law enforcement and the criminal justice system such as gangs, drug trafficking, prisoner re-entry, and domestic violence. A relatively new idea is whether or not community policing can be applied to the phenomenon of terrorism. Community policing techniques may result in increased communication between local law enforcement agencies and the communities they serve, which is a necessary component in the detection and prevention of terrorist attacks.

Since the terrorist attacks on September 11, 2001, there have been drastic changes in the world of policing and law enforcement. Increased advancements in security procedures, strengthened investigation capabilities, and the development or expansion of counterterrorism task forces are just a few of the various different amendments that have emerged in order to fight terrorism. Constant efforts are being made in order to determine the most effective ways for preventing and deterring violent terrorist acts, including policing methods. The Lum, Kennedy, and Sherley (2006) study on the effectiveness of counterterrorism strategies found that there was almost a complete absence of high-quality scientific evaluation evidence on

---

[27] Xu et al. (2005).
[28] Ibid.

counterterrorism strategies. Furthermore, across all the interventions studied, there was no consistent indication of positive effects of counterterrorism policy.[29]

According to Sloan (2002), many law enforcement agencies have shifted toward the localization of intelligence gathering as a response to the threat of terrorism.[30] Intelligence can be defined as the collection, examination, and interpretation of confidential information in an effort to detect and prevent criminal activity. In order to be effective, local law enforcement agencies need to be aware of criminal activity within their jurisdiction. An increase in community involvement through crime watch programs or neighborhood surveillance may help to inform police of criminal activity. Utilizing a strategy such as community policing may provide increased intelligence gathering capabilities at the local police agency level as a result of community partnerships, which may also provide a diffusion of benefits, such as to serve to reduce other forms of crime and disorder, reduction of fear among residents, business owners and frequent visitors of a community, and the sense of ownership by members of the public.

In Ohio, in June 2000, a statewide conference was held, in which representatives from law enforcement agencies located in all of the 88 counties gathered to discuss critical issues involving preparedness in the possible event of a terrorist attack. One issue identified as a valuable factor in preparedness from the perspective of police was the relationship between the police agency and other agencies within the community. Communication and coordination between the different agencies within a community is integral to the effective response to a terrorist incident. The concept of public awareness and education in relation to terrorism was also mentioned as having an effect on the level of preparedness in the event of a terrorist attack. The interaction and ability to exchange information between police and community greatly influence how a police department will respond to and handle a terrorist attack. A police department must maintain communication with community agencies and groups about policies and procedures regarding terrorist attacks, as well as provide citizens education regarding the phenomenon of terrorism. The concept of community policing encourages the exchange of such knowledge as a means of establishing methods to effectively protect society while upholding the law.[31]

Different conditions of community policing, such as the utilization of community involvement and the encouragement to develop positive, trusting relationships between police and the public, can be beneficial for law enforcement agencies in their efforts to regulate and avert terrorism. The significance of community involvement within this policing method is that it provides police with the ability to exchange information with the public as well as collect community intelligence which may have been previously unknown to police. It also informs police of the different groups that exist within the community and the different thoughts and opinions they have regarding a particular issue or idea. The formation of trust between

---

[29]Lum et al. (2006).

[30]Sloan (2002).

[31]Donnermeyer (2002).

law enforcement and citizens that community policing promotes may persuade and facilitate individuals to report information to police. Similar community policing methods that are practiced in other democratic countries, such as the United Kingdom, have been considered constructive in regard to obtaining beneficial information for law enforcement in their efforts to manage terrorism.[32]

The principles of community policing should be utilized when establishing effective methods to address the phenomenon of terrorism, as other policing models, such as the traditional or reactive, may be counterproductive. As Murray (2005) wrote, "community policing has proven to be a dramatic improvement to the traditional model of policing that is essentially reactive."[33] The most important benefits resulting from community policing is the increased communication between the community and police. Eliciting thoughts and opinions of both individuals and groups in a community is extremely important and should be actively pursued, especially from those that are typically reluctant to collaborate with police. As the sense of trust between law enforcement and the community increases, the public will likely be more willing to provide information to police. As a response to the 9/11 attacks and due to increased federal funding for local counterterrorism, many local law enforcement agencies have increased personnel assigned to specialized counterterrorism or special weapons and tactics (SWAT) units, which may signal a shift away from community policing.

A concern with this shift in policing philosophy is impact on the relationship between the police and the public. As Murray (2005) posits, the abandonment of community policing as an overall philosophy would be counterproductive, as it will decrease the "critical facility of prevention and community cooperation which are inherent in community policing."[34] The public will be more likely to voluntarily report information under the following circumstances: when there is an encouragement to do so, both from the community and the police; when there is a sense of trust between the police and the public; and when there is awareness that individual actions by members of the public may impact the interests of the community.

Community policing also entails the utilization of problem solving by police in a proactive approach to law enforcement. Through determining and detecting the fundamental cause or causes of crime and disorder, methods of regulation and prevention for future similar occurrences are created. These proactive efforts such as the SARA model, an acronym for scanning, analysis, response, and assessment, may also be applied to developing plans of monitoring and prevention of terrorism. In addition, these methods can also be useful when analyzing the concept of fear and its ties to terrorist attacks. Public fear associated with terrorism, which may vary in magnitude across communities, may also be addressed through the application of community policing.[35]

---

[32] Innes (2006).

[33] Murray (2005)., p. 347

[34] Ibid., p. 349

[35] Scheider and Chapman (2003).

Although the effectiveness of applying community policing to counter terrorism has not been empirically tested, there are two factors that may provide answers to its potential as a tool for local law enforcement. First, the way in which community policing is defined may range among agencies, as well as the researcher or academic gathering the information and conducting the evaluations. It is important that the definition of community policing is clearly operationalized in order to test whether its application is effective. Second, the expected results also require operationalization in order to consider the utilization of community policing as effective. If a decrease in terrorism indicates community policing as an effective method for the prevention and regulation of terrorism, the extent of the decrease expected to occur should be determined. If effectiveness is viewed as obtaining information or intelligence that results in the apprehension of terrorists and the prevention of terrorist attacks from occurring, then the frequency of such occurrences should be defined.

References

Capowich, G., & Roehl, J. (1994). Problem-oriented policing: Actions and effectiveness in San Diego. In D. P. Rosenbaum (Ed.), *The challenge of community policing: Testing the promises* (pp. 127–146). Thousand Oaks, CA: Sage.

Crank, J. P., & Langworthy, R. H. (1996). Fragmented centralization and the organization of the police. *Policing and Society, 6,* 213–229.

Donnermeyer, J. F. (2002). Local preparedness for terrorism: A view from law enforcement. *Police Practice and Research, 3*(4), 347–360.

Ferreira, B. R. (1996). The use and effectiveness of community policing in a democracy. In M. Pagon (Ed.), *Policing in Central and Eastern Europe: Comparing firsthand knowledge with experience from the west* (pp. 139–149). Ljubljana, Slovenia: College of Police and Security Studies.

Goldstein, H. (1990). *Problem-oriented policing.* New York: McGraw-Hill.

Haberfeld, M. R. (1997). Poland: "the police are not the public and the public are not the police": Transformation from militia to police. *Policing: An International Journal of Police Strategies & Management, 20*(4), 641–654.

Haberfeld, M. R. (2002). *Critical issues in police training.* Upper Saddle River, NJ: Pearson Education, Inc.

Haberfeld, M. R., Walancik, P., & Uydess, A. M. (2002). Teamwork – not making the dream work: Community policing in Poland. *Policing: An International Journal of Police Strategies & Management, 25*(1), 147–168.

Haberfeld, M. R., & Cerrah, I. (2007). *Comparative policing: The struggle for democratization.* Thousand Oaks, CA: Sage Publications, Inc.

Innes, M. (2006, May). Policing uncertainty: Countering terror through community intelligence and democratic policing. *The Annals of the American Academy of Political and Social Science, 605*(1), 222–241.

Kelling, G. L., & Moore, M. H. (1988). The evolving strategy of policing. *Perspectives on Policing, 4,* 1–15.

Lum, C., Kennedy, L. W., & Sherley, A. J. (2006). The effectiveness of counter-terrorism strategies: A Campbell systematic review. *Journal of Experimental Criminology, 2*(4), 489–516.

Maguire, E. R., & Mastrofski, S. D. (2000, March). Patterns of community policing in the United States. *Police Quarterly, 3*(1), 4–45.

Murray, J. (2005, September). Policing terrorism: A threat to community policing or just a shift in priorities? *Police Practice and Research, 6*(4), 347–361.

Office of Community Oriented Policing Services. (2008, April 30). *What is community policing?* Washington, D.C.: U.S. Department of Justice. Retrieved from http://www.cops.usdoj.gov/default.asp?item=36.

Oliver, W. M. (2000, December). The third generation of community policing: Moving through innovation, diffusion and institutionalization. *Police Quarterly, 3*(4), 367–388.

Plummer, L. C. (1999, March). Community policing: Thriving because it works. *Police Quarterly, 2*(1), 96–102.

Reith, C. (1948). *A short history of the British police.* London, UK: Oxford University Press.

Scheider, M. C., & Chapman, R. (2003, April). Community policing and terrorism. *Homeland Security Institute, Journal of Homeland Security.* Retrieved from http://www.homelandsecurity.org/journal/articles/Scheider-Chapman.html.

Skogan, W. G. (2004). *Community policing: Can it work?* Belmont, CA: Thomson Wadsworth.

Sloan, S. (2002, January). Meeting the terrorist threat: The localization of counter terrorism intelligence. *Police, Practice, and Research, 3*(4), 337–345.

Wilson, J. Q., & Kelling, G. L. (1982, March). Broken windows: The police and neighborhood safety. *Atlantic Monthly,* 29–38.

Worrall, J. L., & Kovandzic, T. V. (2007). COPS grants and crime revisited. *Criminology, 45*(1), 159–190.

Xu, Y., Fiedler, M. L., & Flaming, K. H. (2005, May). Discovering the impact of community policing: The broken windows thesis, collective efficacy, and citizens' judgment. *Journal of Research in Crime and Delinquency, 42*(2), 147–186.

Zhao, J. S., Scheider, M. C., & Thurman, Q. (2002, November). Funding community policing to reduce crime: Have COPS grants made a difference? *Criminology & Public Policy, 2*(1), 7–32.

Chapter 3
Methodology

The initial objective of this project in terms of its methodological approach was threefold. First, the team aimed at interviewing police officials in the surveyed countries regarding their training efforts to counter terrorist activities in the post 9/11 era of policing; second, the researchers hoped to be able to generate focus groups within the law enforcement communities to ascertain the level of their preparedness and their perceptions about the level of their preparedness to prevent and counter future attacks; and, finally, they hoped to interview key individuals and also to hold a number of focus groups within the communities policed by the forces that were approached. The key individuals the researchers were aiming at were local politicians, religious leaders, and media moguls who, by the virtue of their social status, were in a position to influence the perceptions and attitudes of the local population toward the phenomenon of terrorism. In this venue, for example, in Turkey the team interviewed a number of minority religious leaders, like the head of the Armenian minority and the head of the Christian minority as well as a director of the local most popular television station, which has a very significant impact on the intensity and scope of the coverage of various terrorist-related events, as well as one of the major movie directors who produces movies on terrorist movements in Turkey.

Although the researchers believed that such an eclectic methodological approach will produce the most insightful view of what has been done on the part of the local law enforcement versus how it was perceived by the local population, they were acutely aware of the threats to the validity of such a medley. Therefore, this report will address, in its methodological section, the advantages and disadvantages of the various methodological approaches that were used, like the focus groups; interview of selected key individuals; and collecting data on the nature of operational training that is not always fully disclosed to the academic researchers, and whatever is disclosed has to be treated in a sensitive manner when it is, in turn, disclosed to the public at large.

Finally, the biggest impediment to the final recommendations of this project and its external validity is reflected in the fact that due to some administrative roadblocks, the researchers were not allowed to complete the focus groups and individual interviews in three out of the six countries, in Sweden, Holland, and the United

Kingdom, and as such the project suffers from the incomplete data collection from half of the countries that were targeted by the team. None withstanding this impediment, the authors feel confident that the findings presented in this report reflect, in an accurate manner, the overall situation and sentiments of both local law enforcement and the community they serve in each of the countries we visited. As with any research study there is always room and need to validate the baseline findings, and the authors would like to caution the readers that this is indeed a baseline contour of the situations and circumstances and perceptions and sentiments of the people they interacted with. By no means the authors aim to present this report as an all-inclusive picture of the local realities.

This part of the report will address, in general terms (that should be taken into consideration by researchers who aim to conduct their studies in foreign countries, using human subject), the advantages and the shortcomings of the methodologies that were used.

3.1 Qualitative Versus Quantitative Data Collection

There are two major processes used when conducting social science research: the qualitative approach and the quantitative approach. Qualitative research is based on in-depth discussions and observations of some type of phenomenon through field or historical research, while quantitative research is based on numerical measurements that represent findings made from studying some type of phenomenon.[1] However, in some research studies both qualitative and quantitative methods can be utilized when obtaining data. This form of multimethod research collection within the same study is often referred to as triangulation.[2] Since our study was originally focused on collecting impressions and attitudes from a multitude of stakeholders, the community and its various human components one side and the law enforcement on the other, we opted to choose the qualitative method, especially given the comparative nature of the study that doesn't always allow for a fair comparison of the same concepts. One of the authors had previous familiarity with conducting both qualitative and quantitative studies in the comparative contexts; it was her experience that the qualitative approach would work much better in comparative and sensitive environments. Some concepts work best when they are talked out among the research participants and do not produce a valid and replicable output through the use of quantitative instruments.

Qualitative research provides a method of analysis for intellectual problems that do not yet have the availability of quantitative measures.[3] Qualitative research is, in a more simplistic sense, the method of making observations. Most individuals engage in some form of qualitative research without even realizing it or having

---

[1] Babbie (2007).

[2] Webb, Campbell, Schwartz, and Sechrest (1966).

[3] Bernard (2000, p. 68).

the intentions of doing so. Observing the occurrence of a particular phenomenon, or participating in some type of social behavior in an attempt to understand such behavior, demonstrates the logic and use of information-gathering techniques that are associated with qualitative research.[4] Researchers conduct qualitative research studies in order to obtain a more profound and comprehensive understanding of the particular phenomenon being investigated. The purpose of qualitative research is to explore and discover rather than make validations. Qualitative studies seek out to answer the questions of how and why regarding the particular topic or occurrence being observed and analyzed.[5] Typically, qualitative research studies are theory generated, in which inductive reasoning is used. The researcher first makes observations and searches for patterns, prior to developing any type of a hypothesis or conclusion.

> Qualitative research is a situated activity that locates the observer in the world. It consists of a set of interpretive, material practices that make the world visible. These practices transform the world. They turn the world into a series of representations, including fieldnotes, interviews, conversations, photographs, recordings, and memos to the self. At this level, qualitative researchers study things in their natural settings, attempting to make sense of, or interpret, phenomena in terms of the meanings people bring to them.[6]

Qualitative research is most appropriate for issues and proceedings that are rather intricate in nature, that are best observed in a natural setting, or that change as time progresses. There are several different paradigms that may be used when performing qualitative research, such as naturalism, ethnomethodology, grounded theory, case studies, extended case method, institutional ethnography, and participatory action research. The phenomenon being studied will determine which paradigm is appropriate and which will be utilized to perform the qualitative research study.[7]

The team chose to utilize a mix of different approaches based on the subjects' availability and sensitivity of the topic. For example, one of the officers in Turkey, a high-ranking Gendarmerie officer, agreed to talk to the researchers about his perception of what local law enforcement is doing vis-à-vis the PKK terrorists only if they came to his apartment. Since there is very little openness on the part of the Turkish Gendarmerie to talk to anybody, including the Turkish National Police, let alone foreign researchers, the team embraced the opportunity and met with him and his family for 2 h, discussing the lack of cooperation and the disconnect between the Turkish National Police and the Turkish Gendarmerie, which in essence proved to the authors that the rhetoric of "information sharing" for the benefit of fighting the common enemy is just a rhetoric that is far away from any field implementation.

The different strengths and weaknesses that correspond with the utilization of qualitative research when conducting studies should always be taken into

---

[4] Babbie (2007).
[5] Ambert, Adler, Adler, and Detzner (1995).
[6] Denzen and Lincoln (2005, p. 3).
[7] Babbie (2007).

consideration. Some advantages that qualitative research studies have are the large amount of information and depth of understanding that can be obtained regarding the phenomenon being studied. Another benefit is the amount of flexibility the researcher has by using a qualitative approach in research. Since qualitative research allows variety among the data collected, researchers are less likely to feel pressure or stress when certain information is unobtainable. Also, in many cases qualitative research studies are a lot less expensive to conduct compared to other methods. In especially cases where the qualitative study consists of mainly observational data, costs that may correspond with conducting surveys, such as the distribution of incentives, would be avoided.[8]

Some disadvantages that may occur when conducting qualitative studies are the amount of coding and interpreting of data a researcher faces when analyzing the information that was obtained.[9] Also, any of the findings that are determined from the study cannot be used in order to form statistical results that could be applied to a larger population. Qualitative research also tends to produce a greater level of validity, yet a lower level of reliability, when referring to the data that are obtained.[10] There is no doubt that the information we obtained from an interview conducted in the Turkish police officer's apartment cannot be applied to a larger population and definitely suffers from a lower level of validity than one that could be obtained in a quantitative manner; however, the opportunity to interview a high-ranking officer in a force that remains largely closed and mystical to the research community cannot be discounted, especially when compared against other data collected from the same country.

Quantitative research involves the investigation of specified variables in order to determine their relationship and establish conclusions based on statistical analysis. This variable-relationship investigation typically is conducted in order to test a particular hypothesis or answer a specific research question.[11] Similar to qualitative research, quantitative research involves the use of interpretation within its application. Some type of interpretation process is used within almost every stage of quantitative research. Since quantitative research uses deductive reasoning, a hypothesis is developed prior to any data collection. Thus, a process of interpretation must be used when creating the survey or experiment that will be employed in order to test the pre-established assumption. Interpretation is also used when constructing and applying numerical codes for the data collected from the research. Once the data are converted, mathematical methods are conducted in order to determine the outcome of the research question or hypothesis in a numerical format. A process of interpretation is also essential in order to analyze the statistical results the study's findings reveal and establish valid conclusions.[12]

---

[8] Ibid.

[9] Wolstenholme (1999).

[10] Babbie (2007).

[11] Ibid.

[12] Kritzer (1996).

Several advantages and disadvantages are often mentioned when conducting research studies using the quantitative approach. Some advantages of using quantitative research studies are the application of statistical analysis toward the data collected, which provides a clear depiction of the results and findings. Mathematical calculations are sometimes deemed more substantial than interpretations of observations; thus many individuals prefer to see statistical evidence when the results of a study are being presented.[13] Also, in some research studies the statistical findings from the sample can be used to describe a larger population, which increases the significance of the study and its results. One of the disadvantages of quantitative research is that a finding of non-significance due to limited statistical power may be misinterpreted to mean that there is no relationship among variables. Quantifying findings from a study may be beneficial for some data, yet inane for others, and by doing so the researcher is reducing the study's substance. Another disadvantage with quantitative research is the possibility of a mathematical error through incorrect calculation or the misinterpretation of statistics indicated by the study's findings. In both situations, any conclusions that may be determined and presented would be incorrect, thus could result in the public being misinformed.[14]

As already indicated, the initial approach in this study was to collect a qualitative data that would serve as a baseline for understanding the attitudes and perceptions regarding the counterterrorist response. It is, however, very much recommended to follow up with a more quantitative approach and distribute a set of very basic questionnaires to the members of the law enforcement agencies in an attempt to glean in a more in-depth and statistically valid manner into the situation and the organizational approach to the problem. This been said, prior attempts of one of the researchers to run some questionnaires within the Turkish National Police were met with rejection. It is extremely hard to collect quantitative data from police organizations, both in the United States and in the comparative context, and based on her experience in comparing the qualitative and the quantitative data that she was able to collect in her prior studies, the researcher found a lot of triangulation between the two methods. This prior experience made it easier to rely on qualitative findings only and opt for collection of data that generated the least resistance within police organizations.

The literature often hints to the notion that when conducting a research study the researcher has one of two options and must select between a qualitative and a quantitative study based on suitability and preference. However, such stipulation is not completely accurate and in many cases, techniques that derive from both approaches are applied within the same study in order to collect the data being sought.[15] The term triangulation, which is used to describe the combination of both qualitative and quantitative techniques within a research study, derives from a military strategy, which utilized multiple reference points in order to determine the exact position

---

[13] Wolstenholme (1999).

[14] Babbie (2007).

[15] Jick (1979).

of a target.[16] In the case of this research, although it was not completely accurate
to say that only one option was available, the qualitative methods employed were
much more convenient in terms of the time frame and the evolving event, as we
lost access to one country (Lebanon) and delayed access to another (the United
Kingdom after the London bombing) due to the nature of the problem that we were
studying. Therefore, it is imperative to make this decision, whether one goes for
the qualitative that is available or wait for the quantitative that might be available
(or not), especially when the subject of the research project is of high sensitivity
and the outcomes might influence policies that are urgently needed to be put in
place.

Social science researchers should be capable of conducting both qualitative and
quantitative research studies effectively, and an inability to do may decrease their
repute as a researcher. Both methods are of equal importance within the field of
research and are considered beneficial tools in the process of data collection. However, both methods have their own limitations and benefits when it comes to their
application within research.[17] Thus, the concept of combining techniques from
both qualitative and quantitative approaches and utilizing them when conducting
a research study seems like a rather intelligent strategy. According to Jick (1979),
using a multimethod research tactic not only allows researchers to feel more confident in their findings but also increases the level of creativity when it comes to developing and testing new approaches to research methods and problem solving. The
combination of qualitative and quantitative techniques also provides more insight
into findings as well as provides better explanations for obtaining certain results that
may have otherwise been unknown.[18] Although the authors agree with the notion
that social scientists should be able to engage in both qualitative and quantitative
research to enhance the validity of their findings, it is important to stress that in
comparative context, when a number of countries are involved, especially when
these countries are experiencing various transformation processes or are exposed to
some existential threats (such as in the case of a major terrorist attack), it is imperative to collect whatever data are available and make use of them while cautioning
about the internal and external validity, due to the constraints, but still make use of
what is available.

The two main research paradigms, quantitative and quantitative, have numerous
methods. When engaging in qualitative research there is an imperative focus on
detail and description; thus in-depth discussions and observations are used when
attaining knowledge regarding the phenomenon being analyzed.[19] Depending on
the intended purpose and objectives for the qualitative study being conducted, the

---

[16]Smith (1975).

[17]Babbie (2007).

[18]Fry, Chantavanich, and Chantavanich (1981).

[19]Babbie (2007, pp. 308–309).

method used to achieve such goals will be chosen accordingly.[20] One technique that may be used when gathering knowledge through interviewing within a qualitative research study is the concept of focus groups.

One of the methods the researchers chose to gather the data was indeed participation in focus groups in a number of countries, primarily in Turkey and Spain, although some focus groups were also held in Ireland and the United Kingdom; these were smaller groups due to the lack of responsiveness at the local level.

3.2 Focus Groups

Focus groups can be defined as a collection of individuals brought together based on some type of prerequisite or certain criteria that connect them to the phenomenon being analyzed in order to participate communally within the research study.[21] As Krueger and Casey (2000) wrote, a "focus group study is a carefully planned series of discussions designed to obtain perceptions on a defined area of interest in a permissive, non-threatening environment."[22] The purpose of using focus groups as a method for data collection within social research is to explore a particular phenomenon rather than describe or explain it. The individuals who make up a particular focus group may not necessarily be representative of a specific population; thus generalizability to a larger population based on information derived from the focus group interview may not be applied.[23]

Focus groups have been used by social scientists to obtain a more complete picture of the phenomenon they are studying. Krueger and Casey (2000) wrote that "the intent of focus groups is not to infer but to understand, not to generalize but to determine the range, and not to make statements about the population but to provide insights about how people in the groups perceive a situation."[24] Focus groups can often produce information that is not accessible through other methods. Morgan (1997) wrote that the "hallmark of focus groups is their explicit use of group interaction to produce data and insights that would be less accessible without the interaction found in a group."[25] Focus groups provide insights into group dynamics. Patton (1990) wrote, "the fact of the matter is that we cannot observe everything. We cannot observe feelings, thoughts and intentions. We cannot observe behaviors that took place in some previous point in time."[26] By employing focus groups, researcher may gain a greater understanding of these factors.

---

[20]Champion (2006).

[21]Kitzinger (1995) and Merton and Kendall (1946).

[22]Krueger and Casey (2000), p. 5

[23]Babbie (2007, pp. 308–309).

[24]Krueger and Casey (2000, p. 83).

[25]Morgan (1997, p. 2).

[26]Patton (1990, p. 278).

Morgan (1997) discusses three basic uses for focus groups in social science. First, in the self-contained method, the group discussion serves as the primary means of collecting qualitative data. The self-contained method requires careful matching of the goals of the research data with the data that the focus group can produce and emphasizes research design. Second, in the focus group as a supplemental source of data, the group discussions serve as a preliminary source of data in a primarily quantitative study. Third, in the multimethod study, the group discussion is one facet of the overall research study, which typically includes other qualitative methods such as participant observation or individual interviews.[27]

In this study, the decision was made to use the focus groups as the third multimethod study, where the group discussions were indeed just one aspect of the overall study that also included individual interviews as well as collections of training curricula and other materials that law enforcement agencies availed to our use. For example, in Northern Ireland the researchers were given an entire training manual that was used by their special counterterrorism unit in training the police officers in recruiting and maintaining a confidential informant (CI), which is included in the final chapter of this report as a recommendation for training to be implemented by other police forces that face the phenomenon of terrorism.

The concept of applicability and relevancy is essential and must be utilized during the selection process of focus group participants, so that their involvement is appropriate as well as valuable toward the research study being conducted.[28] The technique of focus groups involves interaction and communication between both researcher and different members within the group. A key principle behind this method of interviewing is to promote and support discussion among group participants in order to provide a difference in opinions and experiences pertaining to the issue or issues being researched.[29] The use of focus groups relies greatly on the level of group interaction; thus it is important that the individuals chosen are able to communicate effectively and comfortably among each other.[30] In order to guarantee such positive forms of communication among focus group members, Krueger (1994) promotes the use of homogenous groups, in which participants share similar characteristics such as gender, age range, ethnicity, and social background.

Although, especially in police environments, it is definitely an advantageous approach to use homogenous groups in terms of their official ranks, in community groups the researchers found that having mixed groups in terms of gender, age, and social background was extremely beneficial and by itself served as a template for future police–community interactions. For example, in Spain one of the focus groups consisted of college professors, students, journalists, and members of victims' rights groups. It was an extremely dynamic meeting, especially given the polarity of opinions and attitudes. It is rather doubtful that a more homogenous

---

[27] Morgan (1997, pp. 2–3).
[28] Burrows and Kendall (1997).
[29] Kitzinger (1994).
[30] Green, Draper, and Dowler (2003).

group would produce such an intense and solid interaction. This been said, in Turkey a more homogenous focus group (based on the same professional background, all lawyers – members of the local Bar Association) produced a lively discussion, although devoid of the same fire encountered in Spain.

There is no universally accepted minimum or maximum number of participants required within a focus group, and the range varies depending on the researcher and the conducted study. According to Babbie (2007), focus groups usually consist of 12–15 people, with no less than 7, while Krueger and Casey (2000) posit that smaller groups show greater results and suggest between 6 and 8 total participants within a focus group in order to receive the most effective data. The differences in size may also relate to the function of the focus group. Marketing focus groups tend to utilize a larger number of participants than social science focus groups. Small homogenous focus groups, comprised of four to eight members, will allow participants to be more comfortable about discussing their thoughts, which is of great importance in dealing with police officers who are often loathe to share their innermost thoughts with individuals outside the profession.

In the case of this study, although the team opted for a minimum of six participants for each focus group, they did not turn back when less than six arrived for the meeting. It was their experience that if the people who arrived to the meeting were there, the team should have engaged in the conversation due to the fact that the ones who were there showed enough of an interest and represented opinions and attitudes worth recording. If these smaller meetings with less than six participants should be treated more like interviews rather than focus groups, it is hard to establish but the small focus group held in London with the members of the local Muslim Rights group was very powerful and indicative of sentiments that were later observed while visiting one of the police stations in a predominantly Muslim northern London neighborhood. Therefore, the key to the validity of the findings derived from an interaction with smaller focus groups should be the cross-validation with other data, such as participant observation.

A frequent debate among researchers is whether focus groups consisting of individuals with pre-existing relationships or focus groups in which participants are complete strangers provide a more effective setting in order to achieve the most thorough and accurate information from the focus group members within a research study. According to Thomas, MacMillan, McColl, Priest, Hale, and Bond (1995), when participants within a focus group are unfamiliar with one another, the possibility of certain adverse group behaviors, such as an influence among opinions or threats of coercion toward certain responses, is less likely to occur. Unfamiliarity among focus group members may provide the opportunity for participants to respond more honestly and express themselves more freely, which in turn creates a wider range of responses and information for the researcher.[31]

However, pre-existing relationships among focus group members may also be beneficial in that participants can relate to one another, as well as feel more

---

[31] Thomas et al. (1995).

comfortable in questioning each other's responses or challenging opposing opinions. In situations where sensitive or personal issues are being discussed, familiarity among participants may also make responding to questions and engaging in conversations easier by providing a more accepting as well as supportive environment.[32]

It was the team's experience that the pre-existing relationships in focus groups might have had some bearing in law enforcement environments, especially given the rank structure of the participants, but it was not always the case in the community settings. The focus group participants, members of the Human Rights Organization in Turkey, came from the pre-existing personal/work relations and held some contradictory views on certain concepts, even though these concepts were closely related to their daily work environments.

The role of the researcher or interviewer plays a large role with the overall environment of a focus group and the level of comfort participants feel while engaging in the research study, regardless of whether or not focus group members are familiar with one another. Through skillful management and organization, the researcher or individual conducting the interview can help decrease the feeling of uneasiness and discomfort among participants and create a more relaxed environment. The researcher or interviewer also has the ability to encourage participants within a focus group to freely express their thoughts and opinions on the issues being questioned as well as engage in more in-depth discussions among one another if such opportunity arises.[33] Therefore, the role of the researcher is integral to the comparative focus group setting.

When the language is not a barrier, all of the above statements hold true; however, when there is a need to use the local interpreter, which was the case in both Turkey and Spain, the interpreter becomes the key figure in the dynamic between the focus group and the researchers. Choosing the right interpreter is almost as critical as choosing the right participants; therefore substantial attention is required in the decision-making process. Undoubtedly, using interpreters who were law enforcement officers while talking to the law enforcement officials in Turkey was a huge advantage; however, this cannot be said about using the law enforcement interpreter when talking to the civilian subjects. It was the team's experience that the presence of a law enforcement interpreter, no matter how benign, had some subtle yet observable influence on the tenor of our group discussion. On the other end of the spectrum, in Spain, having a civilian interpreter was not always conducive in our exchanges with the local law enforcement, as there were concepts that were not easily translatable. For example, the focus group we held with the Spanish Police (Policia National) in Madrid was a long, nearly 3-h discussion that was slowed down by some misunderstandings of what was conveyed to the researchers and what they were trying to explain. Overall, what could have been accomplished in 2 h lasted an hour longer due to the language barriers.

---

[32] Kitzinger (1994).

[33] Burrows and Kendall (1997).

Utilizing multiple means of recording data during focus groups provides greater reliability of the data collected. Often, having an additional individual available to record information and observe the focus group being conducted can be very beneficial. The researcher then has the ability to compare notes to another source as well as exchange ideas and thoughts on the information that was obtained with another perspective that was present during the same study. In case the researcher missed certain details or important information during the interview, there is the possibility that the other person may have obtained it and can provide the details of such information. The second individual can provide observations, such as nonverbal interaction among group members, that the researcher would not have been aware of nor had the ability to witness while conducting the study, yet may be rather valuable information and contribute to making research conclusions.[34]

During most of the team's interactions, one researcher led the discussion while the other took notes, which was predetermined prior to each interaction. It is advisable to record the focus group's, meetings, but in law enforcement environments can be problematic. Police organizations tend to be very punitive in their orientation, even in the most democratic of countries, and the use of a recording device is not recommended, as it is rarely conducive to honest exchange. Since this research goal was to get some contours of perceptions and attitudes, we were not overly concerned about detailed note taking or verbatim records. The researchers were satisfied with their ability to take notes about the themes that evolved during our interactions. After each focus group meeting, the members of the team met to discuss, in a sort of debriefing mode, the outcomes of the meetings and to make sure that the main themes of discussion were indeed recorded in the notes.

The following section discusses the generic advantages versus disadvantages of focus groups, and the pros and cons of these approaches within the context of this research will be addressed in the country sections when we discuss the specifics of our experiences in a given country. These generic themes serve as an important reminder that data derived from a focus group setting must be compared against other relevant sources of information. For example, a claim by the focus group's, members in London that the police are determined to kill all the Muslims (as per the lesson they [the police] received from the Israeli police force) needs to be validated against some other source of information, not just because of the absurdity of this notion but because of its claim.

If indeed there is some sort of cooperation between the Israeli Police and the Metropolitan Police Force in London, in combating terrorist activities, and the publicity of this cooperation generates real fear within certain communities in London, it is imperative that the British Police address this issue during the community meetings and be aware of the existence of such sentiments. In a way, this example illustrates both the advantages and the disadvantages of holding focus groups meetings. On one end, it provided the researcher with an attitude that

---

[34] Kitzinger (1995).

might have been rather isolated and not indicative of how the others feel, but on the other end, it created an opening into a very deep pocket of irrational fear that might and could immobilize certain community members, and prevent them from cooperating with the local law enforcement, if not addressed properly by the authorities.

3.2.1 Focus Group Advantages

There are several advantages to utilizing focus groups for qualitative research. As Morgan (1997) wrote, "[t]he main advantage of focus groups in comparison to participant observation is the opportunity to observe a large amount of interaction on a topic in a limited period of time based on the researcher's ability to assemble and direct the focus group sessions."[35] Focus groups capture real-life data within a social environment, are relatively low in cost to conduct, thus making them ideal for studies with a rather low budget, and provide a great deal of flexibility for researchers, especially with the use of open-ended questions, which provide the opportunity for in-depth discussions and the exchange of thoughts and opinions. Another advantage the use of focus groups offers is providing high face validity.[36] In other words, because face validity does not depend on any established support, but on whether or not it appears to measure what it intends to measure, thus the technique of focus groups in order to obtain information regarding a particular phenomenon seems like a reasonable method in order to achieve the results being sought.[37]

3.2.2 Focus Group Disadvantages

In comparison to naturalistic observation, which provides the ability to collect data on a large range of behaviors, a greater variety of interaction with participants, and a more open discussion of the research topic, the use of focus groups has several disadvantages. Focus groups are generally limited to verbal behavior, consist only of interaction in discussion groups, and are artificially created and managed by the researcher.[38] Focus groups, when compared to individual interviews, lack the level of control the researcher has over the process, which is necessary to effectively conduct focus groups, as the interaction between participants is an integral part of the process. In addition, as with all field research, there is the potential for reactivity,

---

[35] Morgan (1997, p. 8).
[36] Krueger (1988).
[37] Babbie (2007, pp. 308–309).
[38] Morgan (1997, p. 8).

in which the subjects alter their behavior due to the awareness that they are being studied.[39]

The researcher conducting the groups must employ certain skills such as management and control of the dynamic of the group. In addition, the researcher conducting the focus group needs to allow all subjects within the focus group the opportunity to express ideas, feelings, and experiences about the issues being discussed. Another disadvantage is the difficulty providing a universally conducive setting. Assembling groups in order to conduct interviews can also be rather challenging, and the differences between groups can be problematic. Finding the appropriate individuals to participate within a study may be difficult due to the importance of relevancy such individuals must have toward the phenomenon being studied, as well as the large range of opinions and information that is collected from groups may be difficult to compare to one another.[40]

Another disadvantage of utilizing focus groups for qualitative research is the difficulty associated with analyzing the data collected. Focus groups have the potential to produce a large amount of information within a relatively short period of time, in which a range of ideas and feelings may be presented on a certain topic. Since the technique of focus groups requires participants to discuss or respond to the same issue or question at the same time, contradicting opinions may often occur, as well as detailed replies.[41] Therefore, the researcher may encounter difficulty accurately and precisely recording all of the information that is produced throughout the focus group, which is necessary to properly analyze the data in order to establish conclusions from the research.

Few researchers have utilized focus groups in the study of terrorism. However, one such study was the Davis, LaTourrette, Mosher, Davis, and Howell (2003) RAND report, which convened focus groups to obtain community feedback regarding individual preparedness and response strategies for catastrophic terrorist events. "The overall purpose of these focus groups was to inform the project's recommendations for an individual's strategy for catastrophic terrorism."[42] The objective of the overall study was to provide guidance for individuals so that they will be better able to protect themselves in the event of a terrorist attack, which may involve unfamiliar hazardous conditions – such as with CBRN attacks.

Overall, it can be stated that for the purpose of identifying hidden fears and attitudes, with regard to the understanding of the phenomenon of terrorism and the willingness (or lack of) to cooperate with the local law enforcement, the advantages of holding focus groups regardless of their size and composition (no matter how far they depart from the "ideal" size and composition of the focus group) were clearly

---

[39] Babbie (2007, p. 290).

[40] Krueger (1988).

[41] Krueger and Casey (2000).

[42] Davis et al. (2003, p. 143).

supported by the experiences of the researchers involved in this study. The level of openness, intensity, and sincerity would not have been captured utilizing the quantitative approach.

3.2.3 Institutional Review Board

This study was approved by the John Jay College of Criminal Justice Institutional Review Board (IRB), and the researchers adopted all necessary protocols to protect the health, privacy, and autonomy of the research subjects (see Appendix C for IRB Review Form). The researchers explained to the subjects that the purpose of the study was to help gain a better understanding of the relationship between terrorism and community. Subjects were informed that participation in the study was voluntary, anonymous, and confidential. The subjects were further informed that they were not required to participate and that they were welcome to end their participation for any reason at any time during the study, such as if the participant began to feel upset or uncomfortable. All subjects were shown the consent form, but because of the nature of the situation and the individuals involved, the participants were not required to sign the consent form (see Appendix B for consent form).

References

Ambert, A. M., Adler, P. A., Adler, P., & Detzner, D. F. (1995, November). Understanding and evaluating qualitative research. *Journal of Marriage and the Family, 57*(4), 879–893.

Babbie, E. (2007). *The practice of social research* (11th ed.). Belmont, CA: Thomson Wadsworth.

Bernard, H. R. (2000). *Social research methods: Qualitative and quantitative approaches.* Thousand Oaks, CA: Sage Publications, Inc.

Burrows, D., & Kendall, S. (1997). Focus groups: What are they and how can they be used in nursing and health care research? *Social Sciences in Health, 3,* 244–253.

Champion, D. J. (2006). *Research methods for criminal justice and criminology.* Upper Saddle River, NJ: Pearson Education Inc.

Davis, L. E., LaTourrette, T., Mosher, D. E., Davis, L. M., & Howell, D. R. (2003). *Individual preparedness and response to chemical, radiological, nuclear, and biological terrorist attacks.* Santa Monica, CA: RAND Corporation.

Denzin, N. K., & Lincoln, Y. S. (2005). *The Sage handbook of qualitative research* (3rd ed.). Thousand Oaks, CA: Sage Publications, Inc.

Fry, G., Chantavanich, S., & Chantavanich, A. (1981). Merging quantitative and qualitative research techniques: Toward a new research paradigm. *Anthropology & Education Quarterly, 12*(2), 145–158.

Green, J. M., Draper, A. K., & Dowler, E. A. (2003). Short cuts to safety: Risk and 'rules of thumb' in accounts of food choice. *Health, Risk, and Society, 5,* 33–52.

Jick, T. D. (1979, December). Mixing qualitative and quantitative methods: Triangulation in action. *Administrative Science Quarterly, 24*(4), 602–611.

Kitzinger, J. (1994). The methodology of focus groups: The importance of interactions between research participants. *Sociology of Health and Illness, 16,* 103–121.

Kitzinger, J. (1995, July 29). Qualitative research: Introducing focus groups. *British Medical Journal, 311*(7000), 299–302.

Kritzer, H. M. (1996, February). The data puzzle: The nature of interpretation in quantitative research. *American Journal of Political Science, 40*(1), 1–32.

Krueger, R. A. (1988). *Focus groups.* Newbury Park, CA: Sage Publications, Inc.

Krueger, R. A., & Casey, M. A. (2000). *Focus groups: A practical guide for applied research.* Thousand Oaks, CA: Sage Publications, Inc.

Merton, R. K., & Kendall, P. L. (1946, May). The focused interview. *The American Journal of Sociology, 51*(6), 541–557.

Morgan, D. L. (1997). Focus groups as qualitative research (2nd Eds.). Thousand Oaks, CA: Sage Publications, Inc.

Patton, M. Q. (1990). Qualitative evaluation and research methods (2nd Eds.). Newbury Park, CA: Sage Publications, Inc.

Smith, H. W. (1975). *Strategies of social research: The methodological imagination.* Englewood Cliffs, NJ: Prentice Hall.

Thomas, L. H., MacMillan, J., McColl, E., Priest, J., Hale, C., & Bond, S. (1995). Obtaining patients' views of nursing care to inform the development of a patient satisfaction scale. *International Journal for Quality in Health Care, 7*(2), 153–163.

Webb, E. J., Campbell, D. T., Schwartz, R. D., & Sechrest, L. (1966). *Unobtrusive measures: Non-reactive research in the social sciences.* Chicago, IL: Rand McNally.

Wolstenholme, E. F. (1999, April). Qualitative vs. quantitative modeling: The evolving balance. *The Journal of the Operational Research Society, 50*(4), 422–428.

Chapter 4
The United Kingdom and Ireland

4.1 History

England has been the source of much of the legal history of the Western world. "Our English police system...rests on foundations designed with the full approval of the people, we know not how many hundreds of years before the Norman conquest, and has been slowly molded by the careful hand of experience, developing as a rule along the line of least resistance, now in advance of the general intelligence of the country, now lagging far behind, but always in the long run adjusting itself to the popular temper, always consistent with local self-government, and even at its worst, always English" (Lee, 1971, p. xxvii). The development of our common law system, like that of our modern police, is seated in the English traditions.

Although England has existed since the tenth century, the United Kingdom (UK) of Great Britain and Northern Ireland has only been recognized in its current form for the past 80 years. In 1927, subsequent to the British Government of Ireland Act (1920) and the Anglo-Irish Treaty (1921) that formalized the borders of the nation, the UK formally adopted its current name. The UK, whose population exceeds 60 million, remains a constitutional monarchy. Great Britain has three main contiguous regions, England, Wales, and Scotland, while the fourth region, Northern Ireland, covers about one-sixth of the northeast area of Ireland. The capital of the UK is London, which is located along the Thames River in southeastern England. While not the global power it was in the early twentieth century, the UK is one of the five trillion dollar economies of Western Europe and remains a leading trade and financial center.

As the dominant industrial and maritime power of the nineteenth century, the United Kingdom of Great Britain and Ireland played a leading role in developing parliamentary democracy and in advancing literature and science. At its zenith, the British Empire stretched over one-fourth of the earth's surface. The first half of the twentieth century saw the UK's strength seriously depleted in two World Wars and the Irish republic withdraw from the union. The second half witnessed the dismantling of the Empire and the UK rebuilding itself into a modern and prosperous European nation. As one of five permanent members of the UN Security Council, a founding member of NATO, and of the Commonwealth, the UK pursues a global approach to foreign policy; it currently is weighing the degree of its integration with continental Europe. A member of the EU, it chose to remain outside the Economic and Monetary Union for the time being. Constitutional reform is also

M.R. Haberfeld et al., *Terrorism Within Comparative International Context*,
DOI 10.1007/978-0-387-88861-3_4, © Springer Science+Business Media, LLC 2009

a significant issue in the UK. The Scottish Parliament, the National Assembly for Wales, and the Northern Ireland Assembly were established in 1999, but the latter is suspended due to wrangling over the peace process.[1]

The British have been involved with Ireland since the twelfth century, during an expansion under King Henry II. Between 1801 and 1921, all of Ireland was under the direct control of the British Empire, which is now the United Kingdom of Great Britain and Northern Ireland (UK). In 1916, a failed rebellion led to 5 years of guerilla warfare that led to the British Government of Ireland Act (1920) and Anglo-Irish Treaty (1921), which established the independence of the southern 26 counties on the island of Ireland while the remaining 6 counties comprised Northern Ireland and remained under British rule. Following the establishment of the Irish Free State in June 1921, the IRA established the Irish Republican Police. This force was disbanded in September 1922, and its members were encouraged to join the newly created Garda. Northern Ireland is approximately one-third Catholic, the majority of whom opposed the partitioning of Ireland, and two-thirds Protestant, the majority of whom remain loyal to "the Crown" and the UK. Since that time, there have been numerous incidents between the UK and Ireland in regard to the region in Northern Ireland that remained a part of the UK, although most of the incidents related to "The Troubles" occurred in Northern Ireland.[2]

Celtic tribes arrived on the island between 600 to 150 B.C. Invasions by Norsemen that began in the late eighth century were finally ended when King Brian BORU defeated the Danes in 1014. English invasions began in the twelfth century and set off more than seven centuries of Anglo-Irish struggle marked by fierce rebellions and harsh repressions. A failed 1916 Easter Monday Rebellion touched off several years of guerrilla warfare that in 1921 resulted in independence from the UK for 26 southern counties; six northern (Ulster) counties remained part of the UK. In 1948 Ireland withdrew from the British Commonwealth; it joined the European Community in 1973. Irish governments have sought the peaceful unification of Ireland and have cooperated with Britain against terrorist groups. A peace settlement for Northern Ireland is being implemented with some difficulties. In 2006, the Irish and British governments developed and began working to implement the St. Andrew's Agreement, building on the Good Friday Agreement approved in 1998.[3]

"The Troubles," which began in the 1960s, had four elements: the Protestants, the Catholics, the British government, and the Irish government. The vast majority of Protestants, which comprised approximately two-thirds of the population of Northern Ireland, favored existing links with Britain, despite regular criticisms of the British government, primarily due to fear that a united Ireland would lead to attacks on their political, religious, and economic interests. The vast majority of Catholics, which comprised approximately one-third of the population of Northern

---

[1] US CIA World Factbook: *United Kingdom.* https://www.cia.gov/library/publications/the-world-factbook/geos/uk.html.

[2] US Department of State. (2007, October). Ireland. *Bureau of European and Eurasian Affairs.* http://www.state.gov/r/pa/ei/bgn/3180.htm.

[3] US Central Intelligence Agency (2008, June 19). Ireland. *The World Factbook.* https://www.cia.gov/library/publications/the-world-factbook/geos/ei.html.

Ireland, viewed themselves as Irish, not British, and viewed Northern Ireland as an illegitimate state.[4] Recently, there has been significantly more political than military or paramilitary battles over Northern Ireland, such as the Good Friday and St Andrews agreements.

4.2 Terrorism

Terrorism has been a major issue for the UK, in various forms, for hundreds of years. The occupation of Ireland by the English, starting in the sixteenth century, has been the primary cause of conflict between the Irish and the British. "The Troubles" in Northern Ireland and the separatist movements that utilized tactics, which included extreme violence against both governmental and civilian targets, affected the UK and Northern Ireland for decades. Under a variety of names, such as the White Boys, the Ribbon Society, the Irish Republican Brotherhood, and, most famously, the Irish Republican Army (IRA), the Irish people, predominantly the Catholic segment of the population, have fought against the policies of the Protestant London imposed government, many of which were perceived by the Catholics as oppressive. Most of these separatist movements were under the umbrella of the IRA, and although the IRA wanted to unite the island as one nation, many of the splinter groups of the IRA had different goals. In addition, there were numerous counter groups, mainly Protestant groups that wanted to maintain British control in Northern Ireland, which also used extreme violence against civilian targets. These conflicts were nationalist, religious, economic, and political.

The organization of our modern style of policing, by Sir Robert Peel in 1829, was based largely upon his experiences as the British administrator in Ireland. As Smyth (2002) writes, "the model of policing developed in nineteenth century Ireland, involving a centralized force organized and trained on military lines, became a model for colonial police forces in the British Empire."[5] The activities of these secret societies and the lawlessness they breed gave rise to the idea of an organized force. Indeed, the series of bombings by the Irish Republican Brotherhood in London in the 1860s led to the creation of the Special Branch detective unit, originally called the Special Irish Branch, and the organization of the Criminal Investigation Division. The treaty that ended the Irish revolution in 1921 divided the island of Ireland into two separate political entities. The remaining British entity, Northern Ireland that has a two-thirds majority Protestant population, and Ireland, which is predominantly Catholic.

Although much of the terrorist activity that has taken place in the UK and Ireland in the twentieth century has been associated with Irish republicanism, there has been significant activity on the part of the Protestants of Ulster, who formed groups such as the Ulster Volunteer Force (UVF) and the Ulster Defense Association (UDA),

---

[4]McKittrick and McVea (2001, pp. 1–2).
[5]Smyth (2002, p. 110).

the two largest Protestant unionist and loyalist paramilitary organizations. In the early part of the twentieth century, there was the sense that the government of the UK was planning to give independence, or home rule, to Ireland, which led to the mobilization of the UVF. Over 200,000 people joined the UVF, which was led by members of the Ulster aristocracy and trained by retired British military officers.[6] On May 17, 1974, a series of car bombings by the UVF in Dublin and Monaghan killed 33 civilians and injured hundreds.[7]

Although the First World War (WWI) prevented a civil war in Ireland, as the UVF was incorporated into the British Army, the UVF contributed to the partitioning of Ireland, which gave independence to only three quarters of Ireland, allowing Ulster to remain a part of the UK. After WWI, there was violence in Northern Ireland between Irish republicans and loyalists, some of which was contributed by vigilantism by the UVF. Again, the UVF was incorporated into government service, specifically as members of the "B" Special Constabulary, who were part-time constables in the newly partitioned Northern Ireland.[8] This was in part due to the statement by Sir Edward Carson in response to the fear of attack by Irish republicans. "If... you are yourselves unable to protect us from the machinations of Sinn Fein... we will take the matter into our own hands."[9] Unless the state is in disarray, prostate terrorist organizations are not likely to have longevity, as they are likely, as was the case in Northern Ireland, to be co-opted by the government.[10] The "B" Special Constabulary became a wholly protestant militia that was used to curtail and for retaliation of the Republican Community, but were disbanded in 1969. A 2007 report by the Police Ombudsman for Northern Ireland stated that police colluded with Ulster loyalists in more than a dozen murders in Belfast.[11]

Sinn Fein, the political arm of the IRA, had claimed, in its document *Scenario for Peace*[12] (1987), that the authority of the Anglo-Irish Treaty[13] was invalid due to the United Nations' *Universal Declaration of Human Rights*[14] (1948), *International Covenant on Civil and Political Rights*[15] and *International Covenant on Economic, Social and Cultural Rights*[16] (1966), in addition to the duress from the threat of

---

[6] Bruce (1992, pp. 67–88).

[7] BBC News: *1974: Bombs devastate Dublin and Monaghan.* http://news.bbc.co.uk/onthisday/hi/dates/stories/may/17/newsid_4311000/4311459.stm.

[8] Bruce (1992, p. 67).

[9] The Royal Ulster Constabulary: *History – The B specials.* http://www.royalulsterconstabulary.org/history3.htm.

[10] Bruce (1992, p. 86).

[11] O'Loan (2007); BBC News: *NI police colluded with killers.* http://news.bbc.co.uk/2/hi/uk_news/northern_ireland/6286695.stm.

[12] Sinn Fein (1987). *A scenario for peace.* http://www.sinnfein.ie/pdf/AScenarioforPeace.pdf.

[13] National Archives of Ireland. http://www.nationalarchives.ie/topics/anglo_irish/dfaexhib2.html.

[14] UN: *Universal Declaration of Human Rights.* http://www.un.org/Overview/rights.html.

[15] UN: *International Covenant on Civil and Political Rights.* http://www.hrweb.org/legal/cpr.html.

[16] UN: *International Covenant on Economic, Social and Cultural Rights.* http://untreaty.un.org/English/TreatyEvent2001/pdf/08e.pdf.

war from the British government. These are some of the main factors involved in the justification for violence by Irish republicans.[17] The signing of the *Good Friday Agreement*[18] (1998) led to peace between most Irish republicans and the UK. Many of the larger organizations, such as PIRA, have agreed to pursue their goals through peaceful means and stated that they would "decommission" the weapons formerly used in its armed struggle.[19] However, some IRA splinter groups, such as the Continuity Irish Republican Army (CIRA) and the Real Irish Republican Army (RIRA), have continued to advocate and engage in the use of extreme violence to support their goals, primarily to unite all of Ireland.

Below is a list of dissident groups in Northern Ireland and the year each was founded:

Nationalist-Catholic

1. Official Irish Republican Army (OIRA) – 1916
2. Provisional Irish Republican Army (PIRA) – 1969
3. Irish National Liberation Army (INLA) – 1979
4. Continuity Irish Republican Army (CIRA) – 1986
5. Real Irish Republican Army (RIRA) – 1997

Loyalist-Protestants

1. Ulster Volunteer Force (UVF) – 1912
2. Ulster Defense Association (UDA) – 1970
3. Ulster Freedom Fighters (UFF) – 1980
4. Red Hand Defenders (RHD) – 1985
5. Ulster Democratic Party (UDP) – 1989

Beginning in 1994, with the Provisional Irish Republican Army (PIRA) cease-fires, and continuing through 2004, which signified the end of most terrorist activity between Irish republicans and the British, many of the groups that once fought for nationalist or separatist goals have either begun or continued, to a greater degree, to engage in criminal racketeering. This type of activity has not been limited to IRA splinter groups, but applies to the Ulster groups, such as the Ulster Defence Association (UDA) and the Ulster Volunteer Force (UDF). Over the past decade, agreements between the UK and Ireland have led to a significant decrease in violence; however, the UDA and UDF have been more active in criminal racketeering since 1998. The signing of the *Northern Ireland Act 1998*, also known as the *Good Friday Agreement*, has led to significant progress in healing the wounds caused by more than a century of fighting as a result of "The Troubles."[20] The *Northern Ireland Act*

---

[17] Macfarlane (1990, pp. 35–53).

[18] *Agreement between the Government of the United Kingdom of Great Britain and Northern Ireland and the Government of Ireland* (1998). http://www.nio.gov.uk/agreement.pdf.

[19] Office of the Coordinator for Counterterrorism: *Country Reports on Terrorism.* http://www.state.gov/s/ct/rls/crt/2005/64342.htm#uk.

[20] Achievements in implementation of the Good Friday Agreement, July 14, 2001. http://www.nio.gov.uk/achievements_in_implementation_of_the_good_friday_agreement.pdf.

2006,[21] also known as the *St Andrews Agreement*, further serves to address many of the issues that cause contention within Ireland relating to the UK, including amending the *Northern Ireland Act 1998*.

During the past decade, there has been an increased threat level from religious fundamentalist groups, specifically Islamic extremists. The July 7, 2005, attacks by Islamic fundamentalists, led by Mohammed Sidique Khan and allegedly associated with Al Qaeda, on London's public transportation led to 52 deaths and hundreds of injuries.[22] The attack consisted of three explosive devices detonated nearly simultaneously on London's underground and an explosive device detonated approximately 1 h later on the upper deck of a two-level public bus. Although this was the first successful attack by Islamic terrorists in the UK, in the past many UK citizens have been injured or killed due to Islamic terrorist attacks abroad.

Two weeks after the July 7, 2005, attacks, on July 21, another terrorist attack was attempted in London.[23] Similar to the previous attack, the targets were part of London's public transportation system. Three explosive devices were left on underground trains and one explosive device was left on a bus; however, none of the devices detonated. Police recovered a fifth device 2 days after the incident. These attacks were also attributed to Islamic extremists. Four individuals, Muktar Ibrahim, Yassin Omar, Hussain Osman, and Ramzi Mohammed, all born in East Africa, were found guilty of attempted murder and sentenced to life in prison.[24] The fifth individual, Manfo Kwaku Asiedu, who was born in Ghana, pled guilty to a lesser charge.[25] A sixth individual, Adel Yahya, who was born in Ethiopia and raised in Yemen, pled to a lesser charge of collecting information useful to a person committing or preparing an act of terrorism. Yahya went with Omar, one of the four sentenced to life, to the Finsbury Park Mosque to hear radical preacher Abu Hamza. In May 2004, Yahya joined a training camp in the Lake District with about 20 others, including Muktar Ibrahim, Yassin Omar, Ramzi Mohammed, and Hussein Osman.[26]

On June 29, 2007, an ambulance crew saw smoke coming from a vehicle, a green Mercedes, parked in London, near a nightclub. Police examination revealed a crude explosive device, using gas or propane cylinders, petrol, and nails, which was subsequently disabled by police. The device was probably created by amateur

---

[21] Northern Ireland (St. Andrews Agreement) Act 2006, Chapter 53. http://www.niassembly. gov.uk/transitional/info_office/Act.pdf.

[22] BBC News, *Bombing: Reaction timeline*. London underground releases the timing of events on July 7, 2005. http://www.bbc.co.uk/london/content/articles/2005/07/12/bomb_timeline_feature. shtml.

[23] BBC News, *21 July attacks*. "Four attempted bombings took place exactly two weeks after the deadly 7 July blasts." http://news.bbc.co.uk/1/shared/spl/hi/uk/05/london_blasts/what_happened/html/21_07_05.stm.

[24] BBC News, *21/7 men were 'dedicated' bombers*. http://news.bbc.co.uk/1/hi/uk/6287842.stm.

[25] BBC News, *Man admits 21 July bombing charge*. http://news.bbc.co.uk/2/hi/uk_news/7087302.stm.

[26] For a more in-depth understanding of the July 7th and July 21st 2005 London bombings, see Lieberman & Cheloukhine (2009).

or inexperienced bomb makers.[27] A second car bomb was found in another Mercedes, London's West End, near Piccadilly Circus, parked illegally and towed to a pound by traffic wardens. The explosive device did not detonate and was discovered after staff smelled fumes coming from the vehicle.[28] These recent events have led the UK to reconsider the threat from Islamic fundamentalists in the UK. Although police found no direct links to any organization, simultaneous and coordinated bombs have been a distinguishing feature of Al Qaeda attacks. However, these investigations are ongoing and new information may reveal a connection between the suspects and an organization.

Scotland, however, has not been the target of terrorist attacks, but the police forces in Scotland cooperate with other law enforcement and intelligence agencies in the UK in regard to counterterrorism. Other than the June 30, 2007, suicide attack on Glasgow airport[29] and the December 21, 1988, bomb that detonated on Pan Am flight 103 over Lockerbie,[30] which led to the deaths of all 259 persons on board the plane and 11 in the village where the plane crashed, there have not been any significant associations between terrorism and Scotland. Libya eventually took responsibility for the 1988 Pan Am bomb, handing over two suspects, including the Libyan intelligence officer, Abdelbaset Ali Mohmed al-Megrahi, who was convicted of the terrorist attack in a Scottish court, and paying $2.7 billion to family members of the victims of the attack in exchange for the US agreement to the UN lifting sanctions against Libya.[31]

Terrorism in the Republic of Ireland has taken a different track since the 1970s and the rise to prominence of the PIRA, which has used the Republic as a staging area for support, intelligence, and fund raising. Much of the weapons smuggling form the United States in the 1970s and 1980s were filtered through the Republic. Fund raising by kidnappings and bank robberies were to become the model for this group. Indeed, in 1996 a failed armored car robbery, by a PIRA faction, left Detective Jerry McCabe dead and his partner wounded.

---

[27] BBC News, *Police avert car bomb 'carnage'*. http://news.bbc.co.uk/1/hi/uk/6252276.stm; BBC News, *Police hunting London car bombers*. http://news.bbc.co.uk/2/hi/uk_news/6255452.stm.

[28] Telegraph, *Second car bomb found in London's West End*, http://www.telegraph.co.uk/news/main.jhtml?xml=/news/2007/06/29/nbomb1029.xml.

[29] ABC News, *Investigators: Scotland and London bomb attempts linked to same two men*. http://abcnews.go.com/Blotter/story?id=3342018.

[30] Hoffman (1998, p. 18); Washington Post, *Timeline: The bombing of Pan Am Flight 103*. http://www.washingtonpost.com/wp-srv/inatl/longterm/panam103/timeline.htm.

[31] CNN, *Libya offers $2.7 billion Pan Am 103 settlement*. http://archives.cnn.com/2002/US/05/28/libya.lockerbie.settlement/; US Dept of State press release, *Libya – Pan Am 103*. http://www.state.gov/secretary/former/powell/remarks/2003/23325.htm; UN SC press release 7868, *Security Council Lifts Sanctions Imposed on Libya After Terrorist Bombings of Pan Am 103, UTA 772*. http://www.un.org/News/Press/docs/2003/sc7868.doc.htm; NY Times, Libya Set to Take Responsibility for Pan Am Blast, Envoys Say. http://query.nytimes.com/gst/fullpage.html?res=9E02E2D91E31F930A2575BC0A9659C8B63&n=Top%2FReference%2FTimes%20Topics%2FSubjects%2FP%2FPan%20Am%20Flight%20103.

The four men sentenced today admitted that they had killed Detective Sgt. Jerry McCabe in an attempt to rob a bank van in the western town of Adare. The police said the attack was to obtain money for the I.R.A., which has admitted its responsibility.[32]

Police blamed the IRA for the £26.5 million Northern Bank raid in Belfast. Chief Constable, Hugh Orde, told a news conference in Belfast: "In my opinion the Provisional IRA were responsible for this crime and all main lines of inquiry currently undertaken are in that direction."[33] The IRA denied involvement in the bank robbery and Sinn Fein stated that they believe the denial. Since the cease-fire agreement, much of the PIRA activities in both Ireland and Northern Ireland have been in drug trafficking and in control of the profitable markets in Dublin and Belfast. Additionally, recent investigations by both the Republic and the UK authorities have unearthed money-laundering operations in both real estate transactions and the pub industry worth hundreds of millions in pounds and Euros.[34]

The PIRA has used the Republic as a staging area and as a "back door" to both Europe and the UK. It has successfully used it as a safe haven for its active service units and the structure for its command apparatus. The PIRA's operation and structure has become the model for many other terrorist groups, i.e., ETA in Spain, Hezbollah in Lebanon. While the PIRA is the primary concern of the police in the Republic, increasingly other international terrorist organizations are also establishing themselves in the Republic. The changing immigration patterns have changed the population of Ireland, and increasingly these communities are seen as safe havens for "back room" operations and fund raising. One of the principal advantages to Ireland for these international groups is as a "back door" to the European Mainland.[35]

4.3 United Kingdom Law Enforcement

The UK has numerous governmental agencies, both at national and international levels, associated with addressing the issue of terrorism. The agencies in the UK associated with counterterrorism include the following: The Ministry of Defence, the Home Office, the Foreign Office, MI5, MI6, the Official Committee on Terrorism, the Joint Intelligence Committee, and other police agencies, such as the Police Service of Northern Ireland (PSNI), formerly (until November 2001) known as the Royal Ulster Constabulary (RUC), and the police forces in Scotland.

---

[32]NY Times (1999, February 6th): *4 I.R.A. Gang members sentenced in killing of Irish detective.* http://query.nytimes.com/gst/fullpage.html?res=9F05EEDD173BF935A35751C0A96F958260.

[33]BBC News (2005, January 7th): *Police say IRA behind bank raid.* http://news.bbc.co.uk/2/hi/uk_news/northern_ireland/4154657.stm.

[34]Horgan and Taylor (1999).

[35]Interview by Dr. King of Sean O'Callahan, July, 2005.

The Ministry of Defence[36] (MOD) "is both a policy-making Department of State – like any other central government department – as well as being the highest level military headquarters in the UK, providing political control of all military operations."[37] MOD is responsible for defending the UK and its interests as the military arm of the UK, which maintains one of the best-equipped armies in the world and has been involved in numerous international operations in the past decade, including engagements in the Balkans, Afghanistan, and Iraq. The UK military has been involved in both peacekeeping and regime-change missions.

The Home Office[38] is made up of three components: a central headquarters, which sets goals, develops policies, and provides support services; the National Offender Management Service, which brings together the prison and probation services; and the Immigration and Nationality Directorate, which manages requests to live or work in the UK. In addition, the Home Office is responsible for the police services in England and Wales and a number of other smaller services and public bodies. Below are the six key objectives of the Home Office to protect the public.[39]

1. Protecting the UK from terrorist attack
2. Cutting crime, especially violent and drug-related crime
3. Ensuring people feel safer in their homes and daily lives, particularly through more visible, responsive, and accountable local policing
4. Rebalancing the criminal justice system in favor of the law-abiding majority and the victim
5. Managing offenders to protect the public and reduce re-offending
6. Securing our borders, preventing abuse of our immigration laws and managing migration to benefit the UK

The Metropolitan Police Service (MPS), founded by Sir Robert Peel in 1829, remains one of the most famous and largest police agencies in the world. Peel, often referred to as the founder of "Modern Policing," formed many of his ideas as the Chief Secretary in Ireland. The British Government had used Dublin as an experiment in centralized policing by the Dublin Police Act of 1786.[40] The force that this act created was dissolved after 9 years, because of the cost, although its success was noted by the Irish Administration, which Peel inherited. Because of the continued disorders in Ireland, Peel was successful in the creation of the Peace Preservation Police of 1814.

Upon his appointment as Home Secretary, Peel began a campaign to create a centralized, preventive force to police London. After several rebuffs by Parliamentary

---

[36] UK Ministry of Defence. http://www.mod.uk/defenceinternet/home.

[37] UK Ministry of Defence. *About defence.* http://www.mod.uk/DefenceInternet/AboutDefence/ Organisation/KeyFactsAboutDefence/DefenceOrganisation.htm.

[38] UK Home Office. http://www.homeoffice.gov.uk/.

[39] UK Home Office. *Our objects and values.* http://www.homeoffice.gov.uk/about-us/purpose-and-aims/.

[40] The Law Reform Commission (1985). *Report on offences under the Dublin police acts and related offences.* http://www.lawreform.ie/publications/data/volume4/lrc_33.html.

Committees, Peel, finally in 1829, succeeded in the establishment of the MPS. This idea of the "New Police" spread throughout the Kingdom by a variety of Police Acts. It is interesting to note that Peel was responsible for the founding of both the modern, centralized municipal style police and the paramilitary style of state policing, both popular in the United States. Peel's Peace Preservation Police was the basic for the Irish Constabulary, later christened the Royal Irish Constabulary (RIC), the template for the State police model (for a fuller discussion of the development and evolution of policing and the styles of policing see Palmer (1988) or King (2004).

Historically, the MPS had been involved with counterterrorism (CT) for more than a century, with its response, as early as the 1860s, to the use of bombs by Irish separatists.[41] Some leadership in CT shifted from the MPS to the Security Service,[42] the Counter Terrorism Command (CTC), the branch of Special Operations that combines intelligence analysis and development with investigations and operational support, maintains involvement.

> The Government have now decided that the lead responsibility for intelligence work against Irish republican terrorism in Great Britain should pass from the Metropolitan police special branch to the Security Service. This will bring the arrangements broadly into line with those that already exist for other forms of terrorism. The purpose of this change is to enable the Security Service to use to the full the skills and expertise which it has developed over the years in its work on counter-terrorism. I wish to emphasise that under the new arrangements the Metropolitan police special branch will continue to play an indispensable part in intelligence work against Irish republican groups. The substantial experience and expertise that it has developed will not be lost, and it will continue to work in the closest co-operation with the Security Service.[43]

Although it is a relatively new branch, the Counter Terrorism Command (CTC), also known as SO15, builds on the expertise and professionalism of the former Anti-Terrorist Branch (SO12) and Special Branch (SO13), which it replaced in 2006, which for many years had been at the forefront of the MPS' counterterrorism effort. Below are the responsibilities of the CTC:

- To bring to justice those engaged in terrorist, domestic extremist, and related offences
- To provide a proactive and reactive response to terrorist, domestic extremist, and related offences, including the prevention and disruption of terrorist activity
- Support the National Co-ordinator of Terrorist Investigations outside London
- To gather and exploit intelligence on terrorism and extremism in London
- To assess, analyze, and develop intelligence to drive operational activity
- To engage in partnership with London's communities in order to understand their concerns and to provide reassurance and support where needed
- To provide specialist security advice and services internally and externally

---

[41] Clutterbuck (2006).

[42] On May 8, 1992 the lead responsibility for Irish republican terrorism shifted from MPS to MI5.

[43] http://www.publications.parliament.uk/pa/cm199293/cmhansrd/1992-05-08/Debate-2.html, col. 297.

- To provide an explosive ordnance disposal and CBRN capability in London
- To assist the British Security Service and Secret Intelligence Service in fulfilling their statutory roles
- To be the police single point of contact for international partners in counterterrorism matters
- Assisting in the protection of British interests overseas and the investigation of attacks against those interests[44]

The purpose of the Foreign and Commonwealth Office (FCO) is to "work for UK interests in a safe, just and prosperous world."[45] The FCO develops and delivers the UK's international policies; identifies and influences international developments; provides consular, visa, and commercial services to British nationals, businesses, and others; and maintains a global network of posts, who work closely with international partners. The FCO provides 10 strategic international priorities for the UK, listed below.

1. Making the world safer from global terrorism and weapons of mass destruction
2. Reducing the harm to the UK from international crime, including drug trafficking, people smuggling, and money laundering
3. Preventing and resolving conflict through a strong international system
4. Building an effective and globally competitive EU in a secure neighborhood
5. Supporting the UK economy and business through an open and expanding global economy, science, and innovation and secure energy supplies
6. Achieving climate security by promoting a faster transition to a sustainable, low-carbon global economy
7. Promoting sustainable development and poverty reduction underpinned by human rights, democracy, good governance, and protection of the environment
8. Managing migration and combating illegal immigration
9. Delivering high-quality support for British nationals abroad, both in normal times and in crises
10. Ensuring the security and good governance of the UK's Overseas Territories[46]

In regard to counterterrorism, the main goal of the FCO is to deter, check, and roll back programs for the development of WMD and related delivery systems in countries of concern, and to reduce the supply of, and demand for, such weapons worldwide. An additional goal of the FCO is to reduce the risk from international terrorism so that UK citizens can go about their business freely and with confidence. The four main themes regarding counterterrorism include prevent, pursue, protect, and prepare.

---

[44] Metropolitan Police: *Special operations – Counter terrorism command.* http://www.met.police.uk/so/counter_terrorism.htm.

[45] Foreign and Commonwealth Office. http://www.fco.gov.uk/en/.

[46] Ibid.

Prevention entails an effort to tackle the factors that lead to radicalization, in conjunction with the engaging with the Islamic World group. In particular, the FCO will analyze the drivers of radicalization and counter strategies and examine the relative importance of the various drivers. Pursuit entails support of police agencies in regard to forensics, bomb scene management, hostage negotiation training, strategic leadership training, and crime scene preservation. In regard to terrorism financing, pursuit will also include continuing cooperation with the Charities Commission and the National Terrorist Financing Unit (NTFIU) and the deployment of Terrorist Financing Liaison Officers (TFLOs) to Jordan and Abu Dhabi, who will develop a regional approach to terrorist financing. Pursuit will also include support for the Home Office expansion of the Counter Terrorism Extremism Liaison Officer (CTELO) network through the funding of a dedicated CTELO post in both Pakistan and Turkey. Protection will entail continued support for improvements in aviation and maritime security, VIP protection, and building capacity to protect key installations. Preparation entails the maintenance of programs that assist counties in the development of crisis management response capabilities.[47]

The Secret Intelligence Services (SIS), also known as MI6, was established in 1909 as the Foreign Section of the Secret Service Bureau. The SIS collects secret intelligence, mounts international covert operations, and "provides the British Government with a global covert capability to promote and defend the national security and economic well-being of the United Kingdom."[48] The SIS works in conjunction with the Security Service, Government Communications Headquarters[49] (GCHQ), the Ministry of Defence, the FCO, the Home Office, HM Revenue and Customs, and other UK law enforcement agencies and governmental departments.

The Security Service, also known as MI5,[50] is responsible for protecting the UK against threats to national security. The Security Service accomplishes this task through the collection and dissemination of intelligence, the investigation and assessment of threats and working with other agencies to counter them, advising on protection and providing support. Since the 1960s the Security Service has been involved in combating terrorism, both from national and international threats, and almost 90% of their resources are allocated to counterterrorism and protective security. As previously mentioned, in 1992 the Home Secretary transferred the lead responsibility for Ct regarding Irish republican terrorism from the MPS to the Security Service, presumably due to the increase in availability of resources due to the end of the Cold War.[51] The goals of the Security Service include the following:

---

[47] Global Opportunities Fund Annual Report 2005–2006. *Counter-terrorism.* http://www.fco.gov.uk/Files/KFile/GOFARTerrorism0611clb.pdf.

[48] Secret Intelligence Service. http://www.sis.gov.uk/output/Page79.html.

[49] Government Communications Headquarters [GCHQ]. http://www.gchq.gov.uk/.

[50] Security Service – MI5: *Protecting against terrorism.* http://www.mi5.gov.uk/files/pdf/protecting.pdf.

[51] Clutterbuck (2006).

- frustrate terrorism;
- prevent damage to the UK from foreign espionage and other covert foreign state activity;
- frustrate procurement by proliferating countries of material, technology, or expertise relating to weapons of mass destruction;
- watch out for new or re-emerging types of threat;
- protect government's sensitive information and assets, and the Critical National Infrastructure (CNI);
- assist the Secret Intelligence Service (SIS) and the Government Communications Headquarters (GCHQ) in the discharge of their statutory functions; and
- build Service capability and resilience.[52]

The Joint Intelligence Committee (JIC)[53] is part of the Cabinet Office responsible for providing ministers and senior officials with intelligence assessments. The JIC advises on priorities for intelligence collection, including both overt and covert sources, and assesses performance against them and also responsible for assessing and giving early warning of external developments and threats likely to affect British interests. The following are the responsibilities of the JIC:

- under the broad supervisory responsibility of the Permanent Secretaries' Committee on the Intelligence Services, to give direction to, and to keep under review, the organization and working of British intelligence activity as a whole at home and overseas in order to ensure efficiency, economy, and prompt adaptation to changing requirements;
- to submit, at agreed intervals, for approval by ministers, statements of the requirements and priorities for intelligence gathering and other tasks to be conducted by the intelligence agencies;
- to coordinate, as necessary, interdepartmental plans for activity;
- to monitor and give early warning of the development of direct or indirect foreign threats to British interests, whether political, military, or economic;
- on the basis of available information, to assess events and situations relating to external affairs, defense, terrorism, major international criminal activity, and scientific, technical, and international economic matters;
- to keep under review threats to security at home and overseas and to deal with such security problems as may be referred to it; and
- to maintain and supervise liaison with commonwealth and foreign intelligence organizations as appropriate, and to consider the extent to which its product can be made available to them.[54]

---

[52]MI5, Security Service. http://www.mi5.gov.uk/.

[53]Joint Intelligence Committee (JIC). http://www.intelligence.gov.uk/central_intelligence_ machinery/joint_intelligence_committee.aspx.

[54]Joint Intelligence Committee (JIC). http://www.intelligence.gov.uk/central_intelligence_ machinery/joint_intelligence_committee/jic_terms.aspx.

The Joint Terrorism Analysis Center (JTAC)[55] was established in 2003 as the center for analysis and assessment of international terrorism, both domestically and internationally. JTAC is a multiagency unit, with representatives from the Defense Intelligence staff, the FCO, and the police. Both the JIC and JTAC have an important role in the analysis and assessment of international terrorism; however, "JIC assessments of terrorism are more strategic and place JTAC assessments in a broader geopolitical context for Ministers and senior officials."[56]

As a result of the Belfast Agreement (1998), an Independent Commission on Policing was formed. As a result of that commission, a report, known as the Patten report, was released that provided numerous recommendations about policing in Northern Ireland. As a result of these recommendations, the police in Northern Ireland, formerly known as the Royal Ulster Constabulary (RUC), were given a new badge, uniform, and name, the Police Service of Northern Ireland[57] (PSNI). The PSNI has extensive experience with counterterrorism, while called the RUC during the time of "The Troubles," and continues to work with agencies in the UK to address the IRA splinter groups, such as RIRA and CIRA.

4.3.1 Ireland Law Enforcement

Ireland has numerous governmental agencies, both at national and international levels, associated with addressing the issue of terrorism. The agencies in Ireland that engage in counterterrorist activities include the Department of Defence, *An Garda Siochana*, the Army Ranger Wing, and the Department of Justice, Equality, and Law Reform.

Ireland's Department of Defence[58] (DOD), established by the Ministers and Secretaries Act (1924), is responsible for the military defense forces. Subsequent to the September 11, 2001, attacks in the United States, the government established an Office of Emergency Planning (OEP), which is responsible to take the lead role in emergency planning to meet the new threat from international terrorism and from any escalation in international tensions, including coordination of the responses by the various agencies involved. In addition, the OEP has an oversight role in relation to peacetime planning in order to ensure the best possible use of resources and compatibility between the different planning requirements.

Organized policing in Ireland originated in 1822, with the establishment of the County Constabulary. In 1836, the Irish Constabulary, also known as the Royal Irish Constabulary, and the Dublin Metropolitan Police replaced the County

---

[55]MI5, Security Service. http://www.mi5.gov.uk/textonly/Page63.html; Joint Terrorism Analysis Centre (JTAC). http://www.intelligence.gov.uk/agencies/jtac.aspx.

[56]Joint Intelligence Committee (JIC). http://www.intelligence.gov.uk/central_intelligence_machinery/joint_intelligence_committee.aspx.

[57]Police Service of Northern Ireland. http://www.psni.police.uk/.

[58]Department of Defence, Ireland. http://www.defence.ie/website.nsf/home+page?openform.

Constabulary. In 1922, *An Garda Siochána*[59] was formed and, in 1925, absorbed the Dublin Metropolitan Police. Currently *An Garda Siochána*, whose English translation is the Guardians of the Peace, is the national police service, providing state security services and criminal and traffic law enforcement functions. The Special Detective Unit (SDU) is the unit involved in counterterrorism, in dealing with both national and international terrorism.

The Army Ranger Wing[60] (ARW), which is officially designated *Sciathán Fianóglach an Airm*, was established in 1980. ARW was formed as a result of personnel from the Irish Defence Forces, *Óglaigh na hÉireann*, which received training from the US Army's Ranger school in the later 1960s and then went on to form a training program in Ireland. ARW engages in numerous types of operations, including long-range patrol, training other units, VIP security, antihijacking, hostage rescue, and counterterrorism, although *An Garda Siochána* is the primary response unit in regard to terrorism.

The mission of the Department of Justice, Equality, and Law Reform is to "[m]aintain and enhance community security and equality through the development of a range of policies and high quality services which underpin: the protection and assertion of human rights and fundamental freedoms consistent with the common good; the security of the State; an effective and balanced approach to tackling crime; and progress towards the elimination of discrimination and the promotion of equal opportunities and the accommodation of diversity."[61] The main areas of responsibility include the following: implementing government policy on crime and protecting the security of the state; providing policy advice in relation to the criminal justice system, including *An Garda Síochána*, the Courts, Prisons, and Probation and Welfare Services; continuing reform of the criminal law; implementing core elements in the Good Friday Agreement; cooperating in the EU and international fields and promoting Ireland's interests within our areas of responsibility; implementing and developing national immigration policy; and implementing and developing policy in relation to equal treatment.

In Ireland, as with the UK, numerous governmental agencies are assigned to deal with terrorism, including the Department of Defence (DOD), Ireland's national police service *An Garda Siochána*, the Army Ranger Wing (ARW), and the Department of Justice, Equality, and Law Reform. While these units take on a number of emergency response, intelligence, and international roles in countering terrorism, the national police service, *An Garda Siochána*, is the primary response unit for terrorism (see Department of Justice, Equality, and Law Reform, 2005) through its Special Detective Unit (SDU).[62] SDU engages in monitoring of individuals

---

[59] Garda, http://www.garda.ie/home.html.

[60] Special Operations.com. *Sciathan Fhiannoglaigh an Airm*. The Irish Defence Forces Army Ranger Wing. http://www.specialoperations.com/Foreign/Ireland/Rangers/default.htm.

[61] Department of Justice, Equality and Law Reform. http://www.justice.ie/80256DFD00637EE0/vWeb/pcSSTY5UBER3-en.

[62] Garda, Special Detective Unit. http://www.garda.ie/sdu.html.

suspected of involvement with international terrorist groups. Furthermore, SDU has played a significant role in combating the activities of terrorist groups domestically and has had some major successes against the Real Irish Republican Army (RIRA) and Continuity Irish Republican Army (CIRA). Much of the leadership of both the RIRA and CIRA are in custody, having been convicted or awaiting trial for terrorist-related offences, in part due to the efforts of SDU.

> The Special Detective Unit (SDU) is headed by a Detective Chief Superintendent and forms part of Crime and Security Branch. The primary functions of the Unit are intelligence-gathering and the monitoring and investigation of subversive-related activity. SDU personnel also assist other national units in the investigation of serious organised crime.[63]

4.4   United Kingdom Field Research

The researchers' qualitative observations in the United Kingdom focused primarily upon the Police Service of Northern Ireland as well as efforts by the London Metropolitan Police Service. Terrorism has been a major issue for the United Kingdom (UK) and Ireland for decades, mainly relating to "The Troubles" in Northern Ireland and the separatist movements that have utilized extreme violence against both governmental and civilian targets. While most of these separatist movements were under the umbrella of the Irish Republican Army (IRA), other splinter groups have also existed with a variety of goals. In total, The Troubles can best be described as having a combination of nationalist, political, religious, and socioeconomic roots that have resulted in deep-seated social conflict in Northern Ireland (McGarry & O'Leary, 1995; Tonge, 2002). The law enforcement counterterrorism response in Northern Ireland is a unique case study in itself, as early police responses to countering terrorism were very much intertwined with the conflict itself (see McGarry & O'Leary, 1999), leading to, in a sense, later counterterrorism strategies that involved a series of police reforms (see Independent Commission on Policing in Northern Ireland, 1999). Recently, the UK has also been subjected to "Al-Qaeda inspired" terrorism; the attempted suicide car bombing of Glasgow Airport on June 30, 2007, is but one example.

In Northern Ireland, while the researchers found the counterterrorism response impressive, they also found it was geared specifically toward the IRA and its splinter groups rather than a more general terrorist threat. For example, the PSNI Intelligence and Confidential Informant (CI) units are uniquely designed to hire, cultivate, maintain, and support the confidential informants, who constitute the backbone of the Intelligence Unit. After speaking with the trainers responsible for the CI training, the researchers found it to be a notable enterprise, capable of identifying, penetrating, and dismantling terrorist cells. However, this experience did not seem to translate into a fight against a global terrorist threat, as it appeared that little has been

---

[63] *Annual Report of An Garda Síochána* (2006), p. 17. http://www.garda.ie/statistics/Report2006/annualreport2006.pdf.

done to replicate what appears to be successful practices. Additionally, while coordination with MI5 was emphasized, in practice the local enforcement appeared to be a stand-alone enterprise. There appeared to be very little concern over an Islamic threat or the ties between the IRA and other global terrorist organizations, despite the acknowledgement of the issues.

With regard to the Metropolitan Police Service in London, the researchers interviewed relevant counterterrorism units in the MPS, including the Specialist Operations 13 (SO13) Branch, the Counter Terrorism Command (SO15),[64] and the Muslim Contact Unit. Interestingly relevant to the above discussion on community-based alternatives to countering terrorism was the activities of the Muslim Contact Unit (MCU), which was established to enhance communication between the London Police and the Muslim communities, modeled after the MPS's community policing outreach units. However, although the MPS appeared officially enthusiastic about this unit, it appeared from her observations with various community groups and the police service that there was a significant disconnect between the MCU, the police service more generally, and Muslim communities. A commanding officer from one of the MPS stations informed the researchers that a steady communication flow between these communities and the police had not been effectively established.

The researchers also found that intelligence gathering at the street level appears to suffer from the overlap in jurisdictions between the local police and the security services MI5, as the local police appeared to be under the impression that it was the main concern and responsibility of MI5 to gather such intelligence. Furthermore, there appeared to be a very limited, at best, exchange of information about potential threats between the MI5, SO13, and the rest of the local law enforcement. Efforts to facilitate internal exchange of information between the British police forces have resulted in the formation of a "Rainbow Unit." What appears to be missing is the connection between this unit and other security services that deal with terrorism, both locally and internationally, such as between MI5 and MI6. The research team's impression was that this is a very useful communication tool, but underutilized. One counterterrorism tactic of law enforcement agencies in the United Kingdom is recognized for is its widespread use of closed-circuit television technology (CCTV) to fight crime (see Norris & Armstrong, 1999; Welsh & Farrington, 2003), and more recently, terrorism. The researchers received access to the MPS Communication Center, which revealed over 2500 CCTV cameras located throughout London, constantly monitored by MPS personnel. However, as the effectiveness of this technology can vary by context and location (Welsh & Farrington, 2003), it remains to be seen whether such technology can also be an effective law enforcement tool for both responding to and preventing terrorism.

The researchers received a detailed overview of the Central Communications Complex (CCC), which was created during the early 1990s and has had many

---

[64]"[T]he new Counter Terrorism Command [SO15]. . . has taken over the roles and responsibilities of the Anti-Terrorist Branch [SO13] and Special Branch [SO12] and was launched on October 2, 2006." http://www.met.police.uk/so/counter_terrorism.htm.

official departmental titles during the course of its existence. In early 2001 it became DCC10 (4-3), reflecting its position within the Deputy Commissioner's Command (hence the DCC). It is also referred to as Central Communications. Also forming part of the Communications Branch are Special Operations Room (SOR) and Central Casualty Bureau (CCB), which open as the need arises. Dealing with the latter first, after a serious rail crash in London in 1957, it was felt that a central point was needed for telephone calls to be fielded from people concerned that a friend or relative may be involved in an incident where injuries and fatalities have occurred. CCB is such a point, and can be for incidents anywhere in the United Kingdom. Also, should an event of a similar nature happen abroad, with the possibility of UK nationals being involved, then CCB would open at the request of the Foreign and Commonwealth Office. Special Operations Room will open for the control of a spontaneous or preplanned event. The former would be a rail crash or a terrorist attack, for example. The latter would be such as marches, demonstrations, and ceremonial events.

In March 2002, Central Traffic Control integrated with IR and two different groups within CCC. These two groups were General Support, featuring the telephone call handling, and Operational Monitor, looking after matters affecting greater London, or Pan London as it is referred to, with regard to the radio channels and links with other services.

On January 6, 2003, two new traffic control rooms went live and all traffic control-related matters transferred from DCC10 (4-3) to these new complexes. Both are located in Victoria in Central London, managed by Transport for London (the traffic arm of the Greater London Authority) and are multiagency. Metrocomm, located in Buckingham Palace Road, near Victoria railway station, is the name of the room responsible for the control of traffic patrol units in London. The London Traffic Control Centre (LTCC), just around the corner in Ecclestone Place, is the new home of Area Traffic Control. Casualty Bureau has moved on, and in October 2003, it expanded into larger facilities on the site of the Metropolitan Police Training School, Peel Centre, Hendon. During the visit to the CCC, the researchers were told that the C3i project is driving the Metropolitan Police toward the next generation of communications, all the Borough control rooms of the Metropolitan Police will combine with CCC to provide three control centers, located in Lambeth, Hendon, and Bow, covering a third of London each. This three-center structure is called Metcall/Central Communications Command. The migration from CCC and Borough control rooms commenced in November 2004 and was about to become operational in 2007 (Brayson, 2005).

The impression from this site visit was that the CCC, and especially its CCTV cameras, can be of tremendous use in the aftermath of a terrorist event but not in the preventive stages. However, once the attack commenced such a technological advantage would allow the local police force to quickly close certain escape routes and monitor the crowd control operation, which in the event of another terrorist attack in a city like New York would definitely generate more panic than the one the city experienced during the 9/11 attack; therefore the CCTV technology could be the most valuable asset and life safer in the future. It was the team's view that this particular tool, which was originally put in place to prevent the traditional forms of criminality, could be very well used in its new capacity as one of the monitoring after-the-event developments on the ground and should be seriously considered by large metropolitan cities as one of Incident Management tools. The researchers were shown the specific room, where the London 2005 transit bombings were investigated, and the use of CCTV in this particular investigation was demonstrated and praised as an effective and important tool by the investigators involved.

On the ground level, the researchers also visited a number of police stations in the neighborhoods highly populated by the Muslim minorities. What they observed and what we were told by the local commanders were two different realities. While they were told by the law enforcement officials that they are fully integrated within their community as a legitimate law enforcement body that enjoys a full cooperation of the public they police, we observed very few minorities been actually on the staff of these police stations. Upon the researcher's inquiry if there are many minorities employed by the police, we received a rather amorphous answer of yes and no and the "participant observer" in us barely noticed any uniformed minority officers. However, the waiting area in one particular police station was populated, hugely, by various minority clients who seemed to constitute almost 100% of the population.

In another station, the researchers were given a colorful Power Point depicting the efforts of the local police to respond to the conspicuous activities around a certain Mosque; however, the officers in charge of these responses could not tell us how many minority members they have on the force. The authors of this report do not want to make a claim that in order to have a productive relationship with the community members, the force needs to be more representative of these minorities as the empirical research on this particular angle is inconclusive; however, given the sentiments expressed by members of one of our community focus groups (members of the Muslim Rights Association), who claimed that the local police are involved in a conspiracy to kill all the Muslims as per the training they (the Metropolitan Police Force) received from the Israeli Police force, one needs to wonder what needs to be done to counter these perceptions.

Overall, the perceptions from visiting the local police stations were that there is a disconnect between the law enforcement and the community based on a hugely dominant signs of foreign culture in the neighborhoods, like stores with foreign language signs only; a multitude of religious institutions, schools, and houses of prayer, with signs in foreign languages only; and the presence of people dressed in traditional garbs and attire that is very much removed from the traditional English fashion. It is not farfetched to say that the presence of specifically one police station in one of the neighborhoods, including the demographics of its officers, appeared like an occupying foreign force barricaded in a police compound and not like an office of a legitimate law enforcement government in the friendly or even neutral neighborhood. It was hard for the team to accept that the relationship with the local community is indeed friendly and open and based on trust and cooperation.

One of the aforementioned focus groups, even though composed of only few subjects, was particularly telling. As much as the researchers tried to create a comfortable atmosphere of verbal exchange, the research subjects resented the fact that one of the researchers is a woman and refused to shake hands with her. An important point to be noted here is that it is of tremendous significance to be able to identify the composition of the focus groups ahead of the meeting, with regard to possible biases toward the researchers. It would have been much more conducive to eliminate the unpleasant interaction by maybe having the female researcher not participating in this particular meeting. Even though it appears as a compromise of the research integrity, sometimes this sacrifice is worth taking in order to create a less combative environment of exchange.

In this particular example, the opinions expressed by the focus group members might have been also influenced by the fact that the female researcher was of an Israeli background and this, together with her background in law enforcement, might have created a threat to the internal validity of the encounter. However, based on the triangulation method of comparing the data from this focus group, with participant observation at the police station and the individual interviews of the members of the SO 13, we would like to suggest that there is indeed a significant disconnect between what the police think that it is doing to counter terrorist activities in the city of London and the minority groups that reside in its various neighborhoods.

4.4.1 Ireland Field Research

The research found that although the *Garda* was one of the best-trained police forces in Europe (Haberfeld, 2002), its level of preparedness against terrorism left much to be desired. There was no counterterrorism training provided to the patrol officers and specialized units focus primarily on the IRA or its splinter groups. At the academy where all of the *Garda* are trained, the need for a counterterrorism course for patrol officers was dismissed as premature and unnecessary. Additionally, there was much reluctance to merge the efforts directed against IRA-related activities with the efforts directed against the global terrorist threat, and the researchers were confronted with strong resistance when referring to the IRA and its factions as terrorists groups or connected with other terrorist organizations.

With regard to new threats from Al Qaeda, the Intelligence Unit of Dublin did not employ any Arabic-speaking officers, although researchers were assured that plans to attract some were "on the way." Despite the fact that the ranking officers of the Intelligence Units with whom they spoke were acutely aware of the problem of "open borders" and potential suspects landing in Ireland, there were no plans to create a unit that would monitor the problem and/or gather the possible intelligence. Although the researchers were told that the number of Muslims in Dublin increased rapidly during the recent years, there was, apparently, no response on the part of the *Garda*. It might be farfetched and too presumptuous to state that the increase in the Muslim population should equate with customized response by the local law enforcement, we would like to point to the fact that increase in any type of population in any area should generate some sort of a law enforcement reorganization, as the dynamic and the composition of the community change a law enforcement agency that polices the change must adjust accordingly. To some extent, Ireland appears to be suffering from the same myopic vision as their British counterparts prior to the July 7, 2005, London bombings, in trying to deal with "the threat of the devil that they know" without seeing "the devil on the horizon."

Disclaimer As a disclaimer, prior to the overview the countries that were visited and described based on the team's impressions, it is important to note that the original purpose of this study was to gather impressions and attitudes and training materials that would allow the researchers to create and disseminate training modules for law enforcement agencies in both the US and the countries involved in the research study. Due to this objective, the team committed itself to protect the identities of the individuals who were interviewed, in addition to limiting identifiable details about the specific units and members of the community. The researchers are aware that the information presented here in the Field Research Sections is therefore a more generalized and sanitized version than the one the reader would like to see, but the final format of this report is not the one the team collected the data for.

References

Brayson, J. (2005, October). Call Centre Support Team, DCC 10 (4-3), New Scotland Yard, London SW1H 0BG (Personal communication).

Bruce, S. (1992). The problems of 'pro-state' terrorism: Loyalist paramilitaries in Northern Ireland. *Terrorism and Political Violence, 4*(1), 67–88.

Clutterbuck, L. (2006). Countering Irish republican terrorism in Britain: Its origin as a police function. *Terrorism and Political Violence, 18*, 95–118.

Haberfeld, M.R. (2002). *Critical Issues in Police Training.* Upper Saddle River, NJ: Prentice Hall.

Horgan, J., & Taylor, M. (1999). Playing the 'green card' – Financing the provisional IRA: Part 1. *Terrorism and Political Violence, 11*(2), 1–38.

King, J. (2004). *The development of modern police history in the United Kingdom and the United States.* Lewiston, NY: The Edwin Mellen Press.

The Law Reform Commission (1985). *Report on offences under the Dublin police acts and related offences* (LRC 14 – 1985). Dublin.

Lee, M. (1971). *A history of police in England.* Montclair, NJ: Patterson Smith.

Lieberman, C. A. & Cheloukhine, S. (2009). 2005 London Bombings. In M. R. Haberfeld & A. von Hassel *A New Understanding of Terrorism: Case Studies, trajectories, and lessons learned* (pp. 189–204). New York, NY: Springer.

McGarry, J., & O'Leary, B. (1995). *Explaining Northern Ireland: Broken images.* Oxford: Blackwell Publishers.

McGarry, J. & O'Leary, B. (1999). *Policing Northern Ireland: Proposals for a new start.* Belfast: Blackstaff Press.

McKittrick, D., & McVea, D. (2001). *Making sense of the troubles.* London: Penguin Books.

Macfarlane, L. (1990). The right to self-determination in Ireland and the justification of IRA violence. *Terrorism and Political Violence, 2*, 35–53.

Norris, C., & Armstrong, G. (1999). *The maximum surveillance society: The rise of CCTV.* Oxford: Berg Publishing.

O'Loan, N. (2007, January 22). *Statement by the police ombudsman for Northern Ireland on her investigation into the circumstances surrounding the death of Raymond McCord Junior and related matters.* Belfast: Police Ombudsman for Northern Ireland. Retrieved from http://news.bbc.co.uk/2/shared/bsp/hi/pdfs/22_01_07_ballast.pdf.

Palmer, S. (1988). *Police and protest in England and Ireland, 1780–1850.* New York, NY: Cambridge University Press.

Smyth, J. (2002). Community policing and the reform of the Royal Ulster Constabulary. *Policing: An International Journal of Police Strategies & Management, 25*(1), 110–124.

Tonge, J. (2002). *Northern Ireland: Conflict and change* (2nd ed.). London: Longman.

Welsh, B. C., & Farrington, D. P. (2003). Effects of closed-circuit television on crime. *The Annals of the American Academy of Political and Social Science, 587*, 110–135.

Chapter 5
The Kingdom of the Netherlands (*Koninkrijk der Nederlanden*)

5.1 History

The modern history of the Netherlands dates back to 1579, when the Dutch United Provinces declared their independence from Spain. During the seventeenth century, the Netherlands became a leading seafaring and commercial power, with settlements and colonies around the world. After a 20-year French occupation, the Kingdom of the Netherlands was formed in 1815, which included the region, which is now Belgium, which seceded in 1830 and formed a separate kingdom. The Netherlands remained neutral in World War I but was invaded and occupied by Germany during World War II. Home to the International Courts of Justice[1] (ICJ) and the International Criminal Courts[2] (ICC) at the Hague, the Netherlands was also a founding member of the North Atlantic Treaty Organization (NATO) and the European Economic Community (EEC), which is now known as the European Union (EU), and participated in the introduction of the euro in 1999.[3]

The Kingdom of the Netherlands consists of the Netherlands in Western Europe, bordered by the North Sea, Germany and Belgium, and the Netherlands Antilles and Aruba in the Caribbean. With a population of approximately 16 million, the Netherlands is one of the most densely populated countries in the world, with an average of 459 people per square kilometer. The Netherlands is a constitutional monarchy that has Queen Beatrix acting as the head of state, with a parliamentary system in which the government is formed by the Sovereign and the ministers.[4]

The Netherlands is a coastal European country residing along the North Sea. It is located in the northwestern region of Europe, in-between Belgium and Germany. Approximately, half of the country's land is below sea level, in which the

---

[1] International Court of justice (ICJ). http://www.icj-cij.org/court/index.php?p1=1.

[2] International Criminal Court (ICC). http://www.icc-cpi.int/about.html.

[3] US Central Intelligence Agency (2008, June, 19). Netherlands. *The World Factbook*. https://www.cia.gov/library/publications/the-world-factbook/geos/nl.html.

[4] The Netherlands Ministry of Defence. http://www.mindef.nl/binaries/Facts%20and%20figures_tcm15-46659.pdf.

majority of the terrain is relatively flat.[5] The official name of the country is the Kingdom of the Netherlands, or *Koninkrijk der Nederlanden*. However, the Kingdom of the Netherlands is often used to describe not only this European country, but also the Netherlands Antilles and the island of Aruba as well.[6] The country's population is predominately Dutch, in which 83% of its residents is reported to be of Dutch origin and only 17% is of some other ethnic background. Some of the larger minority communities that consist of 9% of the 17% non-Dutch decedents found within the Netherlands population are Turks, Antilleans, Moroccans, Indonesians, and Surinamese. There are two official languages of this country: Dutch and Frisian. According to statistical findings, 41% of the population is reported to have no religious affiliation; however, of those who are religious, 31% is Roman Catholic, 15% is Dutch Reformed, 7% is Calvinist, 5.5% is Muslim, and 2.5% practices some other type of religion.[7]

Julius Caesar first discovered the region that is presently the Netherlands during the first century B.C. At that time, several Germanic tribes inhabited different portions of the land. This territory was occupied and ruled by many different powers throughout history, prior to the actual formation of the Netherlands and its eventual affirmation as a self-governing country.[8] The modern history of the Netherlands dates back to 1579, when the Dutch United Provinces declared their independence from Spain. However, the nation's independence was not completely ascertained until after the Thirty Years' War, which ended in 1648.[9] During the seventeenth century, the Netherlands became a leading seafaring and commercial power, with settlements and colonies around the world. After a 20-year French occupation, the Kingdom of the Netherlands was formed in 1815, including the region that is now Belgium, which seceded in 1830 to form a separate kingdom. The Netherlands remained neutral in World War I but was invaded and occupied by Germany during World War II. Home to the International Courts of Justice (ICJ) and the International Criminal Courts (ICC) at the Hague, the Netherlands was also a founding member of the North Atlantic Treaty Organization (NATO) and the European Economic Community (EEC), which is now known as the European Union (EU), and participated in the introduction of the euro in 1999.

The Netherlands is a constitutional monarchy that has a hereditary monarch acting as the head of state, with a parliamentary system. The national government consists of three main sections: the Monarch, the Council of Ministers, and the States General. The Netherlands' present monarch is Queen Beatrix, and although the role of the monarch has more of a ceremonial purpose within the country's

---

[5] Information Please Database (2007). *Netherlands*. http://www.infoplease.com/ipa/A0107824.html.

[6] US Department of State (2008, March). The Netherlands. *Bureau of European and Eurasian Affairs*. http://www.state.gov/r/pa/ei/bgn/3204.htm.

[7] US Central Intelligence Agency (2008, June 19). Netherlands. *The World Factbook*. https://www.cia.gov/library/publications/the-world-factbook/geos/nl.html.

[8] US Department of State (2008, March). The Netherlands. *Bureau of European and Eurasian Affairs*. http://www.state.gov/r/pa/ei/bgn/3204.htm.

[9] Tignor et al. (2002).

present-day society, they still have a considerable amount of power and influence within the government. There are also local governments throughout the country, which consists of 12 provinces. The 12 provinces are the first-level administrative divisions that are governed by a locally electrical provincial council as well as an appointed provincial executive.[10]

The country's legal system is based on the combination of civil law practices and French penal theory. There is no jury system within the Netherlands courts, and the administration of justice is delegated solely to judges.[11] Judges are appointed positions, in which, upon being selected, the duration of implementing such duties is lifelong; however, most judges retire at the age of 70. There are a total of 62 cantonal courts, 19 district courts, 5 courts of appeal, and a Supreme Court that has 24 justices.[12] The cantonal courts deal with minor civil and criminal cases. The district courts handle more important cases as well as hear appeals regarding decisions made by the cantonal courts. The five courts of appeal handle any petitions made against district court decisions. The Supreme Court's objective is to ensure consistent and appropriate application of the law throughout the country.[13]

The Netherlands supports the global alliance against terrorism and is a contributor to all 12 United Nations counterterrorism conventions. In 2004, the Netherlands government created a National Counterterrorism Coordinator's Office to restructure and improve Dutch counterterrorism efforts. The country has also donated financial funding as well as deployed troops to Iraq and Afghanistan, in an effort to support the battle against terrorism and assist in the termination of its existence.[14]

5.2 Terrorism

In regard to terrorist attacks, the Netherlands has not been victimized as frequently as many other Western European nations. However, the Netherlands has a history of terrorist attacks, including a number of incidents in the 1970s involving Moluccan nationalists. After the 1945 declaration of independence by Indonesia, formerly the Dutch East Indies, the Christian minority, who lived in the South Moluccan islands, proclaimed an independent Republic of the South Moluccas

---

[10]US Department of State (2008, March). The Netherlands. *Bureau of European and Eurasian Affairs.* http://www.state.gov/r/pa/ei/bgn/3204.htm.

[11]US Central Intelligence Agency (2008, June 19). Netherlands. *The World Factbook.* https://www.cia.gov/library/publications/the-world-factbook/geos/nl.html.

[12]US Department of State (2008, March). The Netherlands. *Bureau of European and Eurasian Affairs.* http://www.state.gov/r/pa/ei/bgn/3204.htm.

[13]Information Please Database (2007). *Netherlands.* http://www.infoplease.com/ipa/A0107824. html.

[14]US Department of State (2008, March). The Netherlands. *Bureau of European and Eurasian Affairs.* http://www.state.gov/r/pa/ei/bgn/3204.htm.

(RMS), *Republik Maluku Selatan*. However, Indonesian armed forces took control of the main island occupied by RMS and fought against the RMS guerilla war until the early 1960s, when the RMS president, Dr. Chris Soumokil, was captured and executed. The execution led to outrage and the first Moluccan action in the Netherlands, a 1966 Molotov cocktail attack against the Indonesian embassy in the Hague.

In 1951, approximately 12,500 Moluccans were relocated to the Netherlands, as a temporary solution, but most would never return. A number of high-profile terrorist attacks occurred during the 1970s. In 1970, 33 armed Moluccans forcibly entered and occupied the residence of the Indonesian ambassador in Wassenaar, during which a Dutch police officer was shot and killed. In 1975, seven armed Moluccans hijacked a Dutch train and took 57 people hostage, killing the engine driver. Both these incidents ended with the surrender of the attackers. However, in 1977, another hijacking of a train by nine armed Moluccans and the takeover of a school led by four armed Moluccans, which lasted 20 days, were ended by a tactical response by Dutch special antiterrorist forces, in which six terrorists and two hostages were killed.[15]

Following the 2004 public murder of the filmmaker Theo Van Gogh,[16] there has been an increase in the debate regarding the existing attitudes and practices toward minorities, specifically Muslim immigrants. Wilkinson (2005)[17] discusses Al Qaeda network building in the Netherlands, citing the murder of Theo Van Gogh as an example of linkages among extremists. The network detected subsequent to the Dutch police investigation linked the murderer to a larger cell of 15 extremists with links to the Al Qaeda movement. A June 6, 2008, Reuters article reported that Dutch police arrested a suspected Islamic militant from Pakistan, who was charged by Spain for planning terrorist attacks in Europe.[18] Commitment to the G-7 Action Plan designed to cut off funding from terrorist organizations has been strong. The reaction to the terrorist attacks on the United States on September 11, 2001,[19] brought together government ministers to form a steering committee, which, among other things, is focused on measures designed to prevent and prepare for attacks from weapons of mass destruction, such as nuclear, biological, or chemical attacks.[20]

According to Sinai (2008), the violent reaction by Dutch Muslims to the anti-Islamic documentary by controversial Dutch politician Geert Wilders further brought attention to the presence of radical Islamic movements in the Netherlands.[21]

---

[15] Janse (2005, pp. 56–61).

[16] BBC News. *Gunman kills Dutch film director*. http://news.bbc.co.uk/2/hi/europe/3974179.stm.

[17] Wilkinson (2005, pp. 22–23).

[18] Reuters. *Dutch seize suspect sought by Spain for attack plans*. http://www.reuters.com/article/latestCrisis/idUSL06913248.

[19] http://usinfo.state.gov/is/international_security/terrorism/sept_11.html.

[20] Rheinheimer (2007).

[21] Sinai (2008).

5.3 Law Enforcement

The Netherlands has a number of organizations that participate in counterterrorism, both at national and international levels. Among the many organizations and agencies involved are the Ministry of Defense, the Military Intelligence and Security Service, the Ministry of the Interior and Kingdom Relations, the General Intelligence and Security Service, the Dutch National Police Agency, and the Royal Netherlands *Marechaussee*.

The *Ministerie van Defense*, the Ministry of Defense, is responsible for the Dutch Armed Forces, the Military Intelligence and Security Service, and the Support Command. Currently the Ministry is headed by two politicians, a Minister of Defense and a State Secretary. The Chief of Defense Staff (CDS) is responsible for the execution of crisis management and humanitarian operations of the four branches of the Armed Forces: the Army, Navy, Air Force, and *Marechaussee*.

The Dutch Armed Forces have three main tasks: the defense of national and allied territory, including the Netherlands Antilles and Aruba; promoting the international rule of law and stability; and supporting and assisting civilian authorities in maintaining law and order, providing disaster relief and humanitarian aid, on a national and international scale. Over the past decades, Dutch military forces have participated in numerous international operations, including the Balkans, Afghanistan, Cambodia, and Iraq. The Dutch Marine Corps, which is part of the Navy, founded a Special Assistance Unit in 1973, *Bijzondre Bijstands Eenheid* (BBE), which was involved in the successful 1977 tactical response to the hostages being held by Moluccan terrorists.[22] The BBE can be brought into action at the request of the Ministry of Justice to combat terrorist activities. The Army Commando Corps has four special-forces units, one of which is designed for deployment as a counterterrorism unit.[23]

The *Militaire Inlichtinge-en Veiligheidsdienst*[24] (MIVD), the Military Intelligence and Security Service, assists the armed forces with important information concerning the viability and proper procedure for various missions abroad. Recently, MIVD has cooperated with *Algemene Inlichtingen-en Veiligheidsdienst* (AIVD) to frustrate terrorist ambitions that threaten Dutch security. Although the current focus of MIVD has been on tracking, monitoring, and disrupting radical Islamist groups prone to violence, other responsibilities include: collecting information about military forces in other countries, collecting information about areas where Dutch troops would be stationed, investigating problems involving officers of the Dutch Armed Forces, collecting information to prevent any harm

---

[22]Janse (2005); http://news.bbc.co.uk/onthisday/hi/dates/stories/may/23/newsid_2503000/2503933.stm; http://www.time.com/time/magazine/article/0,9171,915035,00.html.

[23]The Netherlands Ministry of Defence. http://www.mindef.nl/binaries/Facts%20and%20figures_tcm15-46659.pdf.

[24]Rheinheimer (2007).

to the army, counterespionage, and other military subjects as determined by the government.[25]

The *Ministerie van Binnenlandse Zaken en Koninkrijksrelaties*[26] (BZK), the Ministry of the Interior and Kingdom Relations, is one of the 13 ministries of Dutch central government. BZK is responsible for a wide range of tasks: to uphold the Constitution, guarantee the democratic rule of law, ensure an effective and efficient public administration, coordinate urban policy, promote public order and safety and provide centralized management of the countries police forces, promote the quality of the civil service and coordinate management and personnel policy for all civil servants, and coordinate cooperation with Aruba and the Netherlands Antilles. In addition, BZK developed the Integrated Emergency Center System to facilitate cooperation between various agencies responsible for managing terrorist threats.[27]

The *Algemene Inlichtingen-en Veiligheidsdienst* (AIVD), the General Intelligence and Security Service, is a domestic agency. The primary focus of AVID since the terrorist attacks on the United States on September 11, 2001, has been on radical Islamist networks both in the Netherlands and internationally. AIVD has increased its budget for counterterrorism and laid out a framework for cooperation with military intelligence approved in 2005. In addition to its focus on Islamist terrorist networks, the AIVD also focuses on other terrorist groups in the Netherlands, including the Turkish parties DHKP/C and MLKP-FESK, the Kurdish Kongra-Gel, the Lebanese Hezbollah, the ETA, the IRA, and the Communist Party of the Philippines.[28]

> As a follow-up to the Action Plan for Counter-terrorism that was initiated in 2001, the government again took certain measures in order to improve the combat of terrorism. In some cases these measures triggered debate, because they involve a tension between the protection of constitutional freedoms and enhancement of security. The Minister of the Interior and Kingdom Relations gave a full explanation of the Cabinet's considerations concerning this dilemma in the Second Chamber (Dutch Lower House of Parliament), referring to the memorandum form the Minister of Administrative Reform and Kingdom Relations on constitutional rights in a multiform society.

> The measures include the penalising of recruitment of persons for the jihad. In addition, a legislative proposal by the Minister of Justice to allow the use of AIVD information as evidence in criminal proceedings is now being examined in Parliament. The measures add significance to AIVD information in relation to the tracing and prosecution of persons involved in terrorism. There was a sharp rise in the number of official reports presented by the AIVD to the Public Prosecutions Department in 2004.

> However, the AIVD's efforts are still primarily aimed at gaining insight into current threats for early warning purposes, even if no offence has been committed yet. After all, obtaining information about the preparation of terrorist activities is a crucial part of counter-terrorism,

---

[25] Answers.com. *Intelligence Encyclopedia: Netherlands, Intelligence and Security.* http://www.answers.com/topic/military-intelligence-and-security-service-netherlands.

[26] The Netherlands Ministry of the Interior and Kingdom Relations (BZK). http://www.minbzk.nl/bzk2006uk/.

[27] Rheinheimer (2007, p. 22).

[28] General Intelligence and Security Service, 2004. http://www.fas.org/irp/world/netherlands/aivd2004-eng.pdf.

because it enables the timely frustration of these activities. It was this idea on which the government's decision of April 2004 was based to intensify the monitoring of persons who can in any way be associated with terrorist activities or support to such activities. This has led to a new collaborative structure between the AIVD, the National Police Agency, the Immigration and Naturalisation Service, the Public Prosecutions Department and later also the Defence Intelligence and Security Service. Within this structure, which is referred to as CT (counter-terrorism) Infobox, the information about relevant persons gathered by the various participants is collated as a basis for discussing a possible follow-up.

In September the government announced a new organisational structure for its anti-terrorism policy. A National Counter-terrorism Co-ordinator (Dutch abbreviation NCTb) was appointed, who was to play a co-ordinating role under the responsibility of the Minister of the Interior and Kingdom Relations and the Minister of Justice. The NCTb started his activities on 1 January 2005. The AIVD provides the NCTb with information on both the general threat situation and specific security risks posed to persons, property and services.

Early in 2005 the Minister of Justice and the Minister of the Interior and Kingdom Relations again announced some new, mainly administrative, measures to constrain the activities of persons associated with terrorism.

During the Dutch presidency of the European Union in the second half of 2004, the Netherlands initiated a number of arrangements to improve the European co-operation between intelligence and security services. One of these initiatives was the reinforcement of the Situation Centre, the European co-operative structure within which representatives of European intelligence and security services assemble information and analyses from the services.[29]

The *Politie*, the Dutch National Police Agency, comprised of over 40,000 men and women, is divided into 26 subdivisions based on population size, geographical area, and history of crime. Its National Criminal Intelligence Service works with both Europol and Interpol to track criminal and terrorist activity. Regional divisions are controlled by a police board of local mayors and constables. The *Politie* collaborate with a separate prosecutor's office to ensure the fair implementation of national laws and compliance with procedural rules.[30]

The core tasks of the *Politie* include patrolling the streets and other public places, maintaining public order, investigating criminal offences, and providing assistance in emergencies.[31] Basic units will be responsible for: daily patrols by car, motorcycle, bicycle, on foot, and sometimes on horseback; providing emergency assistance; recording offences reported to the police; keeping in touch with the public and with businesses and institutions, neighborhood associations, and other interest groups; mediating in disputes and providing other forms of assistance; carrying out criminal investigations; preventing crime, for example, by providing advice on burglary prevention; road traffic policing, e.g., conducting vehicle inspections, investigating road accidents, and proposing traffic measures; enforcing the environmental laws; and monitoring observance of statutes such as the Licensing and Catering Act, the Weapons and Ammunition Act, the Betting and Gaming Act, the Shop Trading Hours Act, and the Fisheries Act.[32]

---

[29]General Intelligence and Security Service (2004, pp. 10–11).

[30]Rheinheimer (2007, p. 22).

[31]*Policing in the Netherlands*, p. 11.

[32]*Policing in the Netherlands*, p. 14.

Specialist functions of the *Politie* include: regional crime investigations, investigations in such diverse crimes as drugs trafficking, trafficking in humans, trafficking in arms, fraud, large-scale environmental crimes, and sexual offences; information control, including collecting and processing technical information and information on criminal organizations; immigration services, including regulating the stay of non-Dutch nationals and exercising relevant supervision; and operational supportive tasks for other specialized units, such as the Mounted Police, Canine Units, Riot Police, Computer Crime Units, Special Weapons and Tactics (SWAT) Units, Observation Units, Environmental Teams, and Juvenile and Vice Squads. Special Support Units of the police are called in to deal with hostage taking and acts of terrorism. These units are composed of police officers and the Dutch Armed Forces, such as the specialized personnel from the Marines and Army. These Special Support Units have received highly specialized training for dealing with special situations such as aircraft hijackings and hostage taking. The armed forces and the Royal Military Constabulary also have special support units.[33]

The Royal Netherlands *Marechaussee*[34] is a police organization with military status, comprised of approximately 6400 members. The *Marechaussee* has a wide range of tasks, both civil and military, including carrying out police, security, and courier services for the armed forces; the protection of complexes managed by the *Ministerie van Defense*, places that fall under the Protection of State Secrets Act, and the Royal House; and acting as an organ of the National Police.

5.4 Field Research

The research team interviewed officers in the Aliens Police, the unit of the police force charged to "supervise foreign nationals, with a focus on criminal activity, antisocial behavior, illegal aliens, and the prevention of abuse and exploitation of immigrants."[35] The researchers found that there was an overwhelming feeling among those officers of a lack of preparedness for what was believed to be a real and growing problem of illegal immigrants who are released to the public, after the initial detention, and disappear without a trace into the Muslim communities, some of them display extreme orientation while incarcerated and are perceived by the police as a real terrorist threat. The researchers were told that there were no mechanisms in place that could familiarize local police officers with current terrorism-related issues and that the legal system was not effective in preventing illegal intrusion into the country. Some of the illegal immigrants display extreme attitudes during the detention period and are definitely perceived as a terrorist threat. Additionally, they found no intelligence-gathering efforts at the local level, or counterterrorism training for beat officers or for the Alien Police, who are believed to have the best access to possible sources of intelligence in immigrant communities. As explained above,

---

[33] Netherlands Police [Politie]. http://www.politie.nl/English/.

[34] *The Netherlands Ministry of Defence*. http://www.mindef.nl/binaries/kmar_tcm15-23067.pdf.

[35] Ministry of the Interior and Kingdom Relations (2004, pp. 20–21).

some of the illegal immigrants, detained by the Alien Police, are definitely perceived as a terrorist threat as they display violent attitudes and behaviors while in custody.

The researchers were also able to interview members of the special police unit Korps Landelijke Politie Diensten-Dienst Speciale Interventies (National Police Agency-Service Special Interventions, antiterrorist unit) as well as members of the Police Academy. From the operational standpoint, it was very interesting to see the development of a special counterterrorist unit that was an amalgamation of the local law enforcement and the Dutch Royal Marines. The operational hurdles of having the military working in the same unit with the police were something the authors tried to explore but were met with a rather unclear response, as the unit was not yet tested in the field. The idea for the creation of such a unit came from a college professor who was specifically hired to identify the best possible response to a terrorist incident, and based on his research the unit was created. What was rather amazing was the involvement of a college professor in operational/tactical decisions and the acceptance of his recommendation by the local law enforcement. The inclusion of college professors (with a social science background and not specialist in weapons of mass destruction) in operational deliberations of various law enforcement agencies is a rather novice concept with regard to the topic of counterterrorism and certainly one that could be recommended to other police agencies, regardless of the feasibility of implementation of this specific unit.

From the interviews with the officers in charge of training, it was quite obvious that the need for a revised or innovative training for the foot patrol, with regard to counterterrorist activities, was not yet identified as a major priority. As the Dutch police have an overall very extensive and well-developed specialist training that could serve as a model for many other police agencies (Haberfeld, 2002), it was rather disappointing to discover that the need for a new approach in utilizing the patrol force in a different capacity, as the ones who can potentially gather more intelligence than the specially designated units, was not considered as a viable option. The disconnect between the need to gather intelligence and the lack of preparedness from the training standpoint might have had something to do with the political rather than strictly operational orientation.

As the team was not able to go back to Holland to interview the community members, due to the stop put on the research funds, the researchers were not able to explore the attitudes of the local communities toward the forces that police them. The overall sense was that, given the fact that the Dutch Police have a specialized local unit, the Alien Police that deals with various minority related problems, there is a definite need to assess the role of this unit in a multicultural society. The minority group might become the majority of the community members of the city of Amsterdam in the very near future. The problems inherent in being treated as an 'alien' when your particular minority group represents approximately half the population of the capital city should not be ignored and left to fester without proper attention given to the feelings of the community members referred to as "aliens." Although the Alien Police handle the illegal aliens only, many of them have the direct ties to the legal community members and the way they are treated is definitely not without consequences as far as the legal residents and their attitudes toward police are concerned.

References

Blok, C. (2004). *Policing in the Netherlands*. Amsterdam: Ministry of the Interior and Kingdom Relations. Retrieved from http://www.politie.nl/ImagesLandelijk/politie%20in%20nederland%20engels_tcm31-85725.pdf

General Intelligence and Security Service (AIVD). (2004, June). *Annual report 2004: General intelligence and security service*. The Hague: General Intelligence and Security Service Communications Department. Retrieved from http://www.fas.org/irp/world/netherlands/aivd2004-eng.pdf

Janse, R. (2005). Fighting terrorism in the Netherlands: A historical perspective. *Utrecht Law Review*, *1*(1), 55–67. Retrieved from http://www.utrechtlawreview.org/publish/articles/000004/article.pdf

Ministry of Defence (2004). *The Netherlands Ministry of Defence: Facts and figures on Dutch security policy and the armed forces*. Ministry of Defence, Directorate of general information. Retrieved from www.defensie.nl

Ministry of the Interior and Kingdom Relations (2004). *From dawa to jihad: The various threats from radical Islam to the democratic legal order*. General Intelligence and Security Service. Retrieved from www.aivd.nl

Ministry of the Interior and Kingdom Relations (2006). *Violent jihad in the Netherlands: Current trends in the Islamist terrorist threat*. General Intelligence and Security Service. Retrieved from www.aivd.nl

Rheinheimer, F. (2007). *Counterterrorism in the European Union: A who's who of the agencies involved*. Brussels: World Security Institute Center for Defense Information. Retrieved from http://www.cdi.org/PDFs/EU%20Counterterrorism%20Francis%20Rheinheimer.pdf

Sinai, J. (2008). Terrorism and the Netherlands: The threat and the response. *Journal of Counterterrorism and Homeland Security International*, *14*(2), 38–43.

Tignor, R., Adelman, J., Aron, S., Kotkin, S., Marchand, S., Prakash, G., et al. (2002). *Worlds together worlds apart: A history of the modern world from the Mongol Empire to the present* (pp. 154–155). New York, NY: W. W. Norton & Company, Inc.

Wilkinson, P. (2005). International terrorism: the changing threat and the EU's response. EU-ISS Chaillot Paper no. 84, October 2005.

Chapter 6
The Kingdom of Spain (*Rieno de España*)

6.1 History

Spain is located in the southwestern region of Europe on the Iberian Peninsula and resides between the countries Portugal and France. The official name of Spain is the Kingdom of Spain or Reino de España.[1] Spain's population density is lower than the majority of European countries, although it is one of the larger countries in terms of size.[2] Over 40 million people are estimated to reside within the country. Spain's population consists of both Mediterranean and Nordic-type ethnic groups, more specifically Basques, Catalans, and Galicians. The official language of the country is Spanish, in which 74% of the population speaks it fluently as their first language; however, Catalan, Galician, and Basque are also spoken. Roman Catholicism is the main religion within Spain, in which approximately 94% of the population claims it as their religious affiliation, and a total of 6% of individuals associate themselves with some other religion, such as Protestant or Islam.[3]

Spain is one of the oldest nation states in Europe. The history of Spain can be traced back to the fifth century AD, when the Visigoths established a Germanic successor state in the former Roman diocese of Hispania. The borders of Spain were established through the union between Ferdinand of Aragon and Isabella of Castile in 1469, as the Muslim-controlled lands in the south were subjected to Spanish rule. During the rule of Ferdinand and Isabella, in 1478, the Inquisition, led by the infamous Tomas de Torquemada, enforced religious practices and the sincerity of conversions to Christianity. In the sixteenth century, Spain was one of the premiere European powers and remained involved in international affairs through the eighteenth century, but recurrent political instability, military intervention in politics, frequent breakdowns of civil order, and periods of repressive government led to

---

[1] Information Please Database, *Spain*. http://www.infoplease.com/ipa/A0107987.html.

[2] US Department of State, *Bureau of European and Eurasian Affairs (January 2008) – Spain*. http://www.state.gov/r/pa/ei/bgn/2878.htm.

[3] US Central Intelligence Agency, *World Factbook – Spain*. https://www.cia.gov/library/publications/the-world-factbook/geos/sp.html.

Spain losing power and influence, despite having a constitutional framework similar to the British.

The 1923 military coup that removed King Alfonso XIII did not adequately fill the power vacuum and led to the Spanish Civil War (1936–1939) and more than half a million deaths in Spain. The Nationalist victory led to Franco's authoritarian regime, during which the Franco's semi-fascist regime implemented repressive government tactics that led to the formation of resistance groups that used violence against the governmental forces. After Franco's death in 1975, Prince Juan Carlos took the oath as king of Spain, which led to Spain becoming a parliamentary monarchy.

Spain's government consists of a hereditary monarch, a bicameral parliament, and the Cortes General, which is also known as the General Courts. Executive power is shared among the chief of state, the head of government, and the Council of Ministers, which are designated by the president. The legislature, known as Cortes Generales, consists of two chambers: the lower and upper chambers. The lower chamber comprises the Congress of Deputies, also known as Congreso de los Diputados, and the upper chamber contains the Senate, which is often referred to as Senado. The majority of power lies within the lower chamber, among the 350 members who make up the Congress of Deputies. The judicial system is independent of the other two branches of government. There are a number of different levels and type of courts within Spain's justice system.[4] The highest and most powerful level contains the Supreme Court, which is also known as Tribunal Supremo. The legal system that is utilized within Spain consists of civil law concepts with regional applications.[5]

> Spain's powerful world empire of the 16th and 17th centuries ultimately yielded command of the seas to England. Subsequent failure to embrace the mercantile and industrial revolutions caused the country to fall behind Britain, France, and Germany in economic and political power. Spain remained neutral in World Wars I and II but suffered through a devastating civil war (1936–39). A peaceful transition to democracy following the death of dictator Francisco FRANCO in 1975, and rapid economic modernization (Spain joined the EU in 1986) have given Spain one of the most dynamic economies in Europe and made it a global champion of freedom. Continuing challenges include Basque Fatherland and Liberty (ETA) terrorism and relatively high unemployment.[6]

6.2 Terrorism

Terrorism has been of public concern within the country of Spain for many years. The terrorist group Basque Fatherland and Liberty, often referred to as ETA, has been a major contributor to such threat within the country, since the organization

---

[4]Encyclopedia Britannica, *Spain*. http://www.britannica.com/eb/article-9108580/Spain.

[5]US Central Intelligence Agency, *World Factbook – Spain*. https://www.cia.gov/library/publications/the-world-factbook/geos/sp.html.

[6]US CIA World Factbook, *Spain*. https://www.cia.gov/cia/publications/factbook/geos/sp.html.

was first established in 1959.[7] The ETA's main targets for their violent attacks are Spanish security forces, military personnel, Spanish government officials, and politicians of the Popular and Socialist Parties. Over the years, the government of Spain has been involved in long and ongoing efforts to develop preventative antiterrorist measures against groups such as the ETA. Both legislative and procedural changes have been made as a response to the threat of terrorism. In 1975, legislation was passed dedicated to the Prevention of Terrorism, which introduced antiterrorist laws within the country. In 1985, Spain became a full member of the Terrorism, Radicalism, Extremism, and political Violence Group (TREVI). The group was established to exchange information and develop strategies in an effort to prevent and terminate terrorism.[8]

However, Alvanou (2007), a senior advisor at the Research Institute for European and American Studies (RIEAS), writes that Spain treats terrorism as an aggravated form of crime.[9] Although the penal code states that an act constitutes a terrorist act where the purpose of the act is to subvert the constitutional order or to effect serious disturbances of public order, Spain does not have specific antiterrorism laws. However, in terrorist cases, judges may order suspects be held incommunicado if they believe that knowledge of the detention would prejudice the investigation, such that relatives would not be informed and legal assistance would be provided by the court instead of the suspect having the choice of counsel. In addition, judges may impose secrecy, known as *secreto de sumario*, on an investigation and judicial proceedings, either in whole or in part, in which defense attorneys may not have access to all the evidence used to prosecute a defendant.[10]

Terrorism has been a major issue in Spain since the time of the Franco regime, whose repressive tactics led to the foundation of resistance groups, such as the *Euskadi ta Askatasuna*[11] (ETA), which means Basque Fatherland and Liberty in the Basque language. ETA, which embraced radical Marxist ideologies, was formed in 1959 and began a campaign of bombings in several cities in Spain. The goal of ETA was to form an autonomous Basque state, as the 1978 constitution designated an autonomous Basque region with responsibility for education, health care, policing, and taxation. The Spanish government continues to oppose an independent Basque homeland and has labeled ETA as terrorists.

Grupo de Resistencia Anti-Fascista Primero de Octubre, commonly known as GRAPO, is an urban terrorist group that seeks to overthrow the Spanish Government and establish a Marxist state. It opposes Spanish participation in NATO and US presence in Spain and has a long history of assassinations, bombings, bank robberies, and kidnappings mostly against Spanish interests during the 1970s and 1980s.

---

[7] Alonso and Reinares (2005).

[8] Jimenez (1992).

[9] Alvanou (2007).

[10] UK Secretary of State for Foreign and Commonwealth Affairs (2005).

[11] Council on Foreign Relations. *Basque Fatherland and Liberty (ETA)*. http://www.cfr.org/publication/9271/.

Following the September 11 attacks against the United States, GRAPO publicly supported the airplane attacks in New York and Washington, D.C. GRAPO has appeared increasingly weak over the past decade and, in July 2003, GRAPO's leader was sentenced to 10 years in prison.[12]

The *Grupo Antiterrorista de Liberacion* (GAL), the Antiterrorist Liberation Group, was founded in the 1980s during the Socialist Party administration (PSOE) and operated between 1983 and 1987. GAL was the right-wing force, often referred to as death squads, which began a campaign of revenge killings and bombings among suspected ETA terrorists, primarily in France. More than a third of the people killed by the GAL death squads were alleged to have no connection to ETA. Both agents from *Centro Superior de Informacion de la Defensa* (CESID), the Spanish military intelligence organization, and *La Guardia Civil*, the Civil Guard, were alleged to have been involved in GAL. In the late 1980s, two senior policemen were arrested and later convicted of recruiting hit men and funding GAL attacks. After serving part of their sentences, they provided more information about police involvement. The trial established that GAL was financed by secret funds from the Interior Ministry. The tactics of GAL included kidnapping and murder or assassination. The target of GAL consisted of suspected ETA members and supporters.[13]

After the March 11, 2004, attacks on the Madrid transit system, the focus on separatist or nationalist acts of violence has shifted to the threat from Islamic fundamentalists.[14] Although a purported spokesperson for Al Qaeda claimed responsibility in a videotape that was recovered 3 days after the incident, the extent of coordination and cooperation among the individuals involved remains uncertain.[15] Governmental agencies in Spain continue to investigate the presence and influence of Al Qaeda in Spain, specifically in the areas where the majority of Muslims reside, which is primarily in Southern Spain.

Spanish security officials continue to worry that members of al-Qaeda will take advantage of the clandestine immigration pipeline route by inserting terrorists to make their way to either the enclaves or to the Spanish mainland. To this regard, the Directorate General of National police recently advertised 357 posts for anti-terrorist officers to monitor potential Islamists in areas where the presence of Muslim immigrants is well known, such as Melilla, Ceuta, Granada, Malaga and Alicante.[16]

On February 27, 2008, ABC News reported that a Spanish court convicted 20 out of 30 Islamic radicals of belonging to a terrorist group, but acquitted them of planning to blow up the courthouse, judicial sources said. The 30 individuals were arrested in 2004, subsequent to the Madrid train bombings, and were charged with

---

[12] Haahr (2006).

[13] Woodworth (2001); BBC News (1998, July 9). *Ex-minister jailed in 'dirty war' scandal*; BBC News (1998, July 29). *Spain's state sponsored death squads.*

[14] For a more in-depth understanding of the March 11, 2004 attacks, see Lieberman & Bucht (2009).

[15] BBC News (2004, April 28). *Timeline: Madrid investigation.*

[16] Haahr (2006).

belonging to an Al Qaeda cell that was planning to conduct a terrorist attack.[17] On March 7, 2008, the International Herald Tribune reported that a gunman, suspected of belonging to the Basque militant group, ETA, shot and killed a local politician in Northern Spain.[18]

Haahr-Escolano (2004) predicts that the future threat of terrorism in Spain will be rooted in Islamic fundamentalism, specifically emanating from North Africa. "The role of Algerian Islamists in both the March 11 attacks and the National Court terrorist planning suggests that Spain has become a new locus of operations for North-African based al-Qaeda terrorism."[19] Salafi groups have operated in North Africa, specifically Algeria, Tunisia, and Morocco, for many years and have the potential to reach out to associates in Spain for assistance in the planning, preparation, and execution of terrorist attacks. Citing the EFE News Agency, Haahr-Escolano (2004) stated that, as an example of the potential threat, approximately a third of the mosques in Madrid have some connection to radical Islamic groups or Moroccan extremists. Algeria, Tunisia, and Morocco form a rear base for Al Qaeda, which the Spanish government will need to address in order to prevent or deter future terrorism from groups associated with Islamic fundamentalism.

6.3 Law Enforcement

Spain's armed forces are controlled by the *Ministero de Defensa de España*[20] (MDE), the Defense Ministry of Spain. The armed forces include the Army, *Ejército de Tierra*,[21] the navy, *Armada*,[22] and the Air Force, *Ejército del Aire*.[23]

In addition, the *Centro National de Inteligencia*[24] (CNI), the National Intelligence Center, which is structurally attached to the MDE, is the organization responsible for providing the Prime Minister and the Government with information, analyses, studies, or proposals that allow for the prevention and avoidance of any danger, threat, or aggression against the independence or territorial integrity of Spain, and its national interests. CNI, whose members are not law enforcement agents, is a support body that collects and disseminates information, which may be classified as top secret, secret, or classified.

---

[17] ABC News: *Spain court convicts 20 radicals of terrorism charges.* http://www.abc.net.au/news/stories/2008/02/27/2174682.htm.

[18] International Herald tribune: *Terrorism again intrudes as Spain heads to the polls.* http://www.iht.com/articles/2008/03/07/europe/spain.php.

[19] Haahr-Escolano (2004).

[20] Ministerio de Defense de Espana. http://www.mde.es/Home.

[21] Ministerio de Defense: Army. http://www.ejercito.mde.es/ingles/inicio.htm.

[22] Ministerio de Defense: *Armada Espana* [Navy]. http://www.armada.mde.es/.

[23] *Ejército del Aire* [Air force]. http://www.ejercit-odelaire.mde.es/WebEA/static/ServContenidos?id=home.

[24] Ministerio de Defense: *Centro National Intelligencia.* http://www.cni.es/castellano/index.html.

The Commission investigating the March 11, 2004 terrorist attacks in Madrid recently concluded that since the late 1990s, foreign radical Islamists have been using Spain for jihadist activities in support of al-Qaeda's terrorist operations, particularly al-Zarqawi's anti-Coalition attacks in Iraq. On-going counter-terrorism investigations reveal that Salafist Islamists traveled to Spain in the late 1990s to early 2000s to organize a network of cells for recruiting suicide bombers for operations in Iraq, Bosnia, and elsewhere and, for terrorist training in al-Qaeda camps in Afghanistan and Indonesia. These foreign jihadists played a significant role in creating and organizing the cells that were involved in 9/11, conducted the Madrid attacks (11-M), and planned to bomb the National High Court. Moreover, the National Center of Intelligence (NCI) has identified numerous Muslim immigrants who have recently left Spain to join the insurgency in Iraq.[25]

In 1986, the *Ministero del Interior*,[26] the Interior Ministry, was assigned responsibility for operational matters, pay, assignments, accommodations, and equipment for *La Guardia Civil*, the Civil Guard. "In addition to its rural police functions, the Civil Guard was to be responsible for firearms and explosives control; traffic policing on interurban roads; protection of communication routes, coasts, frontiers, ports, and airports; enforcement of environmental and conservation laws, including those governing hunting and fishing; and interurban transport of prisoners."[27]

La Guardia Civil, the Civil Guard, is a police force that was formed in 1844 and patterned after the French rural gendarmerie. Until 1986, *La Guardia Civil* had been led by an army lieutenant general but now has a civilian director. *La Guardia Civil*, which has more than 70,000 members, contains many subunits that perform specialized functions. Among these units are the *Unidad Especial de Intervencion*, the *Técnicos Especialistas en Desactivación de Artefactos Explosivos*, the *Unidad de Accion Rural*, and the *Guardia Civil del Mar*.

The *Unidad Especial de Intervencion*[28] (UEI), the Special Intervention Unit, is responsible for the following functions: to neutralize situations involving hostages or kidnappings; to respond to situations that involve specific types of dangerous individuals, such as members of terrorist organizations, organized drug traffickers, and in exceptional cases the mentally unbalanced or unstable; to protect the dignitaries and other VIPs; and to respond to criminal activity that requires the specialized expertise of the UEI.

The *Técnicos Especialistas en Desactivación de Artefactos Explosivos*[29] (TEDAX), the Explosive Artifacts Defuser Specialised Technicians, are responsible for the neutralization, decontamination, and intervention of explosive, incendiary, radiological, biological, and nuclear (*explosiva, incendiaria, radiológica, bacteriológica o química*) devices. Also known as the *Servicio de Desactivación de*

---

[25] Haahr-Escolano (2004).

[26] Ministerio del Interior.http://www.mir.es/.

[27] Global Security.org. *Civil Guard*. http://www.globalsecurity.org/intell/world/spain/guard.htm.

[28] Ministerio del interior. *Guardia Civil*. http://www.guardiacivil.org/quesomos/organizacion/operaciones/uespeciales/uei/index.jsp.

[29] Ministerio del interior. *Guardia Civil, Servicio de Desactivación de Explosivos (SEDEX)*. http://www.guardiacivil.org/quesomos/organizacion/operaciones/uespeciales/tedax/index.jsp.

Explosivos[30] (SEDEX), TEDAX was created in 1975 in response to the increasing number of bombing attacks from groups, such as ETA. Since its inception, it has been used as an important tool in Spain's counterterrorism measures. TEDAX has participated in both national and international operations. The *Unidad de Accion Rural*[31] (UAR), the Rural Action Unit, is a specialized unit in the fight against terrorist elements, as well as for other high-risk operations. The *Guardia Civil del Mar* is responsible for Seashore surveillance and security of ports and harbors.

The *Cuerpo Nacional de Policia*[32] the National Police Corps, is the police force that operates primarily in urban areas. It is also controlled by the *Ministero del Interior*. Under the Statutes of Autonomy (1979), the certain regions were granted authority to form their own regional police forces. However, only three of the Autonomous Communities, the Basque Country, Catalonia, and Navarra have set up their own police forces.[33] The police agency for the Basque region is known as *Ertzaintza*[34] the police agency for Catalonia is known as *Mossos d'Esquadra*,[35] and the police agency for Navarra is known as *Policía Foral*. A Security Policy Council was established at the national level to ensure proper coordination between the new regional forces so that these police forces can communicate and cooperate with both *La Guardia Civil* and *Cuerpo Nacional de Policia*.

Other enforcement agencies that also contribute to maintaining the safety of Spain are the *Servicio de Protección de la Naturaleza* (SEPRONA), the Nature Protection Service, which is responsible for environmental protection, and the *Servicio de Vigilancia Aduanera*, the Customs Police.

6.4 Field Research

In their interactions with this law enforcement apparatus, the researchers found that the police forces were first and foremost concerned with the local threat of ETA and not necessarily a broader, global Islamic-based terrorist threat. Participation in the European Task Forces against terrorism was minimal and did not translate into specialized training or the creation of an intelligence apparatus. Similar to Northern Ireland, decades of enforcement against the local threat were not translated into preparedness against the more recent Islamic fundamentalist threat. In larger cities the local law enforcement also played a role; however, from what was learned from interviews with the police in Madrid, this role was more supportive and certainly

---

[30] Ministerio del Interior. http://www.guardiacivil.org/index.jsp.

[31] Ministerio del Interior. http://www.guardiacivil.org/index.jsp.

[32] US Library of Congress Studies.Spain: National Police Corps. http://lcweb2.loc.gov/cgi-bin/query/r?frd/cstdy:@field(DOCID+es0177).

[33] US Library of Congress Studies. *Spain: Other Police Forces*. http://lcweb2.loc.gov/cgi-bin/query/r?frd/cstdy:@field(DOCID+es0178).

[34] The police force from the Basque country.http://www.ertzaintza.net/ingles/html/home.html

[35] Policia de la Generalitat de Catalunya. http://www.gencat.net/mossos/.

not taken into serious consideration. The local police force in the Basque country determines, even further, the very myopic orientation looking at the terrorist threat as a very narrowly defined problem caused by the local terrorists, who are independent in their operations and have no ties to international terrorist groups. Even subsequent to the 2004 Madrid bombings, the realization of the new challenge was somewhat limited.

The lack of training and preparedness at the local level reflected this culture of ignoring the role of the local police in countering terrorism. Informal interviews of the Policia National, in charge of their Community Policing Units, led to the conclusion by researchers that the outreach performed by these units was geared toward other, nonterrorism, criminal activities and little interaction was taken with local municipal police forces with regard to ETA. This despite findings by the researchers, from conversations with the Madrid Municipal police force, that local beat officers were very much aware of the extreme sentiments against the Spanish government and the "West" harbored by local Muslims. However, there are no mechanisms in place to channel this information to the National Police or the Civil Guard. One officer mentioned that he felt it was already "too late" to stop the threat, and each and every day was critical in creating some sort of a constructive response involving local police agencies.

From the focus groups with the members of the local community groups, a very clear picture emerged of some disconnect not just between the communities and the local law enforcement but also between various groups within the community. The mixed focus group, described in the methodology section, was the first one during which we identified the feelings of alienations between the members of the Muslim minority group and the "native" Spaniards. The feeling of alienation expressed by a third-generation Muslim born in Spain was rather astonishing and disturbing. During our focus groups with media representatives and the Bar Association, the feelings of disconnect were reinforced. There were no good explanations for why third-generation minority groups felt the way they did, but the recognition that the problem exists was not denied. The feeling of the local police doing the "right thing" with regard to their dealings with the ETA members emerged as a consensus, something that cannot be said about the feelings toward the Muslim minorities.

Although not perceived as a direct threat, subsequent to the Madrid bombings the orientations started to change, not in a significant manner yet, but certainly the prior awareness of a problem received a new attention and a new focus. It was too early to say if the feelings toward what the local law enforcement is doing to counter terrorism were formed and decisive. The impression was that the way the ETA problem was handled translated into a confidence that any other terrorist problem will be handled with equal professionalism and effectiveness. However, these were the sentiments of the majority members of the Madrid community, which did not match the sentiments of the minority members we spoke to. The level of alienation on the part of the minority members left a great deal of room for concern with regard to future developments of the police–community relations in the area of gathering the relevant intelligence to counter the evolving threat.

Although the researchers were told by the local police officials that there is a significant level of cooperation between the local law enforcement and other police forces in Europe, in the area of counterterrorism activities, the authors were left with an impression that it is not the international cooperation and exchange of the information that is a major challenge for the Spanish police. The major challenge is the disconnect between the local, municipal forces and the minority population that they police. Furthermore, the lack of training in this area will be an evolving and festering problem for the police–community relations with regard to counterterrorism efforts by law enforcement.

References

Alonso, R., & Reinares, F. (2005). Terrorism, human rights, and law enforcement in Spain. *Terrorism and Political Violence, 17*, 265–278.

Alvanou, M. 2007. *Antiterrorism legislation issues in Spain: Terrorism offences and "incommunicado" procedures.* http://rieas.gr/index.php?option=com_content&task=view&id=405&Itemid=41

Haahr-Escolano, K. (2004). Algerian Salafists and the new face of terrorism in Spain. *The Jamestown Foundation Terrorism Monitor, 2*(21), 1–3. Retrieved from http://www.jamestown.org/terrorism/news/uploads/ter_003_013.pdf

Haahr, K. (2006). Emerging terrorist trends in Spain's Moroccan communities. *The Jamestown Foundation Terrorism Monitor, 4*(9), 1–3. Retrieved from http://www.jamestown.org/terrorism/news/uploads/TM_004_009.pdf

Jimenez, F. (1992, Winter). Spain: The terrorist challenge and the government's response. *Terrorism and Political Violence, 4*(4), 110–130.

Lieberman, C. A., & Bucht, R. (2009). Rail Transport Security. In M. R. Haberfeld & A. von Hassel. *A New Understanding of Terrorism: Case Studies, trajectories, and lessons learned* (pp. 189–204). New York, NY: Springer.

UK Secretary of State for Foreign and Commonwealth Affairs (2005). *Counter-terrorism legislation and practice.* Retrieved from http://image.guardian.co.uk/sys-files/Politics/documents/2005/10/12/foreignterrorlaw1.pdf

Woodworth, P. (2001). *Dirty war clean hands: ETA, the GAL and Spanish democracy.* New Haven, CT: Yale University Press.

Chapter 7
The Kingdom of Sweden *(Konungariket Sverige)*

7.1 History

Located between Finland and Norway in Northern Europe, bordering the Baltic Sea, Sweden is a parliamentary democracy. At the national level, the people are represented by the *Riksdag*, the Swedish Parliament, which has legislative power. The full name for Sweden (*Sverige*) is the Kingdom of Sweden (*Konungariket Sverige*). Sweden is a monarchy in which the office of Head of State has been since 1973 held by Carl XVI Gustaf. The title of King or Queen is inherited by the eldest child of the incumbent. Although the Head of State has no political powers, he/she is regularly informed of the affairs and concerns of the realm and chairs the Advisory Council on Foreign Affairs.

A military power during the seventeenth century, Sweden has not participated in a war in almost two centuries, maintaining armed neutrality during both World Wars. Sweden, a member of the European Union (EU) since 1995, combines a capitalist economy with welfare elements and has a population of approximately 9 million. Sweden is also a common destination for refugees and asylum seekers and immigrants make up more than 10% of its population.[1] Sweden has not been the victim of terrorist attacks in the past few decades, but many individuals associated with terrorist organizations have immigrated to Sweden and remain active in their respective organizations. Sweden has been used as a base for propaganda and fundraising and also a place of refuge for terrorists.[2]

Sweden, also known as the Kingdom of Sweden, is located on the Scandinavian Peninsula in Northern Europe, between Finland and Norway.[3] It is the fourth largest country in Europe, yet has a relatively low population density, with an average of 20 people per square kilometer. Sweden has a population of slightly over 9 million people. An estimated one-fifth of the total population of people is either immigrants or has at least one foreign-born parent. The majority of immigrants residing

---

[1] Country profile: Sweden. http://news.bbc.co.uk/2/hi/europe/country_profiles/1021823.stm# overview.

[2] Norell (2005).

[3] Information Please Database (2007). *Sweden*. http://www.infoplease.com/ipa/A0107824.html.

M.R. Haberfeld et al., *Terrorism Within Comparative International Context*,
DOI 10.1007/978-0-387-88861-3_7, © Springer Science+Business Media, LLC 2009

in Sweden come from Finland, Iraq, Serbia and Montenegro, Bosnia-Herzegovina, Iran, Norway, Denmark, and Poland. The primary language spoken in Sweden is Swedish, which is closely similar to Danish and Norwegian.[4] The dominant religion practiced within the country is Lutheranism, in which approximately 87% of the total population reported being Lutheran. However, Roman Catholic, Orthodox, Baptist, Jewish, Buddhist, and Muslim religious affiliation are also found within Sweden's residents.[5]

The first groups of people to inhabit the land, that is present-day Sweden, were hunters and fishermen of the stone age, around 8000 B.C. As advancements occurred within civilization, the individuals residing within Sweden's territory also progressed. The physical demographics of Sweden and its easy access to water made trading resourceful and convenient. Sweden became a kingdom by the ninth century, where kings governed the land and the individuals residing within it. By the eleventh century, the country converted to Christianity, after the Christian baptism of the Swedish king Olaf Sköttkonung.[6] During the sixteenth century, the foundation for modern Sweden was first established, once Gustav Vasa was elected to the throne and endorsed the concept for an independent Sweden. He also broke the country away from the Roman Catholic Church and spread the ideas of Reformation.[7] A military power during the seventeenth century, Sweden has not participated in a war in almost two centuries, maintaining armed neutrality during both World Wars. As time progressed into the nineteenth century, several liberal reforms began to take place within Sweden. The freedoms and rights of citizens began to expand and improve. Internal developments within the country due to economic growth and the demand for Swedish projects, especially following World War I, also occurred during this century. All of which contributed to the establishment of modern-day Sweden.[8]

Sweden is a parliamentary democracy, in which its country's citizens have the ability to elect individuals to represent them. There are three different levels of government within Sweden: national, regional, and local. At the national level, the people are represented by the *Riksdag*, the Swedish Parliament, which has legislative power. At the regional level, citizens within each of the 21 counties within the country elect county councils to represent them and make decisions at the regional level. At the local level, assemblies are elected within each of the 290 municipalities within the country. Elections are held every 4 years, providing Sweden's citizens the

[4] US Department of State (2008, January). Sweden. *Bureau of European and Eurasian Affairs.* http://www.state.gov/r/pa/ei/bgn/2880.htm.

[5] US Central Intelligence Agency. (2008, June 19). Sweden. *The World Factbook.* https://http://www.cia.gov/library/publications/the-world-factbook/geos/sw.html.

[6] Swedish Institute (2008).

[7] Sweden (2008). *Encyclopedia Britannica* online. http://www.britannica.com/eb/article-9108596/ Sweden.

[8] Swedish Institute (2008).

opportunity to vote for the candidates they want in office within each of the three different levels.[9]

Sweden, a member of the European Union (EU) since 1995, combines a capitalist economy with welfare elements. Sweden is also a common destination for refugees and asylum seekers, and immigrants make up more than 10% of its population. Sweden has not been the victim of terrorist attacks in the past few decades, but many individuals associated with terrorist organizations have immigrated to Sweden and remain active in their respective organizations. Sweden has been used as a base for propaganda and fundraising and also a place of refuge for terrorists.

Since the September 11, 2001, terrorist attacks that occurred within the United States, many countries, including Sweden, have increased education and training as well as developed different management strategies in order to better prepare themselves in the event that similar circumstances occur. Departments such as the Swedish Emergency Management Agency and the National Board of Health and Welfare of Sweden have increased their efforts and awareness on the possibility of a terrorist attack transpiring within Sweden. The country also adopted a "Total Defense" strategy in order to defend Sweden and its citizens against an armed attack, as well as maintain peace and security within the country, even when a threat is absent.[10]

7.2 Terrorism

In the past, terrorism in Sweden has included the 1971 Croat activists who killed the Yugoslav ambassador to Sweden and then, a year after, hijacked a domestic flight. Not uncommon for Western European nations at the time, the hijacking resulted in the release of the perpetrators of the embassy murder. In 1975, members of the German Red Army Faction (RAF), *Rote Armee Fraktion*, occupied the West German Embassy in Stockholm, demanding the release of other RAF members imprisoned in West Germany. The incident ended after explosives detonated, leading to the deaths of two hostages, after which the RAF terrorists were expelled to West Germany and imprisoned. In 1977, a plot to kidnap the Minister of Justice, Anna Greta Leijon, with the intent to exchange Leijon for those same imprisoned RAF members, was discovered.

In response to terrorist activity, Sweden has a policy of imprisoning offenders who are citizens, while noncitizens may be deported or extradited to other jurisdictions.[11] In 1975, Japanese activists, tied to the Japanese Red Army (JRA), were expelled after allegations that they prepared attacks on the Libyan Embassy in Stockholm. Also in 1975, two members of the JRA were expelled after planning

---

[9]Swedish Government Offices (2007).

[10]Kulling and Holst (2003).

[11]Hansen (2007).

attacks against Japanese targets in West Germany. Recently, a Jordanian man suspected of plotting to create an Al Qaeda cell in Sudan has been handed over to German authorities after being held in Sweden.[12] On February 28, an ABC News article reported that six people were arrested in Oslo and Stockholm in regard to financing and planning terrorist attacks.[13]

On September 17, 2005, in a statement by Laila Freivalds, Foreign Minister or Sweden, to the 60th UN Assembly, the issue of terrorism was addressed.

> Terrorism has taken the lives of thousands of innocent people. One of our most urgent priorities must be to stop and prevent terrorism. It remains a threat to all of us. We need to address this threat together, with a broad strategy, and with respect for human rights. The outcome of the Summit has given us a platform to build on. The United Nations should now take the lead in developing a comprehensive counter-terrorism strategy based on the Secretary General's excellent work. We must also conclude a comprehensive convention on international terrorism, including a legal definition during the 60th session of the General Assembly.[14]

In a February 2008 article by Carl Bildt, Minister for Foreign Affairs, and Beatrice Ask, Minister for Justice, terrorism, its threat, potential actors, and current limitations are discussed. Bilt and Ask (2008) assert that broad preventative measures are necessary because the traditional measures by the police and the legal system, although a cornerstone of counter terrorism, are not sufficient. Included among the improvements necessary are measures to improve cooperation, education, and operations. Furthermore, the goal is "for Sweden to counter the threat of terrorism through broad preparedness, good coordination and the efficient use of resources."[15] The article presents the issue of global security as interrelated with domestic security.

> We have a responsibility here at home to take necessary measures to stop terrorism, but we also have a responsibility towards other countries. Citizens of other countries should not need to face the risk of terrorism that is planned, assisted or carried out from a Swedish base. Further, we have a responsibility to contribute to the growing international cooperation. Terrorism is a global threat that requires joint solutions.

On February 7, 2008, Sweden's Ministry of Justice released a government communication titled *National responsibility and international commitment: A national strategy to meet the threat of terrorism*, which discusses Swedish counterterrorism. The article focuses on increasing the effectiveness of four areas: pursuit, prevention, protection, and consequence management. On June 19, 2008, the BBC reported that Sweden's parliament approved controversial new laws that allow government

---

[12] The Local: *Sweden hands over Jordanian suspected of terror links*. http://www.thelocal.se/6921/20070405/.

[13] ABC News: *Six nabbed in Norway, Sweden 'terrorism' swoop: Police*. http://www.abc.net.au/news/stories/2008/02/28/2175836.htm.

[14] Foreign Minister of Sweden statement to the UN http://www.un.org/webcast/ga/60/statements/swe050917eng.pdf.

[15] Government Offices of Sweden: *Comprehensive Swedish strategy to combat terrorism*. http://www.sweden.gov.se/sb/d/7960/a/97770.

agents to scan international communication, such as telephone calls, faxes, and email.[16]

7.3 Law Enforcement

Sweden has a number of organizations that participate in counterterrorism, both at national and international levels. Among the many organizations and agencies involved are Sweden's Ministry of Defense, Military Intelligence and Security Service, Armed Forces, Ministry of Justice, Security Police, Police, and National Board of Psychological Defense. In addition, the Justice and Home Affairs (JHA) Council deals with such issues as police cooperation, cooperation against terrorism, criminal justice cooperation, and issues involving civil justice.

The goal of *Försvarsdepartementet*,[17] Sweden's Ministry of Defense, is to fulfill the objectives of the Government and *Riksdag*, primarily relating to defense policy, protection and preparedness against accidents, and preparedness for severe peacetime emergencies. Led by the Minister of Defence, Mikael Odenberg, *Försvarsdepartementet* is responsible for introducing the rules of international humanitarian law in Sweden. In addition, *Forsvarsdepartementet* is responsible for intelligence activities designed to identify external military threats and to support foreign, defense, and security policy.[18]

The *Militara underrattelse-och sakerhetstjansten* (MUST), Sweden's Military Intelligence and Security Service, is responsible for collecting and analyzing information vital to the security of Sweden and presenting that information to the head of *Försvarsmakten*, the Armed Forces. In addition, MUST cooperates with *Försvarsdepartementet*, Sweden's Ministry of Defense, and *Utrikesdepartementet*,[19] Sweden's Ministry for Foreign Affairs, which is responsible jointly with foreign diplomatic missions for handling Sweden's relations with other countries.

The goal of *Försvarsmakten*,[20] Sweden's Armed Forces, is to prepare in peacetime to defend Sweden in war against armed attacks that could threaten Sweden's freedom and independence. *Försvarsmakten* also takes part in international peace-promoting and humanitarian operations. In addition, in cooperation with the Civil Defense Organization, *Försvarsmakten* also acts to prevent or assist in managing

---

[16]BBC News: *Sweden approves wiretapping law*. http://news.bbc.co.uk/2/hi/europe/7463333.stm.

[17]Government Offices of Sweden: *Ministry of Defence*. http://www.sweden.gov.se/sb/d/2060; Ministry of Defence: Government Communication 2007/08:64: *National responsibility and international commitment: A national strategy to meet the threat of terrorism*.http://www.sweden. gov.se/content/1/c6/10/51/27/64e294b3.pdf   http://www.sweden.gov.se/content/1/c6/10/66/84/ 36f8afde.pdf.

[18]Government Offices of Sweden: *Areas of Responsibility of the Ministry of Defence*. http://www.sweden.gov.se/sb/d/2060/a/21983;jsessionid=aR-8a4sicfb6.

[19]Government Offices of Sweden: *Ministry of Foreign Affairs*. http://www.sweden.gov.se/sb/ d/2059.

[20]The Swedish Armed Forces. http://www.mil.se/?lang=E.

civilian disasters and crises, such as natural disasters, environmental accidents, acts of terrorism, and large influxes of refugees.

> The Swedish Armed Forces are currently undergoing a process of comprehensive transformation to create smaller, but more focused, mission-oriented defence forces. The political decision to undertake this reform is a consequence of the radically altered threat picture and the emerging common approach to European security as well as the rapid pace of development, both in technology and in European society at large.[21]

Försvarsmakten has four main components: the Army (*Armen*), Navy (*Marinen*), Air Force (*Svenska Flygvapnet*), and Home Guard.[22] The Home Guard, whose duties are to protect Swedish infrastructure against sabotage, constitutes the greater part of Sweden's territorial defense forces. Home Guard personnel are locally recruited volunteers. In regard to potential terrorist attacks, the Army has Chemical, Biological, Radiological, and Nuclear units (CBRN), which are trained to deal with threats and incidents, including detection, identification, monitoring, warning, reporting, physical protection, and risk management.[23] Following a decision by the *Riksdag*, *Försvarsmakten* units have to be prepared to take part in international military operations.

The goal of *Justitiedepartemenet*,[24] Sweden's Ministry of Justice, is to address legislation concerning the constitution and general administrative law, civil law, procedural law, and criminal law. In addition, *Justitiedepartemenet* handles matters relating to migration and asylum policy and takes part in efforts to lay the groundwork for international cooperation against cross-border crime. Among *Justitiedepartemenet's* 18 divisions that are related to phenomenon of terrorism are the Divisions for Crime Policy, Penal Law, and Criminal Cases and International Judicial Cooperation.

The Division for Crime Policy is responsible for criminal policy issues, including issues related to the prison and probation services, crime prevention efforts, and victims of crime. The Division for Penal Law is responsible for legislation relating to central matters of penal law, the Public Camera Surveillance Act, and international cooperation on penal law matters. The Division for Criminal Cases and International Judicial Cooperation is responsible for legislation and negotiations concerning international judicial cooperation in criminal cases, including extradition, the European Arrest Warrant, mutual recognition and enforcement of sanctions, and coercive measures.[25]

The *Polisen*, Sweden's Police,[26] with more than 22,000 employees working at the national or local level, is one of the largest government services in Sweden. The *Polisen* have a National Laboratory of Forensic Science, which performs laboratory

---

[21] The Swedish Armed Forces: *Försvarsmakten*. http://www.mil.se/article.php?id=15694.

[22] The Swedish Armed Forces: *The Home Guard*. http://www.mil.se/article.php?lang=E&id=15708.

[23] The Swedish Armed Forces: *The Army*. http://www.mil.se/article.php?lang=E&id=15699.

[24] Government Offices of Sweden: *Ministry of Justice*. http://www.sweden.gov.se/sb/d/584.

[25] Government Offices of Sweden. http://www.sweden.gov.se/sb/d/2876/a/16348.

[26] National Police Board (2005).

analyses of evidence from various types of suspected crimes. The National Criminal Investigation Department (NCID) provides investigation and criminal intelligence support for cases involving crimes with nationwide or international ramifications.[27]

The *Sakerhetpolisen* (SAPO), Sweden's Security Police – also known as the National Security Service, are responsible for the protection of sensitive objects, counterespionage, antiterrorist activities, protection of the constitution, and protection of diplomats and royals. In regard to counterterrorism, the Security Service works to prevent attacks in Sweden and attacks against Swedish interests through intelligence activities, prevent and detect the illegal trade of products that could be used in the production of WMD's, and prevent foreign nationals with terrorist ties from obtaining visas, residence permits, or citizenship. In addition, the Security Service provides intelligence, resources, and methodological knowledge to other governmental agencies.[28]

> The National Police Board is the central administrative agency for the police authorities and the chief agency for the National Body of Forensic Science. The National Police Board includes the National Criminal Investigation Department, the Swedish Security Service and the Police College.[29]

The Swedish Emergency Management Agency (SEMA) coordinates and develops the preparedness of Swedish society to manage serious crises. SEMA works together with municipalities, county councils, and government authorities, as well as with the business community and several organizations, to reduce the vulnerability of society and improve the capacity to handle emergencies. SEMA has recently planned to conduct a simulated exercise to assist in the preparation for the response to a large-scale terrorist attack.[30]

Styrelsen för psykologiskt försvar (SPF), Sweden's National Board of Psychological Defense, is responsible for defense of Swedish society against the devices of psychological warfare to provide advice and guidance regarding contingency planning and the media's capacity for dealing with critical strains on society in peacetime, and to disseminate information about security policies and total defense.[31] Norell (2005) analyzes Sweden's counterterrorism policies using a comparative context and discusses the flaws in the Royal Commission findings regarding the impact of "nine-eleven." Norell (2005) argues that the existing structural flaws, involving the limitations on coordination and information sharing, undermine the effectiveness of existing counterterrorism policies and provide seven recommendations to counter the flaws, focusing on research, communication, and cooperation.[32]

---

[27] The Swedish Police Service. http://www.polisen.se/inter/nodeid=10232&pageversion=1.jsp.

[28] Swedish Security Service (2006). http://www.säpo.se/download/18.79f4d0a71125247256 d800035/swedishsecurityservice2006.pdf.

[29] Government Office of Sweden, Police Authorities. http://www.sweden.gov.se/sb/d/2708/a /15125.

[30] The Local: *Stockholm prepares for terror attack.* http://www.thelocal.se/7103/.

[31] Sweden's National Board of Psychological Defence. http://www.psycdef.se.

[32] Norell (2005, pp. 32–33).

The Swedish National Council for Crime Prevention (Brottsfo˙rebyggandera det, BRA) is a centre for research and development work within the justice system that provides assistance to criminal justice system agencies to improve knowledge and assist in the development of methods to combat and to prevent crime. In 1998, BRA was involved with support for municipal local crime prevention councils that could function as contact points for individuals who are interested in, and are able to contribute to, reducing crime and increasing levels of safety in the local community. These local crime prevention councils have come to assume a central and strategic role in the work of crime prevention. Initially, there were slightly fewer than 40 municipal local crime prevention councils in Sweden. As of 2005, according to Andersson (2005), "the agency [BRA] was in possession of information showing that there are now local crime prevention councils in over 80% of the country's 290 municipalities."[33]

7.4 Field Research

The law enforcement efforts related to terrorism in Sweden were felt by the research team to be best described as still in an embryonic stage. Within Sweden's police force (the *Polisen*), a National Criminal Investigation Department (NCID), assists in investigations of cases of national or international importance while the Sweden's Security Police (also known as the National Security Service or *Sakerhetpolisen* [SAPO]) also has antiterrorist responsibilities.[34] Because of the relatively new threat of terrorism in Sweden, law enforcement agencies, in particular, the Emergency Service Units (ESU) are the only "professional" response to the possible terrorist threat. From the team's interviews with officers in Stockholm's National Agency, it was apparent that they are not yet concerned with the need to establish counterterrorism units or Intelligence units, and the perception is that the Security Service has a good grasp of the terrorism situation and should be responsible in providing the relevant information to the National Police. The potential risk of a terrorist event or suicide terrorism was not taken too seriously and therefore, very little preparedness or intelligence-gathering efforts were under way.[35] The Swedish Security Services did not appear to have much of a contact with the local, neighborhood police forces.

At the academy level, the researchers interviewed the officer in charge of the tactical training, who felt that although it would be a good idea to implement more counterterrorism training, from the conceptual perspective, and integrate it to the presently offered tactical training, it was just a polite recognition of what might

---

[33] Andersson (2005, p. 82).

[34] A general description of the organization and responsibilities of the Polisen can be found in the police service's general report, *A Presentation of the Swedish Police Service* (National Police Board, 2005).

[35] A couple of weeks after the researchers completed their data collection, a Muslim immigrant attempted to blow himself up with explosives tied to his waist.

be done but without a sense of real urgency. Similar to the findings from the focus groups with the Stockholm SWAT team members, the level of tactical prepared-ness seems to be the more important one that the proactive prong of gathering the field intelligence and translating it into preventive techniques. When the researchers visited a police station in the neighborhood heavily populated by legal and illegal immigrants, it was clear that there is no real plan as to how to reach out to this community in terms of mobilizing them for some sort of cooperation with the local police.

The researchers were informed that there is significant pressure on the police to treat criminal cases that involved members of the minority communities or immi-grants with special attention. When the team members inquired as to the nature of this "special attention," they were told that basically the officers felt pressured not to investigate the crimes the way they would investigate the same crime involving a native Swede, in order not to alienate the minority community. This was a rather disturbing finding that the authors wanted to explore further in the meetings with the local communities but, again, due to the administrative problems, the second visit to Sweden did not occur and therefore the findings were not cross-validated with regard to the feelings of the community itself. It was rather apparent thought that there is a high level of frustration, on the part of local law enforcement, in terms of their inability to treat certain populations in a professional manner and investigate the crimes the way they were taught to do. The lack of close ties with this specific community and the overall impression of the researchers was that this is, yet again, a source of major concern for the future relations between the police and the minor-ity members, and the possibility of mobilizing the latter to fight the terrorist threat appears to be very remote.

References

Andersson, J. (2005). The Swedish National Council for crime prevention: A short presentation. *Journal of Scandinavian Studies in Criminology and Crime Prevention, 6,* 74–88.

Hansen, D. (2007). Crisis and perspectives on policy change: Swedish counter-terrorism policy-making (Doctoral dissertation, Swedish National Defence College, 2007). *Universiteit Utrecht.* Retrieved from http://igitur-archive.library.uu.nl/dissertations/2007-0403-200232/full.pdf

Kulling, P. E. J., & Holst, J. E. A. (2003, July–September). Educational and training systems in Sweden for prehospital response to acts of terrorism. *Prehospital and Disaster Medicine, 18*(3), 184–188.

Ministry of Defence. (2008, June 4th). *This is the Ministry of Defence.* Stockholm: Government Offices of Sweden Records Centre.

National Police Board. (2005). *A Presentation of the Swedish Police Service.* http://www.polisen.se/mediaarchive/4347/3474/4637/Polis_05_eng.pdf

Norell, M. (2005, April). *Swedish national counter terrorism policy after 'nine-eleven': Prob-lems and challenges.* Stockholm: Swedish Defence Research Agency. Retrieved from http://www.foa.se/upload/pdf/foi-norell-r-1618.pdf

Swedish Government Offices. (2007, October 30). *How Sweden is governed.* Information Depart-ment. Retrieved from http://www.sweden.gov.se/sb/d/575

Swedish Institute. (2008, February 15). *The history of Sweden: Fact sheet* (pp. 1–5). Stockholm, Sweden: Swedish Institute.

Chapter 8
Republic of Turkey *(Turkiye Cumhuriyeti)*

8.1 History

The country of Turkey is located in the southeastern region of Europe and the south-western region of Asia, with two of its coasts resting along the Mediterranean and Black Sea. Although the majority of the country resides within the Asian continent, a small proportion of it is located in European territory, near Greece and Bulgaria.[1] The official and formal name of Turkey is the Republic of Turkey. The land that constitutes Turkey is one of the more earthquake-prone regions in the world. Approximately, there are over 71.8 million people residing within the country, in which 80% of the population is Turkish and an estimated 20% is Kurdish or some other ethnic origin. The official language of the country is Turkish, yet Kurdish, Zaza, Arabic, Armenian, and Greek are also frequently used. Over 99% of the individuals living in Turkey is practicing Muslims, while less than 1% is affiliated with some other religion, such as Christian, Bahai, and Jewish.[2]

The Indo-European Hittites first occupied the land that now comprises Turkey in 1900 BC.[3] Several empires reign power over Turkey's territory throughout history, such as the Persian Empire, Roman Empire, and Byzantine Empire. One of the last empires to rule Turkish land was the Ottoman Empire, which was finally overthrown in 1922, thus initiating the development of present-day Turkey.[4]

Modern Turkey was founded in 1923 in the region of Anatolia, which was at once part of the Ottoman Empire, when Mustafa Kemal led a national war of independence, which ended with the Lausanne Peace Treaty and the Republic of Turkey *(Turkiye Cumhuriyeti)*. Kemal, who later became known as Ataturk, which means father of the Turks, instituted a secular nation and many reforms intended to modernize the state, abolishing both the sultanate and caliphate. The Turkish government follows the 1982 constitution, which replaced the constitution of 1961. Both the

---

[1] Encyclopedia Britannica online. *Turkey*. http://www.britannica.com/eb/article-9111078/Turkey.

[2] Kinzer (2001); Mango (2004, 2005); US Central Intelligence Agency, *World Factbook – Turkey*. https://www.cia.gov/library/publications/the-world-factbook/geos/tu.html.

[3] Information Please Database, *Turkey*. http://www.infoplease.com/ipa/A0108054.html.

[4] Tignor et al. (2002, pp. 380–381).

constitution of 1961 and the constitution of 1982 were drafted and adopted during the periods of military rule, the latter following the September 1980 coup.

Turkey utilizes a democratic, secular, and parliamentary system of government. The head of the state is the President of the Republic, which is an elected position with a term of 5 years. Executive power is shared among the president, the prime minister, and the council of ministers, while the Grand National Assembly of Turkey exercises the legislative power. The legal system that is practiced within the country of Turkey is based on several different European civil law structures. The judiciary branch is deemed independent from the other two sectors, and the Constitutional Court is responsible for making sure the laws and rulings of the constitution are being complied within the country.

Some areas controlled by Turkey have been the subject of much dispute. Territorial control of islands in the Aegean Sea, specifically Cyprus, continues to be an issue of dispute with Greece. In 1974, the island was divided into two autonomous entities, with Greek Cypriots controlling the southern part of the island and the Turkish Cypriots controlling the Northern part of the island. The UN Peacekeeping Force in Cyprus (UNFICYP) has served in Cyprus since 1964 and maintains the buffer zone between north and south.[5]

The country of Turkey has been experiencing the threat of terrorism for many years. In the 1960s, an Islamic movement began to occur in Turkey along with terrorist activity. Many leaders of the Islamic Liberation Party were imprisoned as a result of their radical attempts of promoting the Islamic State Constitution to the country.[6] During the 1970s, Armenian terrorists started targeting Turkish diplomats. After the 1973 attack on a Turkish consul-general in Los Angeles, California, as a form of revenge, terrorist attacks became a rather frequent occurrence. Ten years following that first attack, more than 30 Turkish diplomats were murdered throughout the world and several more were wounded. Members of the Armenian Secret Army for the Liberation of Armenia were deemed responsible for these violent acts targeted toward Turkish citizens.[7] Terrorist attacks continued through the 1980s and 1990s within the country of Turkey, up until the present time. After the United States declared War on Terrorism, many countries have joined in the effort to terminate terrorism. Turkey has also gotten involved through the use of different antiterrorism measures. In the spring of 2007, a Turkish military force of over 1000 soldiers had stationed themselves along the northern Iraq border in order to collect intelligence and monitor actions.[8]

Modern Turkey was founded in 1923 from the Anatolian remnants of the defeated Ottoman Empire by national hero Mustafa KEMAL, who was later honored with the title Ataturk or "Father of the Turks." Under his authoritarian leadership, the country adopted wide-ranging social, legal, and political reforms. After a period of one-party rule, an experiment with

---

[5] UN Peacekeeping Force in Cyprus. http://www.un.org/Depts/dpko/missions/unficyp/.

[6] Karmon (1998).

[7] Zurcher (2004, p. 277).

[8] McGregor (2007).

multi-party politics led to the 1950 election victory of the opposition Democratic Party and the peaceful transfer of power. Since then, Turkish political parties have multiplied, but democracy has been fractured by periods of instability and intermittent military coups (1960, 1971, and 1980), which in each case eventually resulted in a return of political power to civilians. In 1997, the military again helped engineer the ouster – popularly dubbed a "post-modern coup" – of the then Islamic-oriented government. Turkey intervened militarily on Cyprus in 1974 to prevent a Greek takeover of the island and has since acted as patron state to the "Turkish Republic of Northern Cyprus," which only Turkey recognizes. A separatist insurgency begun in 1984 by the Kurdistan Workers' Party (PKK) – now known as the People's Congress of Kurdistan or Kongra-Gel (KGK) – has dominated the Turkish military's attention and claimed more than 30,000 lives. After the capture of the group's leader in 1999, the insurgents largely withdrew from Turkey mainly to northern Iraq. In 2004, KGK announced an end to its ceasefire and attacks attributed to the KGK increased. Turkey joined the UN in 1945 and in 1952 it became a member of NATO. In 1964, Turkey became an associate member of the European Community; over the past decade, it has undertaken many reforms to strengthen its democracy and economy enabling it to begin accession membership talks with the European Union.[9]

8.2 Terrorist Groups

Turkey and Armenia continue to have poor relations, primarily due to the "Armenian Genocide" (1915–1917), in which approximately 1.5 million Armenians were killed during their deportation from Turkey. Although these events occurred before the establishment of the current government, Turkey continues to deny the magnitude of the events, stating that the deportation was due to the Armenian cooperation with the enemies of the Ottoman Empire during World War I. Two Armenian groups, the Armenian Secret Army for the Liberation of Armenia (ASALA) and the Justice Commandos of the Armenian Genocide,[10] had been engaged in violent conflict with Turkey in Eastern Turkey. After Hagop Hagopian, leader of ASALA, was killed in Greece in 1988, the organization had ceased operational activity.[11]

Left-wing Marxist groups have also been active in Turkey over the past few decades. The Turkish Peoples Liberation Army split in the late 1970s, and the group Dev Sol was formed. The goal of Dev Sol, which is against both NATO and the United States, is to foster a popular national revolution among the Turkish working class. In 1994, the organization was renamed Revolutionary People's Liberation Party/Front (DHKP/C). During the Gulf war, the DHKP/C conducted attacks against US and NATO military, commercial, and cultural facilities in Turkey. In addition to assassinations and bombings, in 2001 DHKP/C added suicide bombings to its tactics.[12]

---

[9] CIA World Factbook, https://www.cia.gov/cia/publications/factbook/geos/tu.html.

[10] Library of Congress, http://lcweb2.loc.gov/cgi-bin/query/r?frd/cstdy:@field(DOCID+tr0112).

[11] FAS: *Armenian Secret Army for the Liberation of Armenia (ASALA); Orly Group; 3rd October Organization*, http://www.fas.org/irp/world/para/asala.htm.

[12] FAS: *Revolutionary People's Liberation Party/Front (DHKP/C); Devrimci Sol (Revolutionary Left); Dev Sol*, http://www.fas.org/irp/world/para/dev_sol.htm.

Southeastern Turkey has been a major area of conflict in regard to the Kurdish population, estimated between 12 and 15 million, from which a significant portion of the terrorist incidents in Turkey can be attributed. Although the Kurdistan Workers' Party (PKK) has changed its name and form many times over the past few decades, the PKK is the primary organization related to the Kurdish movements that advocate and engage in violent activities to pursue their goals of an independent Kurdish state in Eastern and Southeastern Turkey.

Founded by Abdullah Ocalan in 1974 as a Marxist-Leninst separatist movement, Kongra-Gel became known as the PKK in 1978. Since 1984, when the PKK began utilizing violence as a means of achieving its goal to form a separate Kurdish state, over 3000 deaths have been attributed to the conflict, though some estimates are substantially higher up to 20,000 deaths.[13] While their tactics began with rural-based insurgent activities, in the early 1990s the PKK began to engage in urban terrorism, including bombing civilian targets. The 1999 capture of Ocalan led to a decrease in the attacks, as Ocalan announced a peace initiative that would involve a refrain from violence and the use of political dialog to address the grievances of the Kurdish population. In 2002, the PKK changed its name to the Kurdistan Freedom and Democracy Congress (KADEK) and proclaimed a commitment to peaceful tactics to support Kurdish rights. In 2003, KADEK changed its name to Kongra-Gel again and claimed to promote peace, while refusing to disarm and defending violence as self-defense. In 2004, the People's Defense Force (HPG) took control of the organization and renounced the cease-fire.[14]

The Turkish Revenge Brigade (TIT), *Türk İntikam Tugayı*, is an ultranationalist group that has used violence against those individuals or groups perceived to be insulting Turkey. TIT has claimed responsibility for attacks on politicians, journalists, and human rights activists. The conviction of a former gendarmerie officer, with links to TIT, for the 1998 attempted murder of Akin Birdal, president of the Turkish Human Rights Association (HRA), has led to many to question the possibility of the government being involved with, supporting, or neglecting to properly investigate TIT.[15] During the 1990s, when the Kurdish populations began becoming involved in local politics, hundreds of political activists, human rights activists, and journalists were killed. The police were not effective in identifying the offenders, who were alleged to have been death squads that had been supported by governmental agents, such as police.[16]

Turkey, whose population is 99% Muslim, has fundamentalist Islamic groups, such as Turkish *Hezbollah*[17] ("Party of God"), which was founded in Southeast Turkey in the 1980s. The goal of Turkish *Hezbollah* is to overthrow the Turkish

---

[13]FAS: *The Kurds in Turkey*. http://www.fas.org/asmp/profiles/turkey_background_kurds.htm.

[14]FAS: *PKK*. http://www.fas.org/irp/world/para/pkk.htm.

[15]Human Rights Watch: *Turkey: Condemn threats on human rights defenders*. http://hrw.org/english/docs/2005/04/20/turkey10516.htm.

[16]Van Bruinessen (1996).

[17]MIPT – Memorial Institute for the Prevention of terrorism. http://www.mipt.org/.

secular government and introduce a strict Islamic state and Sharia law. Turkish *Hezbollah*, which is believed to be funded entirely by Iran, utilizes assassinations and bombings as its primary tactics. According to Jenkins (2008), Turkish *Hezbollah* was founded in the 1980s in Turkey in the southeastern city of Diyarbakır by Hüseyin Velioglu, an ethnic Kurd and former student activist. Jenkins (2008) further states that, during the 1980s, members of Turkish *Hezbollah* traveled frequently to Iran, where they received training from elements in the Iranian intelligence services.[18]

8.3 Law Enforcement

The two main police agencies in Turkey are the National Police and gendarmerie, *Jandarma*, both of which are headquartered in the capital, Ankara, and both are administered by the Ministry of the interior. The National Police, which have more than 50,000 men and women, handle police functions, including traffic control, in the urban areas, such as cities and towns. The gendarmerie is the military security force, which during wartime or in areas placed under martial law, functions under the army. Turkish police have received criticism for human rights violations.

> The performance of the Turkish police has been the subject of persistent criticism for violations of fundamental human rights. These problems, which have received growing international and domestic attention, involve torture during questioning, incommunicado detention, politically motivated disappearances, "mystery killings," and excessive use of force. Successive governments have repeatedly promised to curb abuses by the security forces, but little if any improvement has been recorded.[19]

The gendarmerie, which has more than 70,000 men and women, is primarily a rural police force, maintaining public order outside municipal boundaries of cities and provincial towns and guarding Turkey's land borders against illegal entry and smuggling. Military conscription provides the Gendarmerie's recruits and its officers, and noncommissioned officers (NCO's) are transferred from the Army. In 1982, the maritime wing of the gendarmerie was formed, but is now a separate agency; the coast guard, which also reports to the Ministry of the Interior. The coast guard is responsible for maintaining the security of the coast and territorial waters. *Jandarma Istihbarat ve Terorle Mucadele* (JITEM) is a special unit of the gendarmerie, responsible for gathering antiterrorist intelligence.[20]

Intelligence gathering is the primary responsibility of the National Intelligence Organization (MIT), *Milli Istihbarat Teskilati*, which combines the functions of both internal and external intelligence agencies. Each branch of the military, the army,

---

[18] Jenkins (2008); Wilkinson (2005).

[19] Library of Congress: *Turkey – Police system.* http://lcweb2.loc.gov/cgi-bin/query/r?frd/cstdy: @field(DOCID+tr0113).

[20] Rheinheimer (n.d.); Alliance for Liberals and Democrats in Europe: *JITEM – Jandarma Istihbarat ve Terorle Mucadele.* http://www.organisedcrime.info/index.php?mode=11&id=94.

navy, and air force, has its own intelligence arm, as does the National Police and the gendarmerie. MIT has no police powers and is only authorized to gather intelligence and conduct counterintelligence abroad. In addition, MIT is responsible to identify internal communist, extreme right-wing, and separatist groups. In the past, MIT has been charged with failing to notify the government of intelligence relating to plots and complicity in military coup attempts.[21]

8.4 Field Research

Since the original research project commenced in Turkey, the researchers had a disproportionate amount of data from this country, in comparison to the other countries visited based on securing additional funding. Due to this disproportionate "wealth," this section is arranged in a slightly different manner than the Field Research sections described in the other chapters. In this chapter, the authors grouped various themes that emerged from the focus groups and individual interviews and present them in a bullet-point format rather than just as generalized concepts. The bullet points actually accompany the more generalized sentiments and impressions derived from the interactions with many research subjects. It is certainly recommended that precisely such an extensive interaction takes part in each and every country subject to a comparative research, but it is, of course, dependent upon the local contacts and other situational impediments, like the bombings that occurred in London, while the team was en route to conduct the research.

In conversations with the TNP and its counterterrorism and intelligence chiefs, the research team found that the approach to terrorist suspects was very different from the approach to other criminals. In regard to terrorism, the main goal is to maintain effective surveillance of the leaders and active supporters, who according to their estimates constitute a rather small number that can be easily contained by effective enforcement, and to prevent the hundreds of passive supporters from becoming involved with active engagements. The TNP argued that its most effective tool to achieve this goal was in the way it conducted investigations and interrogations of terrorist suspects, which was described to the researchers as handling suspects with "velvet gloves" out of fear of spreading the rumor that the "freedom fighters" are oppressed by the police force and haunted by the government. It was not clear to the observers, however, if the relatively "new breed" of the Turkish Al-Qaeda was treated in the same manner, as they do not have a large number of local supporters and the police do not feel constrained by the same consideration they face with the PKK suspects.

Although the number and the strength of the counterterrorism units appears to be adequate, the researchers found limited cooperation between the TNP and the Gendarmerie, who are also involved in the fight against the domestic terrorists. When

---

[21]Library of Congress: *Turkey – Gendarmerie*. http://lcweb2.loc.gov/cgi-bin/query/r?frd/cstdy:@field(DOCID+tr0114).

speaking anonymously to ranking members of the Gendermarie, they shared with the researchers their feelings of a lack of cooperation and exchange of intelligence with the TNP. Although they felt confident in their ability to target the terrorist threat, but, similar to the TNP, their knowledge of the Turkish Al-Qaeda was limited in comparison to other groups, thus making cooperation and information more critical in their view.

Finally, the researchers found that patrol officers did not receive specialized training in the area of counterterrorism and were told that "they know enough" based on the long history of police efforts against the PKK. When the evolution of a new and much global threat like the Turkish Al-Qaeda and the possible lack of knowledge about their ideology and modus operandi were pointed out, the reseachers were assured that this is also "under control." Nevertheless, based on conversations with patrol officers in Istanbul, it was not apparent that they know what they are dealing with, not from the perspective of intelligence gathering, surveillance, or any other relevant aspect of policing the threat.

In the conversations with various police officials (who are not identified by the authors for the purpose of preserving their anonymity), the following points illustrate the factual and perceptional picture in Istanbul and Ankara, as expressed by these high-ranking officials.

- Involving community in training and various projects in certain neighborhoods is institutionalized, although not equally in each neighborhood.
- There is no formal training with respect to community mobilization for counterterrorism
- There is a strong recognition that terrorism has to be targeted in a nontraditional way involving both law enforcement and the public.
- The overall impression was that terrorism was not a major problem for the Turkish law enforcement, although it is certainly recognized as such by the authorities.
- What happened in the Istanbul bombing of the synagogue in 2004 was not indicative of a need to deal with the issues in a different way from the field perspective.
- The number of individuals that the Istanbul police were concerned with can be summarized as follows: up to 100,000 passive supporters; 200 active supporters; 50 terrorists ready to deploy upon command by leadership; and about 15 in leadership positions. This represents a concentric circle, which generates a fear of the movement of passive to active supporters and represents a major concern in terms of dealing with the active suspects, during the investigative and interrogative stages, and this is where the "velvet glove" approach is utilized.
- The need to treat the passive supporters within the framework of the human rights themes in order to prevent progression from passive to active is strongly recognized.
- There is a fear that various NGOs provide support for terrorism at minimum at the passive level.
- The need to network with religious leaders for information and intelligence is of major importance.

- Traditional intelligence work, very effective in capturing the core involved in Istanbul attacks, will not prevent the further progression of the circles.
- The intelligence units acknowledged the fact that Turkey has been struggling with terrorism for the last 30 years, so they have a significant experiential base.
- The intelligence units felt that there is a need for training to enhance their intelligence capabilities, but did acknowledge the importance of community mobilization skills.

The focus groups with the community members, as well as individual interviews, included subjects from the Bar Association, the Center from Human Rights, media representatives, film directors, and religious minority leaders; following are the major themes the team was able to record from the interactions.

8.4.1 The Center for Human Rights

- Since center for Human Rights was established there is a dramatic increase in complaints against the police.
- They do some training of both the Gendarmerie and the National Police, although not enough.
- The public has more grievances with the Police than the Gendarmerie because of the urban centers.
- There are problems with the training of gendarmerie because they are soldiers, and usually only for a couple of years.
- Community trusts the gendarmerie more than the National Police.
- Linkage blindness exists between the Gendarmerie and the National Police, translated in plain terms into lack of cooperation and exchange of information between the two agencies.

8.4.2 Bar Association

- Desire to take control over the police was expressed by the participants, maybe through some of a prosecutorial police force that would ensure accountability and more transparency.
- All suspects are treated as terrorists by the police, and the definition issue of who is and who is not should be clearly operationalized.
- Confusion with regard to effectiveness and efficiency of police was clearly stated, while there was a sense of overall effectiveness, but paired with a lot of grievances.
- Gendarmerie is perceived to be a much more professional presence in the fight against the terrorism phenomenon.
- There was a sense of an overall willingness to cooperate with the police, however, subject to an equal partnership level.

8.4.3 Turkish National Police Graduate Students

- Agreement that there is no connection between the police and the public.
- Very little training exists with respect to how to deal with the community.
- No community meetings or other mobilization techniques, they are open to integration with the community for police work, but require directions on how to accomplish this goal.
- Confusion over Community Policing American style and community mobilization as the researchers operationalized it with regard to the terrorist threat, therefore the need to clarify and operationalize the term "Community Oriented Policing" for the Turkish customized version.
- Overall, there was expressed enthusiasm for new ideals and professionalization with respect to how to police better.

8.4.4 The Media and Film Producer

- Realized the responsibility they have toward informing and forming the public's opinion; however, their political orientation was not always in tune with the official government policy, and this definitely influenced the way they transformed the images related to terrorist activities.
- Overall, there was a strong realization of the ability to shape perceptions but little desire to work together with the police or any other government agencies to de-escalate the tensions and to better inform the public of the level, scope, and intensity of the threat.

8.4.5 The Minority Leaders

- Satisfaction was expressed with regard to the way police handled minorities, and the desire to cooperate with the police was rather transparent.
- The level of cooperation and interaction on a daily basis appeared to be satisfactory, and the feeling of respect was mutual and acknowledged as the only way to deal with the minority populations.

The researchers' perceptions were however a bit skewed toward skepticism, since the interviews took place in the presence of an active duty police officer who served as the team's interpreter. It was very much conceivable to assume that the opinions and statements given to the team by the minority leaders were heavily influenced by the presence of the law enforcement officer. It is also important to note that the researchers have not interviewed the leaders of the Kurdish minority, due to the lack of proper contacts, and there is little doubt that the latter would have expressed a different perspective about the nature of their interactions with the local law enforcement. That been said, credit needs to be given to the Turkish Police for maintaining close relationships with the minority leaders the team managed to interview, even if the nature of this relationship is not as proper as was presented to the team.

References

Jenkins, G. (2008, January 24th). Back with a vengeance: Turkish Hezbollah. *The Jamestown Foundation Terrorism Monitor: In-Depth Analysis of the War on Terror, 6*(2), 9–11.

Karmon, E. (1998, Winter). Islamic terrorist activities in Turkey in the 1990s. *Terrorism and Political Violence, 10*(4), 101–121.

Kinzer, S. (2001). *Crescent & star: Turkey between two worlds.* New York, NY: Farrar, Straus and Giroux.

Mango, A. (2004). *The Turks today.* New York, NY: The Overlook Press.

Mango, A. (2005). *Turkey and the war on terror for forty years we fought alone.* New York, NY: Routledge.

McGregor, A. (2007, July 3). Turkey's evolving anti-terrorism measures on the Iraqi border. *Terrorism Focus, 4*(21), 1–7.

Rheinheimer, F. (n.d.). Counterterrorism in the European Union: A who's who of the agencies involved. World Security Institute. Retrieved from http://www.cdi.org/PDFs/EU%20Counterterrorism%20Francis%20Rheinheimer.pdf

Tignor, R., Adelman, J., Aron, S., Kotkin, S., Marchand, S., Prakash, G., et al. (2002). *Worlds together worlds apart: A history of the modern world from the Mongol Empire to the present* (pp. 380–381). New York, NY: W. W. Norton & Company, Inc.

Van Bruinessen, M. (1996). Turkey's death squads. *Middle East Report, 199*, 20–23. Retrieved from http://www.jstor.org/view/08992851/di011540/01p0007d/0

Wilkinson, P. (2005). *International terrorism: The changing threat and the EU's response.* Institute for Security Studies. Retrieved from http://www.iss.europa.eu/chaillot/chai84.pdf

Zurcher, E. J. (2004). *Turkey: A modern history* (p. 277). London: I. B. Tauris & Co. Ltd.

Chapter 9
Germany

Andre Konze*

9.1 History

9.1.1 The Federal Republic of Germany

In 1945, subsequent to being defeated twice, World War I and World War II, in the first half of the twentieth century, Germany was occupied by the United States (USA), the United Kingdom (UK), France, and the Union of Soviet Socialist Republics (USSR). With the advent of the Cold War, two separate German states were formed in 1949: the western Federal Republic of Germany (FRG) and the eastern German Democratic Republic (GDR). The democratic FRG embedded itself in key Western economic and security organizations, including the EC, which became the EU, and the North Atlantic Treaty Organization (NATO).[1] While the GDR was on the front line of the Soviet-led Warsaw Pact, the decline of the USSR and the end of the Cold War allowed for German unification. October 3, 1990, is now known as the national day of the reunified republic.[2] All four allied powers formally relinquished rights March 15, 1991.

With a population of approximately 82,000,000, the unified Federal Republic of Germany consists of 16 states, 11 states from the FRG and 5 states from the GDR: Baden-Wuerttemberg, Bavaria, Berlin, Brandenburg (former GDR), Bremen, Hamburg, Hesse, Mecklenburg-Western Pomerania (former GDR), Lower Saxony, North-Rhine Westphalia, Rhineland – Palatinate, Saarland, Saxony (former GDR), Saxony – Anhalt (former GDR), Schleswig-Holstein, and Thuringia (former GDR). Reunification included the GDR states into the Federal Republic of Germany and its legal framework. The FRG constitution initially went into effect on May 23, 1949. The legal and governmental framework imbedded and implemented through that construction consists of three branches: legislative, judicial, and executive.[3]

---

*Guest Author: Andre Konze, State Police of North Rhine Westphalia, Düsseldorf, NRW, Germany

[1] EU: http://europa.eu/index_en.htm; NATO: http://www.nato.int.

[2] http://www.germany.info/Vertretung/usa/en/Startseite.html; http://www.ena.lu/.

[3] CIA World Factbook: Germany. http://www.cia.gov/library/publications/the-world-factbook/geos/gm.html.

9.1.2 Three Branches of the Federal Republic of Germany

The federal legislative branch is bicameral. The parliament consists of the Federal Assembly (*Bundestag*)[4] with usually 614 seats, elected by popular vote under a system combining direct and proportional representation. Due to extraordinary voting results it may happen that the number of seats increases. A party must win 5% of the national vote or three direct mandates to gain proportional representation and caucus recognition. Angela Merkel was elected by the Bundestag as Germany's first female Federal Chancellor on November 22, 2005. The Federal Assembly serves for 4-year terms. The other component of the legislative branch is the Federal Council (*Bundesrat*),[5] which has 69 votes. These votes proportionally represent state governments. Depending on population, each state has three to six votes; however, each state is required to cast all votes together as a block. As the members of Federal Council are representatives of the states, it does not have a term, indeed it is "eternal" – at least as long as the Federal Republic of Germany exists. The three Central functions of the Bundesrat are:

- Defend the interests of the Länder vis-à-vis the Federation and indirectly vis-à-vis the European Union.
- Ensure that the political and administrative experience of the Länder is incorporated in the Federation's legislation and administration and in European Union affairs.
- Like the other constitutional organs of the Federation, the Bundesrat also bears its share of the overall responsibility for the Federal Republic of Germany.

One of the main bodies of the federal judicial branch is the Federal Supreme Court (*Bundesverfassungsgericht*).[6] Half the judges of the Federal Supreme Court are elected by the Federal Assembly and half by the Federal Council. A second superior court is the Federal Criminal Court (*Bundesgerichtshof*).[7] Here, cases of criminal law find their final decision if they are not taken to the Federal Supreme Court. The third important federal court is the Federal Administrative Court (*Bundesverwaltungsgericht*).[8] Under certain circumstances, administrative cases will be decided there. The federal executive consists of several agencies. Important bodies are the Custom Service and other financial departments. The only pure law enforcement bodies are the Federal Police (*Bundespolizei*) and the Federal Criminal Police Officer (*Bundeskriminalamt*).[9]

---

[4] German Bundestag: http://www.bundestag.de/htdocs_e/index.html.

[5] German Bundesrat: http://www.bundesrat.de/EN/Home/homepage__node.html.

[6] German Bundesverfassungsgericht: http://www.bundesverfassungsgericht.de/en/index.html.

[7] German Bundesgerichtshof: http://www.bundesgerichtshof.de/.

[8] German Bundesverwaltungsgericht: http://www.bverwg.de/enid/dbd778f1bb9e5ee5146ed87644 ac81b0,51519f6d6f6465092d09/BESONDERE_SEITEN/Startseite_2.html.

[9] German Federal Police: *Bundespolizei.* http://www.bundespolizei.de/; and Federal Police Officer: *Bundeskriminalamt.* http://www.bka.der/.

The structure of each of the 16 German states incorporates the three branches, whose responsibilities are described both in the constitution of the Federal Republic of Germany and in the constitutions in each of these states. The general rule that the states are responsible for all governmental issues and which is stated in the constitution was undermined during the 60 years of existence of the Federal Republic of Germany. This was possible due to the fact that Articles 72 and 74 of the constitution states that in cases when common legislation is necessary in all states, the federal parliament can take responsibility. What can be stated here is that the federal parliament used this article extensively. Fortunately and wisely the constitution excludes certain issues like education and policing. For policing, an exception from the exception was made, as the Federal Criminal Police Office received special responsibilities also by the constitution. The fundamentals for the establishment of the Federal Police Office are codified in Article 73, nos. 10 and 87, Section 1 of the constitution. Furthermore, the issue of terrorism primarily is the responsibility of the Federal Criminal Police Office.

9.1.3 Schengen Agreement

Posted in the center of Western Europe, Germany has borders to nine countries: Austria, Belgium, Czech Republic, Denmark, France, Luxemburg, The Netherlands, Poland, and Switzerland. This causes advantages and disadvantages as well. The advantages mainly can be seen in economic factors. As Europe's largest economy, Germany is depending on trade good infrastructural connections with its neighbors. This openness created the necessity of the Schengen Agreement, which allows all citizens of the zone to travel within the countries that have signed the agreement without any border controls and implemented law enforcement measures, which should ensure that safety and security can be sustained within the zone.[10] The measures taken are described below under "Law Enforcement."

9.2 Terrorism

9.2.1 The Red Army Faction

Scrutinizing contemporary terrorism usually means analyzing the 9/11 attacks and hundreds or thousands of strikes committed under the same or similar objective targets like religious fanaticism or anti-Americanism. The reasons for these are as manifold as the ways to combat it. Doing a disquisition of terrorism and its abatement in the Federal Republic of Germany after WWII, it shows up immediately that it has a totally different appearance than terrorism nowadays. Even if this form of

---

[10]Schengen Agreement. http://www.migrationsverket.se/infomaterial/om_eu/schengen_en.pdf; BBC News: Schengen Agreement. http://news.bbc.co.uk/1/hi/in_depth/europe/euro-glossary /1230052.stm.

appearance of terrorism is not omnipresent in Germany any more, it has essentially informed the legislation and the law enforcement response. To get an understanding how Germany's suppression of terrorism was built up in the 1970s, 1980s, and 1990s, the crucial incidents have to be addressed.

The Red Army Faction or RAF (German *Rote Armee Fraktion*) was postwar West Germany's most violent and prominent militant left-wing terrorist group. The RAF was formally founded in 1970 by Andreas Baader, Gudrun Ensslin, Horst Mahler, Ulrike Meinhof, Irmgard Möller, and others. The origins of the group can be traced back to the student protest movement in West Germany. Like other industrialized nations in late 1960s experienced massive social upheavals stemming from dissatisfaction with capitalist society among both workers and students. RAF described itself as a communist "urban guerrilla" group engaged in armed resistance. The conservative media were considered biased by the radicals, as they were owned and controlled by conservatives such as Axel Springer, who was implacably opposed to student radicalism.

It is claimed that property destruction during the Watts Riots in the United States in 1965 influenced the practical and ideological approach of the RAF founders. Many of the radicals in Germany felt that lawmakers were continuing authoritarian policies.[11] The Federal Republic of Germany was exporting arms to African dictatorships, which was seen as supporting the war in Southeast Asia and engineering the remilitarization of Germany with the US-led entrenchment against the Warsaw Pact nations. Public perceptions of state and police brutality and widespread opposition to the Vietnam War, many young Germans became a rallying point for the West German New Left. A quote made by one of the later RAF members made that time is: "If you set a car on fire – that is a criminal offence. If you set hundreds of cars on fire – that is political action."

The Red Army Faction operated from the late 1960s to 1998, committing numerous operations, especially in the autumn of 1977, which led to a national crisis that became known as "German Autumn."[12] It was responsible for 34 deaths, including many secondary targets – such as chauffeurs and bodyguards – and many injuries in its almost 30 years of activity. Although more well known, the RAF conducted fewer attacks than the Revolutionary Cells (RZ) (296 bombs, arson and other attacks 1973–1995). The activities of RAF have recently returned after many years of absenteeism subsequent to the release of a recent film and book.[13] While it is nearly impossible to expose the complexity and scale of incidents connected to RAF and its subgroups, this book attempts to highlight some of the more significant acts committed to provide an overview of this part of contemporary German history.[14] Below is an image of a wanted poster for the Baader Meinhoff Gang, circa 1972.[15]

---

[11]Crenshaw (1995); Dershowitz (2002).

[12]Red Army Faction: A Chronology of Terror. http://www.dw-world.de/dw/article /0,,2763946,00.html.

[13]Guardian.co.uk: *The Baader Meinhof Complex*. http://www.guardian.co.uk /; Aust (2008).

[14]Wunschik (1997).

[15]Wanted Poster: "Baader/Meinhof Gang". http://germanhistorydocs.ghi-dc.org/sub_image.cfm? image_id=2395.

On May 11, 1972, RAF ("Kommando Petra Schelm") conducted an attack in Frankfurt, Germany, in which three explosive devices, homemade pipe bombs, were simultaneously detonated at 6:59 PM and 7:02 PM in front of the headquarters of the 5th US Army Corps, killing 1 US soldier and injuring 13 other people. RAF released a communiqué, stating the attack was in response to the US blockade of North Vietnam. On May 15, 1972, the RAF was responsible for the detonation of an explosive device placed in the car of the judge who had signed most of the arrest warrants for members of the RAF. The device detonated when the judge's wife turned on the ignition, causing her serious injuries.[16]

On May 19, 1972, several homemade bombs detonated in the Axel Springer Headquarters, which is one of the biggest newspaper enterprises in Germany. Unfortunately, the phone calls providing advance warning of the bombs were not taken seriously, the building was not evacuated and 17 people were injured seriously. In the letter sent to the Axel Springer Verlag by RAF blamed them to be an enemy of the people. On May 24, 1972, at around 6 PM, the RAF conducted an attack, a bombing attack on the European headquarters of the US Army in Heidelberg, Germany. The explosive devices were detonated in front of a casino, killing three and injuring five US soldiers. RAF characterized this assault as a reaction on the announcement of a US General to continue bombing Vietnam. On November 10, 1974, a shooting during an attempt of RAF to kidnap the President of the Superior Court of Justice in Berlin led to the death of the intended target. RAF released a communiqué that expressed their delight about the execution.

Another startling action of the RAF was the April 25, 1975, occupation of the German embassy in Stockholm, Sweden, in which 12 employers of the embassy were held hostage. The demands of the hostage takers included the release 26 "political prisoners" jailed in Germany, important members of RAF such as Andreas Baader, Ulrike Meinhof, Gudrun Enslin, and Jan Carl Raspe. This and other demands, such as the payment of $20,000 to each of the political prisoners, were denied by the Chancellor of Germany, Helmut Schmidt. The hostage takers reacted on by killing a hostage after having shot dead another person to keep Swedish police away from the embassy. The event ended as a result of the accidental detonation of an explosive device by one of the hostage takers, which killed one hostage taker and injured another, who expired later at a prison hospital.

On April 7, 1977, the attorney general of the Federal Court of Justice of Germany was driven to work in his car accompanied by two people. While waiting at a red signal, members of the RAF approached via motorbike and fired automatic weapons, killing all three passengers. "Revolutionaere Zellen," a subgroup of the RAF, released a communiqué subsequent to the attack. On July 30, 1977, the chief executive officer of the Dresdner Bank was killed in his house by two members of RAF, who called themselves "Aktion Roter Morgen." The remarkable fact, in this case was, that the terrorists got access to the house using the acquaintanceship of one of the RAF members.

---

[16]Tucker (2000, pp. 95–98).

On September 5, 1977, Hans Martin Schleyer, the head of two influential organizations, the Confederation of German Employers' Associations (BDA) and the
Federation of German Industries (BDI), was kidnapped by the RAF, during which
two police officers, his driver, and his body guard were killed. The RAF demanded
the German government to release imprisoned members of their group. According
to Kurbjuweit (2008), Schleyer was hidden in a high-rise near Cologne, Germany.
Later, he was taken across the border into the Netherlands, and subsequently moved
to Belgium, where he spent the majority of his time in captivity. The German police
came very close to finding Schleyer, but due to lack of internal communication could
not rescue him. Several local police officers were convinced that he was held in the
aforementioned high-rise close to the Autobahn. One police officer had even rung
the doorbell of the apartment in question, but nobody had conveyed this information
to the crisis center of the Federal police.

After 43 days, the German government had not given into the demands of the
kidnappers. Hours after the German antiterror unit GSG 9 ended the Palestinian
hijack of Lufthansa Flight 181 (see below), three RAF members were found dead in
their prison cells in Germany, the result of suicide. After the kidnappers of the head
of BDA and BDI received the news of the deaths of the imprisoned RAF members,
he was taken to Mulhousem, France, and executed. The kidnappers phoned the location of the car to the Deutsche Presse-Agentur, after which his body was recovered
in the trunk on October 19, 1977.[17]

9.2.2 "Landshut" Kidnapping

On October 13, 1977, during a flight from Palma de Mallorca/Spain to Frankfurt,
Germany, the Lufthansa airplane "Landshut," containing 91 passengers and crew,
was hijacked by four militants belonging to "Commando Martyr Halima," led by
Mohair Yourself Akache, AKA "Captain Martyr Mahmud." "Landshut," the name
of the airplane, became a synonym of that hijacking.[18] The "Landshut" had to
change course and had to ground in Rome/Italy for refueling. Mahmud demanded
the release of 11 RAF terrorists imprisoned in Germany, and US $15 million. The
"Landshut" continued its journey, landing in Larnaca/Cyprus, Bahrain/United Arabic Emirates and Dubai/UAE, following a series of denied landing clearances at
other airports across the Arabian Peninsula. On October 15, 1977, in Dubai, the
captain of the "Landshut" was able to radio the number of hijackers onboard. In
an interview with journalists, this information was given away by the then Minister of Defense. The hijackers learned about this, with Mahmud threatening to kill
the flight captain. The "Landshut" then flew to Salalah/Oman, where it was denied
landing and changed course to Aden/Oman.

---

[17] Kurbjuweit (2008).

[18] Landshut, a city in the southern part of Germany, was also the name of the hijacked Lufthansa
airplane. Lufthansa airplanes are named for German cities.

As the main runway was blocked by vehicles and the plane was running low on fuel, the captain had to land on a sand strip nearby. In order to verify the condition of the landing gear following the rough landing, he was allowed to temporarily leave the plane. He did not immediately return to the plane after the inspection, even after numerous attempts to recall him and a threat to blow up the plane on the ground. Some reports indicate that flight captain asked the Yemeni authorities to inhibit the continuation of the flight and to respond to the terrorists' demands. He voluntarily returned to the airplane in face of his probable execution. He was shot in the head by one of the terrorists in the main passenger cabin. His body was thrown out of the airplane in Mogadishu/Somalia. The plane was refueled and took off at 2 AM on October 17, 1977, piloted by the copilot. It later landed in Mogadishu. After pouring the duty-free spirits over the hostages in preparation for destroying the plane, the hijackers were told that prisoners were to be released and that the transfer to Mogadishu required several more hours, they extended the deadline to the next morning, at 12:30 AM local time.

By order of German Chancellor Helmut Schmidt, a team of GSG 9 commandos assembled in Dubai and continued the flight in a white-painted Luftwaffe airplane to Mogadishu. The team stormed the airliner at 11:05 PM local time on October 18, 1977. In the 7-minute operation, four terrorists were killed while one GSG 9 member and a flight attendant were injured. All the remaining 86 hostages were rescued. After the "Landshut" crisis, the German government stated that it would never again negotiate with terrorists. The German Chancellor of the time was widely praised for his decision to have the plane stormed.

9.2.3 Continuous RAF Terrorism

Even if the RAF core members committed suicide while in prison, the story of the RAF continued another 20 years. It pursued with spectacular trials and court hearings of arrested RAF members, bank robberies and hunger strikes of imprisoned RAF members to be put together in one prison. The execution of the chairman of the board of the engine and engine union (MTU) and chairmen of the Federal association of German air and space industry registered association (BDLI) was committed February 1, 1985. Until today the offenders are unknown. On August 8, 1985, a US soldier was killed by a female RAF member to get his ID card. On the same day she was involved in the bombing of the US Air Base in Frankfurt/Germany, where 2 US employers have been killed and 11 have been injured. On July 9, 1986, a member of the Siemens Board of Directors of research and technology and chairman of the "atomic energy board" of the Federal Union of German industry and his driver were killed by a subgroup of the RAF called "Commando Mara Cagoll."

On October 10, 1986, a high-ranked representative of the German Ministry of Foreign Affairs was killed by the RAF. Three years later on November 30, 1989, the chief executive officer of the Deutsche Bank was shot dead in front of his house. On April 20, 1998, in an eight-page-long letter sent by the RAF to the press association Reuters, the annulment of RAF was expounded. Indeed no crimes are

reported since then committed by the RAF. In 2007, amid widespread media controversy, the German president had considered pardoning one of last still living RAF
member Christian Klar, who filed a pardon application several years ago, but on May
7, 2007, this was denied. However, on November 24, 2008, parole was granted. Two
other RAF members were released in 2007.

9.2.4 Munich Massacre

On September 5, 1972, at 4 AM, five of eight Arab terrorists began executing their
plan to scale the six-foot six-inch fences at the Olympic Village apartments of the
Israeli Olympic athletes in Munich/Germany. Although they were seen by several
people, the gunmen made their way to apartment one and inserted a stolen key.
The Israeli wrestling referee began reacting to the sound of Arab voices behind his
door. He quickly alerted his roommates and pushed his 275-pound body against
the door in an attempt to deny the Arabs' entrance. His efforts were effective for
only a few seconds, but allowed his roommate, the weightlifting coach time, to
escape successfully. The Arab terrorists entered apartment one, immediately taking
five Israeli team members including the track coach, the fencing master, the rifle
coach, the weightlifting judge, and the wrestling referee as hostages. The terrorists
expanded their search throughout the complex, capturing six additional athletes in
apartment number three.[19]

The wrestling coach, who was away from the complex during the initial assault,
arrived back at the apartment while the terrorists continued their search for additional Israeli game participants. Upon entering the apartment, he struggled with two
assassins, striking one and knocking him unconscious. The second Arab terrorist
shot him in the face. Although critically wounded, he rendered another attacker
unconscious before being shot repeatedly in the chest by a third terrorist. Despite his
efforts to defend himself and his colleagues, the Arab terrorists killed him with gun-
shot to his head. As the attack continued, two weightlifters tried to escape through
an open kitchen window. One of them, failing to make his way through the window,
located a kitchen knife and stabbed one gunman in the forehead. A second Arab
moved forward and killed him. By approximately 5 AM, the Arab terrorists had
killed two Israeli team members and captured nine. Due to the unanticipated battle
and chaos, the terrorists failed to locate eight additional team members in apartments two, four, and five. Two Israeli athletes had escaped, made their way to safety
and alerted the authorities to the incident. Within the next hour, the Arab terrorists
had issued a set of demands written in English.

The Palestinian Black September Organization claimed responsibility for the
attacks. Their demands included the release of 234 Arab and German prisoners held
in Israel and West Germany. The terrorists provided a typewritten list of prisoners for release; these included Ulrike Meinhof and Andreas Baader, the founders
and leaders of the German-based RAF. The terrorists also demanded that the police
provide three planes for their escape. Upon receiving confirmation on the release

---

[19] Bard, 2008.

of the prisoners, the terrorists would select one of the planes to transport them to a safe destination. Manfred Schreiber, the Munich Police Commissioner, became the de facto command authority over the hostage incident. He was also the officially appointed chief of the Olympic Security Forces. His superiors in the capital, in 1972, Bonn, established communications with Israel's Prime Minister, Golda Meir, as well as coordinated the possible release of the RAF members with German authorities. The Interior Minister of Bavaria acted as Munich Police Commissioner's superior officer, and West German Chancellor Willy Brandt conducted discussions with the Israeli Prime Minister. Meir maintained her position that the Government of Israel would never negotiate with terrorists.

The West German police negotiators successfully extended three deadlines originally imposed by the terrorists. The Black September Group requested a jet to transport them to Cairo where the prisoners demanded for release by Israel would meet them. However, the government of Egypt refused to provide assistance in support of any West German police action during the crisis. This development, in combination with Golda Meir's absolute refusal to negotiate, forced Munich Police Commissioner to conclude that a rescue attempt was his only option. He determined that in order to conduct a successful hostage rescue, he must confine the terrorists to Germany. To initiate a rescue, he decided the best option was to isolate the terrorists at the airport. Once at the airfield, West German sharpshooters would attempt a hostage rescue operation.

It is important to note that the then Mossad Chief had traveled directly to Munich to discuss the ongoing incident with the West German authorities. He tried to negotiate permission for specially trained Israeli commandos to conduct the hostage rescue. Although Chancellor Brandt might have acquiesced, the local state officials refused. According to the German federal constitution, these decisions are in the hands of the state officials. German police that time lacked the expertise and experience in conducting actions like this. It was only after the arrival at the airport that the West German Police realized there were eight terrorist members, not the five originally estimated. The police deployed only five German snipers at the airport to initiate the rescue. This was far short of the sniper requirements for this type of ambush scenario. In addition, other police officers involved in the rescue attempt were without radio contact with the command post or other police units.[20]

After the Munich Police Commissioner ordered the police snipers to open fire, a full gun battle ensued. The Israeli captives were still sitting bound in the helicopters which had transported them to the airfield. The initial firefight between the terrorists and police lasted approximately 75 minutes. The German Police decided to initiate an attack to move the terrorists from the vicinity of the helicopters. As the attack began, one Arab terrorist jerked a grenade into one of the helicopters holding five of the Israeli athletes. The helicopter exploded, killing all five athletes. Shortly thereafter, another terrorist entered the second helicopter and killed the last four hostages. The police captured three terrorists during the ensuing firefight. At approximately 1:30 AM, the last of the Arab terrorists that were still exchanging

---

[20]Calahan, 1995.

gunfire with the German police were killed. Through the miserably failed operation of the German police, which was neither trained nor equipped for such actions, nine hostages and one police officer were killed. Three kidnappers were detained and five of them were killed. The action subsequently was called the "Munich Massacre." A widely viewed 2006 film titled "Munich" was widely criticized because of several reasons. As this paper only deals with terrorism in Germany, the Israel response to the Munich Massacre should not be scrutinized here.[21]

9.2.5 Contemporary Terrorism

In December 2006, the Federal Office for the Protection of the Constitution became aware of two men observing two US facilities in the city of Hanau, Germany. In August 2007, these two men, with a third person, with false identities and paying cash in advance, rented an apartment in a remote rural area in North-Rhine Westphalia. In this apartment, they collected material to build several bombs with the weight of almost one ton. On September 7, 2007, the three men were stopped by traffic police because they committed an administrative offence. Although they were observed and intercepted permanently in the car and the apartment, the police officers from the Federal Criminal Police Office were not able to impede the stop through the traffic police. The investigators were worried that the stopping through the local police can cause acting of the terrorists. And indeed, although the police control did not cause any problems for the terrorists, while back in the apartment they started discussing, if they better should now conduct the attacks. They started preparation of the bombs through collate of the chemistry to attain the explosives. They already had bought the vans to be used to place the bombs. So the police were forced to take action and to seize the potential terrorists.

On September 7, 2007, 2:20 PM, the road leading to the apartment was blocked by the special forces of GSG 9, who entered the house. Two of the suspects were taken into custody by special forces immediately after entry, while another was captured shortly thereafter while attempting to escape through a window in the back of the house. The terrorists belonged to a group that called themselves Jihad Union. They had planned to kill hundreds of people through suicide bombings with the homemade bombs.[22]

This incident was one of the very few considerable attempts of Islamic terrorism to perform an attack which came to the awareness of German authorities. Although about 700 people are under surveillance of German Secret Services because of their activities related to Muslim homegrown terrorism, not more than 300 of them are assessed to be potential acting terrorists. Only 50 are under concrete suspicion to plan or perform terror-related crimes.[23] These figures create a lively discussion

---

[21] Melman (2006); Jonas (1984); Israel 1967–1991 Olympic Team Murder (n.d.).

[22] Kellner, Lambeck, and Uhlenbroich (2007); Kemmesies (2006).

[23] Bedrohung der Sicherheit in Deutschland durch Terrorismus und Organisierte Kriminalität (n.d.).

between liberal and conservative politicians about the likelihood of an attack conducted through Islamic terrorists living or staying in Germany. Although conservative prognoses are reduced to statements about "an increasing tendency of a terrorism danger," liberal parliamentarians argue that these statements create fear and panic within the population.[24] They use their parliamentarian rights to request detailed numbers of concrete warnings published by the responsible authorities. And indeed these figures do not justify a concrete danger of an attack performed through Muslim home-grown terrorists in the near future.[25] The fact that all official statements are vague and not underlined with any concrete evidence supports liberal assessments that Germany still is not within the focus of homegrown terrorism. On the other hand, it cannot be assessed here if official statements include all knowledge collected by secret services or law enforcement agencies.

There is one considerable development which became evident through several cases. Increasingly greater numbers of German citizens or residents convert to Islam and become Muslims, some of whom are recruited to join the global jihad against Western nations. Some of those recruited go to foreign countries such as Chechnya, Bosnia, Iraq, Afghanistan, or other countries, in which the war on terrorism is present every day.[26] There have not yet been any confirmed cases in which a German who converted to Islam has been involved in an attack in Germany, but there are several cases in which individuals have committed terrorist attacks, including, but not limited to suicide attacks, in the countries mentioned above.[27] With their knowledge about Germany, its security system, and their German identity, it probably is only a matter of time before one or a few of them will be used to conduct or support a serious attack on German soil.

9.3 Law Enforcement

9.3.1 Federal German Police

Due to the federalist system in the Federal Republic of Germany, each Federal State (16) in general holds responsibility for policing the very state. This became manifest in the German constitution in May 1949. Although within the Federal Police services and each Federal State, several re-organizations took place and, due to political and technical development, the services were reduced enormously; this task sharing stayed valid until today. Even if police organizations are quite complex and cross-linked, this chapter attempts to give an understandable overview of the two Federal Police Services, the German Federal Police (*Bundespolizei*) and the Federal Criminal Police Office (*Bundeskriminalamt* or BKA), and to exemplify the organization of the State Police of the State of North-Rhine Westphalia. In 1951, the German

---

[24] Ibid.

[25] Deutscher Bundestag (2008a, 2008b); Wintrobe (2003).

[26] Rushton (1995).

[27] Kämpfer aus Deutschland für den Heiligen Krieg im Irak (2004).

government established a Federal Border Protection Force (*Bundesgrenzschutz* or BGS) composed of 10,000 men under the Federal Interior Ministry's jurisdiction. The force replaced allied military organizations such as the US Constabulary then patrolling Germany's international borders. The Federal Border Protection Force was described as a mobile, lightly armed police force for border and internal security, despite fears that it would be the nucleus of a new West German army. In 1953, the Federal Border Protection Force took control of the German Passport Control Service. In 1976, the state police grades replaced the military ranks to reflect its transition to a multifaceted police agency. The West German Railway Police, formerly an independent service, and the East German *Transportpolizei* were restructured under the Federal Border Protection Police in 1990. A law enacted on July 1, 2005, renamed the Federal Border Protection Force to Federal Police (*Bundespolizei*). The German Ministry of Interior reviewed the structure of the Federal Police in 2007 and, in March 2008, made the structure leaner to get more officers out of offices and into patrol. In addition, the training of the Federal Police was modified to closely match that of the state police forces.

The Federal Police have the following missions:

- border security, to include passport control and the provision of coast guard services along Germany's coasts;
- protection of federal buildings and foreign embassies in the Federal capital Berlin and the former Federal capital Bonn; they also protect the two highest German courts: the Federal Constitutional Court of Germany (*Bundesverfassungsgericht*) and the Federal Court of Justice of Germany (*Bundesgerichtshof*) in Karlsruhe;
- provide the federal government's mobile response force for internal security events;
- provide transportation security at international airports and on the German railways;
- provide counterterrorism forces (GSG 9);
- provide air (or sky) marshals;
- support international police missions;
- document adviser for airlines around the world;
- in-house security for German embassies in several countries; and
- provide rescue helicopter service.

The Federal Police can also be used to reinforce State Police if requested to do so by a state government. It maintains these reserve forces to deal with major demonstrations, disturbances, or emergencies to supplement the capabilities of the State Operational Support Units. Several highly trained detachments are available for crisis situations requiring armored cars, water cannon, or other special equipment. The Federal Police consists of around 40,000 personnel, including 30,000 fully trained police officers and 10,000 salaried civilian (unarmed) support personnel. Among the specialized units within the German Federal police are the GSG 9 (*Grenzschutzgruppe* 9 or Border Guard Group 9), an elite counterterrorism and special operations unit. GSG 9 was officially established on April 17, 1973, subsequent to the Munich Massacre, a terrorist attack at the 1972 Munich Summer Olympics by Black September, a Palestinian militant group, and the deaths of 11 Israelis and 1 German police officer.

In 1972, the Munich Massacre was mainly caused through poor equipped and trained German police services (Federal and State Police). As a consequence of the incident's mismanagement, German officials created the GSG 9 of the then Federal Border Protection Force. Similar situations like in Munich 1972 in the future since then could be responded adequately and professionally. Each of the 16 state police services has implemented similar units trained and equipped on the same standards like GSG 9. Training and competitive exercises are conducted between the Special Intervention Units (*Spezialeinsatzkommandos*) and GSG 9 to ensure the collaboration in times of emergency. After renaming the Federal Border Protection Force into Federal Police in 2005, the abbreviation GSG 9 was kept due to the fame of the unit. Its first mission, which is still one of the most well known and established the GSG 9's reputation as an elite unit, was carried out in 1977 when Palestinian terrorists hijacked the Landshut, a Lufthansa plane on the way from Palma de Mallorca/Spain to Frankfurt/Germany.[28]

9.3.2 The Federal Criminal Police Office (*Bundeskriminalamt – BKA*)

In March 1951, the "Law on the Establishment of a Federal Criminal Police Office" came into force. A short time afterward the "Criminal Police Office for the British Zone" became the *Bundeskriminalamt* (Federal Criminal Police Office), abbreviated BKA. Legislators thus acted on the authority granted by the German Constitution to set up central agencies at Federal level for police information and communications as well as for criminal police work. Wiesbaden was designated as the headquarters for the new criminal police agency that same year. The Bonn Branch of the Federal Criminal Police Office moved into a new building in Meckenheim in October 1981. In July 1988, another location of Federal Criminal Police Office was established in Wiesbaden-Bieberich, and after the re-unification and Berlin becoming the capital of the reunified Federal Republic of Germany, the Protection Division was created in Berlin. The third location in Wiesbaden on a former US Military Camp was allocated in September 1994. The duties of the Federal Criminal Police Office nowadays are performed by more than 5500 employees from 70 different professional groups.

In the 1970s and 1980s, the terrorist activities of the Red Army Faction not only had a decisive influence on the work of the Federal Criminal Police Office but also kept the entire country in suspense. As of the mid-1980s, besides continuing its battle against terrorism, the Federal Criminal Police Office concentrated above all on dealing with the growth of international drug trafficking and the spread of organized crime. At the beginning of the new millennium, the Federal Criminal Police Office,

---

[28]Neuorganisation Bundespolizei (2008).

like police agencies all over the world faced the challenge posed by progress in the fields of information and communications technology, which criminals and terrorists also use for their purposes. Since the terrorist attacks in the United States on September 11, 2001, the battle against international terrorism has become a focal point of security policy throughout the world. The resulting new organization of the state security division of the Federal Criminal Police Office distinctly strengthened the investigative potential in the fight against international terrorism. With the creation of the "Joint Counter-Terrorism Centre" (GTAZ) in Berlin in December 2004, in which information on international terrorism is collated and analyzed by various agencies, the fight against terrorism has taken a major step forward. The GTAZ will be described more specifically later on in this paper. These measures are supplemented by the newly founded division "International Coordination" in January 2005, which was a contribution to the cooperation with international partners.

The responsibilities and powers of the Federal Criminal Police Office are regulated by a federal law and can be described by the following five functions:

1. Function as a central agency;
2. Investigative functions;
3. International functions;
4. Protection tasks and prevention; and
5. Administrative function.

The Federal Criminal Police Office, comparable to the Federal Bureau of Investigation (FBI), is a national investigative police agency subordinate to the Federal Ministry of the Interior. The diversity resulting from the principle of federalism in Germany should not lead to uncoordinated activity of the 16 state and 2 federal police services. To coordinate crime suppression and avoid duplication of effort at national and international levels, the Federal Criminal Police Office was established as the central office for police information and communications as well as for the German CID. By acting as information and communications center and maintaining centralized systems and facilities of the German police, it should provide support to the police forces of the federation and of the states in connection with the prevention and prosecution of crimes. All official communications between the German police and other countries are routed through the Federal Criminal Police Office. The Federal Criminal Police Office also acts as the national central office for Interpol, Europol, and the Schengen Information System. The Federal Criminal Police Office investigates outstanding cases of international crime as defined by law.

Besides its function as a central agency, the Federal Criminal Police Office also has to carry out law enforcement tasks in certain cases of international and serious crime and terrorism. In this respect, it will conduct investigations either on the basis of its own (original) jurisdiction or if it is tasked to do so. The Federal Criminal Police Office has primary jurisdiction to conduct investigations in cases of transnational organized trafficking in weapons, ammunition, explosives, or drugs; transnational organized production, or passing, of counterfeit currency; transnational organized money laundering; and, since the year 2002, in cases of transnational organized terrorism. When investigation of terrorist attacks of the RAF or of persons involved in the terrorist attacks of September 11, 2001, in New York and Washington is concerned, the Federal Criminal Police Office that takes charge of the law enforcement activities in Germany, usually at the direction of the Federal Prosecutor General.

In Germany, terrorism is defined as a politically motivated crime. That means that the ST Division of the Federal Criminal Police Office can get competency for law enforcement in cases of terrorist crimes if the offender(s) committed offences which can be abstracted under Section 129 a, Subsection 1 (1 and 2), of the German Penal Code (formation of terrorist organizations) and Section 129 b of the German Penal Code (criminal and terrorist organizations abroad). In this respect, extremist and terrorist offences constitute the most serious manifestations of politically motivated crime. The prevention and suppression of such offences have top priority in the execution of the Federal Criminal Police Office's duties. The continued threat of international terrorism is particularly clear since the attacks in the United States (September 11, 2001), in Madrid/Spain (March 11, 2004), and in London, United Kingdom (July 7 and 21, 2005). In addition, the attempted attacks on local trains in Koblenz and Dortmund, Germany (July 31, 2006) provided evidence of the linkage of terrorism to Germany. On September 4, 2007, German police arrested suspected members of the Islamic Jihad Union (IJU) in Medebach-Oberschlehdorn, Germany, resulting in the seizure of considerable quantities of explosives.

In Berlin in December 2004, the "Joint Counter-Terrorism Centre" (GTAZ) was created as a response to the threat of terrorism, including Islamic fundamentalism. GTAZ, which includes the Federal Criminal Police along with 40 other partner services, is responsible for gathering intelligence in order to detect and deter terrorism. In addition to Federal Criminal Police, the Federal Office for the Protection of the Constitution, and the Federal Intelligence Service, other partners include representatives of the local State Criminal Police Offices, State Offices for the Protection of the Constitution, the Federal Police, the Central Office of the German Customs Investigation Service, the Federal Office for Migration and Refugees, the Military Counter-Intelligence Service, and the Federal Prosecutor General.

The inclusion of the Federal Prosecutor General intensifies the cooperation between law enforcement and prosecution. With the presence of the representatives of the authorities on site, information can be quickly pooled, compounded, and jointly assessed. Therefore, all available sources of information are included in order to be able to recognize possible threat scenarios expeditiously, enabling coordination of operational measures on an ad hoc basis. The officers responsible strive for as much proximity and cooperation as possible, while observing the legally prescribed principle of separation. The international and national tasks performed by the Federal Criminal Police Office are not limited to combat terrorism, but since worldwide terrorism became a crucial issue, they are linked to this issue as well:

1. "Interpol Wiesbaden," which is nothing else than the Federal Criminal Police Office, as the National Central Bureau for the International Criminal Police Organization (ICPO), uses the most modern means of communication to exchange messages with its counterparts throughout the world.

2. At European level, EUROPOL – the "European Police Office" in which all EU
   member states are represented – is a central partner for cooperation. As the
   national unit for Europol, the Federal Criminal Police Office also performs central duties for Germany.
3. Germany's national central office for the Schengen Information System (SIS),
   known as SIRENE (Supplementary Information Request at the National Entry),
   was set up at the Federal Criminal Police Office as well. After the elimination of
   checks on persons at the internal borders of the Schengen countries, persons who
   are wanted by individual Schengen states, or who are to be refused entry into the
   Schengen area, are now circulated at transnational level in the SIS. The Federal Criminal Police Office is the German partner for the police forces of other
   European countries and the rest of the world, and it currently maintains a global
   network of 64 liaison officers serving in 50 countries, who obtain information of
   significance for law enforcement in Germany.[29]

9.3.3 State Police of North-Rhine Westphalia

As mentioned at the beginning of this chapter, the organization and main responsibilities of one state police should be explained on the example of the state
police of North-Rhine Westphalia. As it is the largest police service by number of
police officers (45,000) of all police services – it has even more than the Federal
Police (40,000) – it is probably unique in its organization. Smaller services cannot
provide all services available within the police service of North-Rhine Westphalia,
which serves a population of about 19,000,000 people. Among the NRW operational
police authorities, there are 47 constabularies and the Crime Investigation Authority
(*Landeskriminalamt* – LKA). The 21 urban constabularies are headed by a President
of Police appointed by the state government, and the 26 rural constabularies headed
by the very County Chief Admin Officer elected for 5 years by municipal elections.
Hence, chief of police is always a civilian assisted by a chief police officer responsible for all operational law enforcement which reads prevention and prosecution.
The only ranking police officer with some operational police authority is the Director of Crime Investigation Authority reporting to State Home Office directly. The
State Home Office holds responsibility for operation, training, and standards related
to the development of police excellence. Beside the operational authorities, there are
mainly three police institutions supporting operation and development of policing
excellence. As the Crime Investigation Authority is the most important one concerning the issue of terrorism, it will be the only unit of the state police of North-Rhine
Westphalia, which needs to be described here in a more detailed manner.

    The departments within the Crime Investigation Authority act as a central author-
ity, dealing with all sorts of crime. In doing so they investigate, evaluate, search

---

[29] Das Bundeskriminalamt Fakten und Zahlen (2008).

and collate evidence, collect and analyze intelligence, support operations through coordination and advice, develop police tactics, engage in forensic research, and coordinate intelligence among law enforcement agencies. This is performed within the following departments:

- The Central Department provides administration, equipment, and medical service;
- Department 1 investigates and analyzes organized crime;
- Department 2 handles state security protection, including certain cases of terrorism;
- Department 3 deals with evaluation of crime, search, and prevention;
- Department 4 supports investigations through special technical support units, including surveillance teams and target search units; and
- Department 5 incorporates the Forensic Institute.

Though, in principal, all law enforcement is within responsibility of the very regional police force of that area, the Crime Investigation Authority investigates and prosecutes crime due to the Police Organization Act if Home Office, Ministry of Justice, a court of justice, or a public prosecutor's office ask for it or statutory orders say so. Crime Investigation Authority automatically may be the responsible authority or performs the expert support function. However, in any case the authority becomes the mandatory contact for all law enforcement agencies inside and outside national borders. Department 2 is responsible for state security protection. As a central state office, it is responsible for all crime against state security.[30]

9.4 Field Research

The federal structure of Germany as implemented in the constitution experienced several exceptions since 1949. Specifically, in cases where a common solution to all states is needed, the constitution allows the federal government and parliament to take responsibility. This went so far that the exception became the rule in most of the fields of governmental responsibilities. In contrast, daily policing remained in the hands of the states, but only as long as it does not concern issues that endanger the existence of the Republic as a whole – such as with the threat of terrorism.

The development of all police services within the Federal Republic of Germany was influenced, if not formed, as an outcome of the occurrences and evolution of terrorism in Germany. Even when it was aimed against Germany directly, the Munich Massacre in 1972, as described above, provided evidence that the Federal Republic of Germany was not prepared for tactics employed by terrorists. First, serious incidents were always followed by reactive actions by government agents responsible for security within Germany. Second, most frequently, the federal government took

---

[30]General Introduction of NRW Police (n.d.).

over the case claiming that terrorism endangers the stability of the republic. Third, most measures implemented to combat terrorism were concentrated in specialized units, such as Special Forces. Local police officers are neither aware about the provisions and measures introduced nor involved in the performance of these, which was supported by the research (see below).

After the single incident of the Munich Massacre in 1972, the long-lasting period of RAF and its subgroups terrorism, which culminated in the German Autumn in 1977 went along and formed politics, legislation, and law enforcement in Germany for almost three decades. It led to consequent decisions and consequences. The laws necessary to punish terrorists, such as Article 129 of the penal code, were implemented, and the budgets needed for equipping police adequately with personnel and equipment especially in special forces and units of the Federal Criminal Police Office, the GSG 9, the Crime Investigation Authorities and the Special Units of state police services were supplied. This again did affect ordinary parts of all services if it supported the work of the special units, for example, through installing computer systems to deliver information. Officers from nonspecialized units utilizing these systems are not aware what happens with the information provided by them.

After RAF released a communiqué that declared the organization dissolved in 1995, the fear of terrorism among the German public decreased. However, after the attacks against the United States on September 11, 2001, this perspective changed. In addition, the March 11, 2004, attack in Madrid and the July 7 and 21, 2005, attacks in London also had a significant impact on the public fear of terrorism. While scrutinizing the consequences of German politics, legislation, and development of law enforcement, essential differences between the history of the 1970s and 1980s are still discernible today. As Germany was not affected by a serious Islamic (successful) assault until today, consequences are mainly performed in very specialized units within the Federal Criminal Police Office as described above. The measures performed mainly aim to prevent an assault in Germany, to support other countries, which have been successfully targeted by Islamic terrorists, and to collect and exchange information.

During interviews with police officers conducted with the North-Rhine Westphalia police service, it was confirmed that the officers were only intermittently informed or involved in the preventive or proactive measures with regard to the phenomenon of terrorism. Local police were not informed regarding any operation by Special Forces, in which individuals suspected of terrorism were under observation for months and subsequently detained. The reluctance to involve or inform local police about surveillance or detention of individuals suspected of terrorism was a function of the confidential nature of investigations involving terrorism. Local police may have vital information, but due to the limited interaction between federal and local agencies, that information is not likely to be passed from the local to the federal. Much of the information secretly collected by federal agents investigating terrorism may already be available within the local police service.

While conducting the field research, these facts had to be taken into consideration. The interviews conducted attempted to cover all groups of law enforcement officials involved or potentially involved in combating terrorism. The research encompassed interviews of law enforcement officials from several levels of the hierarchy within the Federal Criminal Police Office and the State Police of North-Rhine Westphalia, including the Crime Investigation Authority. The interview, which focused on the subject's current position, training received, experiences in regard to combating terrorism, cooperation within the police service and between police services, and involvement of communities or other agencies than police, while combating terrorism, was conducted either in person or via the telephone. The interview also employed some open-ended questions, including the solicitation of proposals for enhancing quality of information collection or intelligence. The results of these interviews are reported below utilizing two separate groups: subjects working with the Federal Criminal Police Office and subjects working with the North-Rhine Westphalia State Police.

9.4.1 Federal Criminal Police Office

Officers serving in counterterrorism units within the Federal Criminal Police Office tended to be very well trained, including intelligence and investigation skills. There is strong cooperation between the units within the Federal Criminal Police Office, with foreign police services, and specialized units and forces within the different State Police agencies. None of the subjects reported a need for greater cooperation with external agencies. Subjects reported practically no institutionalized cooperation with local communities, which was expected, as communities are not represented at the federal level.

9.4.2 State Police of North-Rhine Westphalia

The responses provided by subjects from the Crime Investigation Authority were very similar to responses provided by subjects from the Federal Criminal Police Office; however, assessments provided by officers from the constabularies were very different. Terrorism for local officers was not reported to be a major problem in daily policing. Despite these findings, there is significant interest by local officers to be better informed and more involved with regard to terrorism, which is summarized in the following points:

- Primarily, only senior officers received special education or (in-service) training on terrorism issues;
- The involvement of communities into combat terrorism is very limited if at all notable; and
- There is a strong recognition that an in-service training, an involvement of communities and other agencies, and a better cooperation between special units in combat terrorism are needed.

Although at the state level – at least in the State of North-Rhine Westphalia – there are several possibilities to involve communities in fighting terrorism, until today these possibilities have not be used intensively. For example, it would be possible to use the Council of Cities and Towns (Deutscher Staedte- und Gemeindetag) to find common solutions how to combat terrorism. Additionally, even if they are not under the same authority as the communities, the police constabularies as part of the Ministry of Internal Affairs command chain could use their connections with the local authorities. These agencies are under the command of several ministries depending on the issue dealing with. However, both the local police constabularies and the communities dispose of a margin of possible measures, which could be used for a more effective strategy in fighting terrorism. This missing cooperation could at least partially be explained through the controversial debate.[31]

The political debate in Germany about the likelihood of a terrorist attack motivated by Islamic fundamentalism is very controversial. As a wealthy industrial society, involved and connected with the United States on many issues, such as politics, culture, and economy, the fact that no assault was successfully conducted against Germany through early 2009 seems remarkable. The risk of Germany being targeted should initiate all measures feasible to prevent and prepare for a terrorist attack. However, the fact that there has not been a successful terrorist attack in Germany since the September 11th attacks makes it very difficult, if not impossible, to increase or implement measures, which may have an impact on civil rights or broaden police powers, designed to deter or prevent a terrorist attack.

An example which represents the nature of this paradox can be seen in the passage of an aviation security act, Article 14 (*Luftverkehrssicherheitsgesetz*), which provided authorization to Secretary of Defense to order an airplane under control of terrorists and is used as a weapon against an innumerable number of people to be shot down. Although there were several restrictions prior to implementation, the German Supreme Court declared Article 14 unconstitutional on February 15, 2006.[32] The reasoning of the court was that the state does not have the right to decide about the killing of innocent people as a result of the order by a government agent to shoot down the airline. The Supreme Court did not mention how a situation like the described one could be solved in another way or how the state could justify letting hundreds or thousands of people, including the ones in the airplane, die through the attack. The support given to the court's decision showed that currently in Germany the preparedness to make extensive decisions continues to be problematic. It is difficult to assess whether public opinion would change subsequent to a terrorist attack within German borders with numerous casualties, similar to the recent attacks in Madrid and London. During the most violent actions perpetrated by members of the RAF, risky and momentous decisions were made by German officials, such as the decision by Chancellor Helmut Schmidt to take action in Mogadishu.

The current model in Germany, which employs highly specialized law enforcement units of the Federal Criminal Police Office and other agencies, has been suc-

---

[31] Zwick (2004).
[32] BverfGE 115, 118.

cessful, to date, in preventing a major terrorist attack against the Federal Republic of Germany. However, this model may not be sufficient as it does not address local law enforcement, which could be a significant resource in the prevention of terrorist attacks due to the potential for local police to have relationships with members of the community. These relationships may yield valuable intelligence, which is a necessary component in preventing terrorism in its planning and preparation stages. The other limitation to the existing model is the lack of any community involvement, which, as previously discussed, may provide valuable information necessary to implement proactive counterterrorism tactics.[33]

References

Aust, S. (2008). *Baader-Meinhof complex*. London, UK: The Bodley Head Ltd.

Backes, U. (1991). Bleierne Jahre, Baader-Meinhof und danach, Erlangen.

Bard, M. (2008). The Munich Massacre. The American-Israeli Cooperative Enterprise. Retrieved December 18th, 2008, from http://www.jewishvirtuallibrary.org/jsource/Terrorism/munich.html

Bedrohung der Sicherheit in Deutschland durch Terrorismus und Organisierte Krimiinalität. (n.d.). Zukunftsforum Öffentliche Sicherheit, Bedrohung durch Terrorismus und OK. Retrieved March 3, 2009, from http://www.zukunftsforum-oeffentliche-sicherheit.de/download/22/

Bernholz, P. (2004). Supreme values as the basis for terror. *European Journal of Political Economy, 20*, 317–333.

Bundesverfassungsgericht – Pressestelle (2008). Urteil vom 27. Februar 2008 – 1 BvR 370/07; 1 BvR 595/07.

Calahan, A. B. (1995). The Israeli Response to the 1972 Munich Olimpic Massacre and the Development of the Independent Covert Action Teams. Retrieved February 4th, 2009, from http://www.fas.org/irp/eprint/calahan.htm

CIA World Factbook. (n.d.) Germany (last updated – February 24th, 2009). Retrieved January 16th, 2009, from https:// www.cia.gov/library/publications/the-world-factbook/geos/gm.html

Crenshaw, M. (1995). *Terrorism in context*. University Park, PA: Penn State Press.

Das Bundeskriminalamt Fakten und Zahlen (2008), Bundeskriminalamt Oeffentlichkeitsarbeit, Wiesbaden.

Dershowitz, A. M. (2002). *Why terrorism works: Understanding the threat, responding to the challenge*. New Haven, CT: Yale University Press.

Deutscher Bundestag (2008a). Drucksache 16/10007 – 18.07.2008, Das Gemeinsame Terrorismus-abwehrzentrum.

Deutscher Bundestag (2008b). Drucksache 16/10724 – 30.10.2008, Anzahl der Terrorwarnungen.

General Introduction of NRW Police. (n.d.). Polizei des Landes Nordrhein-Westfalen. Retrieved December 18th, 2008, from http://www.polizei-nrw.de/lka/

German Bundestag. (2008). Basic Law for the Federal Republic of Germany. Retrieved from http://www.bundestag.de/interakt/infomat/fremdsprachiges_material/downloads/ggEn_download.pdf

German Bundestag. (2009). Rules of Procedure of the German Bundestag. Retrieved February 28th, 2009 from http://www.bundestag.de/interakt/infomat/fremdsprachiges_material/downloads/goEN_download.pdf

Israel 1967–1991 Olympic Team Murder. (n.d.). Who murdered the athletes of the Israeli 1972 Olympic Team in Munich? *Palestine Facts*. Retrieved February 4th, 2009, from http://www.palestinefacts.org/pf_1967to1991_munich.php

---

[33] Rees (2003).

Jonas, G. (1984). *Vengeance: The true story of an Israeli counter-terrorist team.* New York, NY: Simon & Schuster.

Kämpfer aus Deutschland für den Heiligen Krieg im Irak. (2004). Spiegel online. Retrieved March 4, 2009, from http://www.spiegel.de/schulspiegel/0,1518,druck-296401,00.html

Kellner, B., Lambeck, M. S., & Uhlenbroich, B. (2007). Drei Bombentransporter standen schon bereit. Retrieved January 17th, 2009 from www.bild.de

Kemmesies, U. E. (2006). Terrorismus und Extremismus – der Zukunft auf der Spur, Bundeskriminalamt (BKA) Kriminalistisches Institut.

Kurbjuweit, D. (2008), Bilder der Barbarei, Der Spiegel, Nr. 37/8.9.2008, Spiegel-Verlag, Hamburg.

Melman, Y. (2006, January 17). Munich: fact and fantasy. Retrieved December 18, 2008, from http://www.theguardian.co.uk

Neuorganisation Bundespolizei (2008). Bundesministerium des Innern.

Rees, M. (2003). *Our final hour: A scientist's warning: How terror, error, and environmental disaster threaten humankind's future in this century – on earth and beyond.* New York, NY: Basic Books.

Rushton, R. M. (1995). The Rushton report – Right-wing extremism in the Federal Republic of Germany 1973–1995. Retrieved January 16th, 2009, from http://www.nizkor.org/hweb/people/r/rushton-reginald/rushton-report-2.html

Tucker, J. B. (2000). *Toxic terror: Assessing terrorist use of chemical and biological weapons (BCSIA Studies in International Security).* Cambridge, MA: MIT Press.

Wintrobe, R. (2003). Can suicide bombers be rational? Department of Economics, University of Western Ontario, London (Canada). Retrieved January 16th, 2009, from http://cas.uchicago.edu/workshops/cpolit/papers/suicide.pdf

Wolff, A. (2002). When the terror began. *Sports Illustrated.* Retrieved February 4th, 2009, from http://sportsillustrated.cnn.com

Wunschik, T. (1997). Baader-Meinhofs Kinder: Die zweite Generation der RAF, Opladen.

Zwick, M. M. (2004). Terrorism as perceived by the German public, *Disaster and Society – from Hazard Assessment to Risk Reduction*, 359–367, Berlin.

Chapter 10
United States

10.1 History

The United States of America (US), the third largest country in the world, both in population[1] and in size,[2] was established subsequent to the American Revolutionary War and the signing of declaration of independence by 13 states along the Eastern coast of North America from British rule in 1776. Following the Treaty of Paris in 1783 the US was recognized as a new nation.[3] During the nineteenth and twentieth centuries, the US expanded westward across North America, increasing the number of states through 1959 and the addition of its 50th state, Hawaii. In addition to the 50 states, the US has a number of dependent areas.[4] The United States experienced a civil war from 1861 to 1865, during which the northern states defeated a confederacy of secessionist southern states. The current government is based on the US constitution, which was drafted by revolutionaries that had learned from their experiences with the British that governmental power in the hands of unelected officials not accountable to the people they govern can readily lead to abuses.

The framework for the current US government was created in 1787 when the North American colonists replaced the Articles of Confederation with the Constitution of the United States of America. The US constitution established a representative democracy that strictly divides federal power among three branches of government: the legislative branch is represented by the two Houses of Congress, the House of Representatives and the Senate; the executive branch is represented by the Presidency; and the judicial branch is represented by the Supreme Court.

---

[1] US population is over 300 million; only China and India, with populations over 1 billion each, are larger.

[2] Only Canada and Russia have more area, although all have areas that are primarily uninhabited in the Arctic circle.

[3] "The Treaty of Paris was signed by U.S. and British Representatives on September 3, 1783, ending the War of the American Revolution." http://www.state.gov/r/pa/ho/time/ar/14313.htm.

[4] US dependent areas: American Samoa, Baker Island, Guam, Howland Island, Jarvis Island, Johnston Atoll, Kingman Reef, Midway Islands, Navassa Island, Northern Mariana Islands, Palmyra Atoll, Puerto Rico, Virgin Islands, Wake Island. https://www.cia.gov/library/publications/the-world-factbook/geos/us.html.

M.R. Haberfeld et al., *Terrorism Within Comparative International Context,* 123
DOI 10.1007/978-0-387-88861-3_10, © Springer Science+Business Media, LLC 2009

In addition, the US constitution provides flexibility to allow for amendments that reflect the evolving will of the people.

The American colonists were reluctant to revolt, and did so only after numerous unsuccessful attempts to negotiate some measure of independence and self-governance from the British government across the Atlantic, which had imposed heavy taxes on the colonists, denied them the right to participate in their government, and suppressed the civil liberties that were provided to British subjects living in England. The Revolutionary War began on April 19, 1775, when colonial militias engaged British troops that were searching for caches of weapons, and those who might wield them, in the towns of Lexington and Concord, Massachusetts. At that time, a majority of the American colonists opposed war, the Continental Army had not been formed, nor had the Declaration of Independence been drafted. During these early engagements, the colonial militias adopted tactics that were considered "unconventional" and inappropriate by eighteenth century standards of warfare – the Americans refused to fight in the open, they engaged the British troops from hidden positions using "sniper attacks," and they continued these sniper attacks as the British soldiers marched home to their barracks in Boston.

After the colonists won independence from Great Britain, they drafted a proposed "Constitution for the United States of America," which, after much debate, was unanimously ratified by representatives of the 13 colonies in 1787. The US constitution is, by its own terms, the "supreme law of the land" (Article VI). As such, it is binding on all elected and appointed officials working for the various state governments and the federal government – explicitly including the president, members of congress, judges, and all elected or appointed officials – who must each swear or affirm that they will support the constitution (Articles II and VI). The drafters of the constitution, who had learned to be mistrustful of governmental officials, divided power into three "branches": the legislative branch (the Two Houses of Congress), the executive branch (the Presidency), and the judicial branch (the Supreme Court and the lower federal courts). A system of checks and balances among the three branches of government were designed to impose accountability and limit the abuse of power by any one branch.

The legislative powers of the United States are detailed in Article I of the constitution, which states that proposed federal legislation must be approved by a majority of elected members of both Houses of Congress (the House of Representatives and the Senate). If a law approved by both Houses of Congress is signed by the president, it becomes law. Article I also sets forth the means by which each of the individual states elects their federal legislators, the lengths of the legislators' terms of office, and the respective and shared powers of the two "Houses." Thus, Members of the House of Representatives are elected to serve 2-year terms in office; each state is granted at least one seat and the total number of representatives from any one state is based upon its total population, so that more populous states have a greater number of representatives. Each state is permitted two Senators, who each serves 6-year terms. In addition to the power to approve federal legislation, Article I of the constitution specifically empowers the two Houses of Congress with the authority to declare war; to raise, fund, and regulate the military; to control all federal taxation and spending; to borrow money; to regulate interstate commerce; to coin money; to control immigration and naturalization; to "constitute" the lower federal courts; to suspend the "writ of habeus corpus" (under which imprisoned individuals may challenge their imprisonment in federal court); and to override a presidential veto (upon the votes of two-third of the members of both Houses) and enact legislation rejected by the president.

Article I of the constitution also details powers unique to the House of Representatives, including the power to "originate" tax laws and the power to "impeach" elected and appointed officials for serious misconduct (impeached officials are then tried by the Senate, which decides whether they should be removed from office). Powers unique to the Senate's include the right to "advise and consent" – i.e., review and then approve or reject – presidential appointments of federal officials and Supreme Court justices; the right to "advise and consent" to treaties proposed by the president; and the power to conduct trials of officials impeached by the House of Representatives (with the Chief Justice of the United States presiding).

Presidential powers are set forth in Article II of the constitution, which limits the president to a 4-year term of office and explains how the president is elected. Under Article II, the president is commander-in-chief of the armed forces and "shall take care that the laws be faithfully executed." Article II empowers the president, with the "advice and consent" of the Senate, to appoint federal officials, including officers of the United States, military officers, ambassadors, and Supreme Court justices. Finally, Article II empowers the president to pardon any federal offense except impeachment and to fill vacancies in positions occupied by federal officials when Congress is in recess.

Article III of the constitution sets forth the powers of the federal judiciary, which refers to the "one Supreme Court, and. . . such inferior courts as the Congress may establish." Federal judges are appointed for life, and "shall hold their offices during good behavior" (i.e., may only be impeached for serious misconduct). Article II limits the jurisdiction of the Supreme Court to disputes involving the constitution, federal laws, treaties, matters in which the federal government is a party, cases involving ambassadors, controversies between states, and controversies involving foreign governments.

Finally, Article V of the constitution (which contains other provisions beyond the scope of this overview) provides flexibility by authorizing amendments to the constitution itself, subject to a fairly high threshold involving two steps: (1) a two-thirds vote of both Houses of Congress, or approval by two-thirds the state legislatures, approving the proposed amendment; and (2) ratification of the proposed amendment by vote by either three-quarters of the state legislators or conventions in three-quarters of the states. The first 10 amendments, which set forth various civil liberties and were passed soon after the constitution itself was ratified, are collectively known as the "Bill of Rights." The amendment process under Article V has been used to amend the constitution 27 times to, among other things, prohibit slavery and ensure the equal protection of law to citizens of all states.

10.2 Terrorism

In most western democratic countries, acts of terrorism are ultra-low frequency events when compared with other criminal activities or other more common causes of injury and death, such as vehicular accidents. The issue with terrorism and its potential risk to modern society is the increasing level of lethality. The September 11, 2001, attacks against the US dramatically changed the perception of terrorism worldwide.[5] Although the number of terrorist attacks in Western countries may have decreased over the past decades, the lethality of the attacks has increased substantially. This recent trend in conjunction with the technological advances and availability of materials necessary to develop and employ a weapon of mass destruction (WMD) has led many countries to allocate much greater resources to the phenomenon than the frequency of such events would warrant. Recent events, such as the arrest of three individuals in possession of enough enriched uranium to build a radiological or dirty bomb, provide the evidence necessary to believe that there is a reasonable probability that a nonstate actor will be able to obtain material necessary to develop a WMD.[6]

The threat of terrorism is a major source of concern for police officers, regarding international as well as domestic terrorists. Although much of the focus on terrorism has been on international actors, such as Al Qaeda, the domestic threat, as shown by individuals such as Timothy McVeigh, Theodore Kaczynski (the unabomber),[7] is real and significant. In the United States, domestic terrorism attacks outnumber international attacks by a ratio of 7:1.[8] With regard to the potential of violence due to interaction between police and domestic terrorists, at least 65 domestic far-right extremists died as a result of confrontations with police. In addition, the far-right was responsible for the deaths of over 20 law enforcement officers, 4 of which occurred in 2007.[9]

While terrorism remains one of the greatest threats to modern society, the ability of law enforcement agencies to respond to the threat continues to be problematic, despite major increases in funding and resources for counterterrorism (CT). A May

---

[5] For a more in-depth understanding of the 9/11 attacks and the response by law enforcement, see Shane (2009).

[6] BBC News: Slovak raid nets bomb uranium. http://news.bbc.co.uk/2/hi/europe/7119172.stm; BBC News: Arrests in Slovak nuclear plot – "Police in Slovakia and Hungary have arrested three people for allegedly trying to sell 1 kg (2.2 lb) of radioactive material, officials said... International agencies have repeatedly warned of the risk of radioactive material from the former Soviet Union passing into the hands of criminals or terrorists. A police raid in the Czech Republic in 1994 uncovered an attempt to sell 2.73 kg (96 ounces) of enriched uranium illegally. Police in the same year confiscated 2.97 kg (105 ounces) of enriched uranium intended for illegal sale in the Russian city of St Petersburg". http://news.bbc.co.uk/2/hi/europe/7117758.stm.

[7] See DeSa & McCarthy (2009).

[8] LaFree, Dugan, Fogg, and Scott (2006).

[9] See the National Consortium for the Study of Terrorism and Responses to Terrorism (START) at http://www.start.umd.edu/start; DHS (2009); McGarrell, Freilich & Chermak (2007).

2007 US Government Accountability Office (GAO) report, which examined law enforcement efforts to assist foreign nations to identify, disrupt, and prosecute terrorists, found that:

> most [Law Enforcement Agencies (LEAs)], with the exception of the FBI, have not been given clear guidance, they lacked clearly defined roles and responsibilities on helping foreign nations identify, disrupt, and prosecute terrorists. In one country we visited, the lack of clear roles and responsibilities between two U.S. LEAs may have compromised several joint operations intended to identify and disrupt potential terrorist activities, according to the U.S. and foreign nation LEAs. In addition, we found LEAs generally lacked guidance on using resources to assist foreign nations in addressing terrorist vulnerabilities and generally lacked performance monitoring systems and formal structures for sharing information and collaborating. We also found that, because comprehensive needs assessments were not conducted, LEAs may not be tailoring their full range of training and assistance to address key terrorism vulnerabilities in foreign countries.[10]

Given the low frequency of terrorism and the fact that most local law enforcement agencies have multiple responsibilities, many law enforcement agencies are severely limited in their ability to have personnel assigned full time to CT duties. Most local law enforcement agencies will be hard pressed to justify shifting personnel from more traditional assignments when communities are more concerned by local issues that have a greater probability of impacting them in the near future. In comparison to other serious criminal activity, communities in the United States have rarely been subjected to successful terrorist attacks.[11]

A 2007 report by the National Intelligence Council (NIC), which judged that the terrorist threat to the United States is in a heightened threat environment, assessed that globalization and technological advances will continue to enable individuals to mobilize resources without requiring a centralized organization, training camp, or leader. Furthermore, the NIC report concluded that detection of terrorist plotting will "require greater understanding of how suspect activities at the local level relate to strategic threat information and how best to identify indicators of terrorist activity in the midst of legitimate interactions."[12]

Although larger agencies have developed or increased resources for CT, the greatest potential for identifying individuals or groups involved in planning a terrorist attack may lie with local law enforcement agents through communication with the communities they serve. Community policing may be the greatest asset to decreasing the threat posed by the phenomenon of terrorism in the new millennium. By increasing the cooperation and communication between the community and the police, the ability of individuals planning a terrorist attack to maintain the covert nature required for success can be significantly impacted. The plans of a terrorist must remain hidden from law enforcement in order to be able to be successful

---

[10]GAO. Combating terrorism: Law enforcement agencies lack directive to assist foreign nations to identify, disrupt, and prosecute terrorists. http://www.gao.gov/new.items/d07697.pdf.

[11]US Senate (2007); National Commission on Terrorist Attacks Upon the United States (2002); National Intelligence Estimate (2007).

[12]US National Intelligence Council (http://www.dni.gov/press_releases/20070717_release.pdf).

in carrying out an operation. Effective community policing can serve to promote intelligence gathering and identification of individuals and groups planning terrorist attacks. As found in the Smith, Damphousse, and Roberts (2006) study, a significant proportion of individuals planning an attack both reside and engage in preparatory acts in relatively close proximity to the location of the planned attack; therefore it is likely that the individuals will come into contact with members of the community and local law enforcement prior to an attack.[13]

What is terrorism? Terrorism is at least as old as the Common Era, with the oldest known historical terrorist group, *the Sicarii*,[14] a religious sect that consisted of men of lower order in the Zealot struggle in Palestine, dating back to the first century. The definition of terrorism is a major component of any policy related to combating terrorism, but terrorism has not been clearly and concisely defined, at either national or international level.[15] There has not yet been, nor is there ever likely to be, an academic consensus on the definition, which creates a major limitation for the consistent operationalization of terrorism. Neither is there a consensus among nation states on the definition of terrorism.

Historically, many liberation struggles have employed violence, but it is questionable whether violence is a necessary component of self-rule or self-determination. India gained its independence primarily through nonviolent resistance, although at great cost and suffering to its people. Rather than blaming violence on state oppressors and thereby justifying violence, especially violence against civilians, as a legitimate means, India's success could be used as a model for other liberation movements worldwide, which would be much more likely to gain international support. Although, as Crenshaw (1995) states "[i]f terrorism seems to be the only effective means of armed struggle, then resistance and terrorism become synonymous."[16]

Some terrorist experts echo this issue, in that the policies enacted by governments may be counterproductive in nature, further alienating segments of the population or increasing sympathy for the causes promoted by individuals or organizations utilizing terroristic tactics and increasing the base from which to draw resources. Crenshaw posits that "[c]oercive or repressive policies designed to destroy or contain the terrorist threat in the immediate, even if successful in achieving that end, may alienate and aggrieve others who sympathize with the claims of those resorting to violence. . . Thus, the response to terrorism must be legitimate if the government is to defeat a group without expanding its support base. Violations of human rights in the pursuit of counter-terrorism will be counterproductive."[17]

The US research employs a violence matrix, Table 10.1 below, to determine the classification for acts of violence that attempt to coerce a target audience to implement a political, economic, religious, or ideological change, examining two variables, the actor and the target. An act of violence committed by a nonstate actor

---

[13] Smith et al. (2006).

[14] Barghothi (1996).

[15] Hoffman (1998); Schmid (2004); Schmid & Jongman (2005).

[16] Crenshaw (1995, p. 16).

[17] Crenshaw (2005, p. 16).

Table 10.1 Violence matrix: Actor v. target

	Target	
Actor	*Government or military*	*Civilian*
State	Act of war	War crime *or* crime against humanity
Nonstate	Guerilla warfare *or* revolution	Act of terrorism

that targets military or governmental facilities would be operationalized as guerilla warfare or revolution. An act of violence committed by a state actor that targets civilians would be operationalized as a war crime or crime against humanity. An act of violence committed by state actor that targets foreign military or governmental facilities would be operationalized as an act of war. An act of violence committed by a nonstate actor that targets civilian would be operationalized as an act of terrorism. There are gray areas that involve some crossover, but the four categories presented provide a clear framework from which to exclude situations that obscure the operationalization of terrorism.[18]

There is no inclusion of freedom fighter, the controversial term often associated with terrorism, because the groups and individuals associated with the above four categories of acts can declare themselves as freedom fighters. A freedom fighter is a subjective label describing the group or individual, while in Fig. 10.1 the specific act is the determining factor. A state actor may simultaneously engage in acts that are war crimes and acts of war. An example is Iraq in the 1980s, in which the military conflict with Iran would be categorized as an act of war, while the use of chemical warfare against civilian Kurdish populations in Northern Iraq would be categorized as a crime against humanity or possibly genocide. A nonstate actor may also simultaneously engage in both guerilla warfare and acts of terrorism. An example of this is the IRA, whose operations against government targets would be categorized as guerilla warfare, while an operation that targeted civilians, such as the 1983 Harrods bombing in London,[19] would be categorized as terrorism.

The exclusion of state actors provides for a definition more likely to be accepted by the leaders and government representatives of nation states. The Rome Statute of the International Criminal Court (ICC) provides for acts committed by nation states, such as the crime of genocide, crimes against humanity, war crimes, and the crime of aggression. Calling these same acts terrorism does not provide any additional benefit. Saddam Hussein, the former leader of Iraq, was sentenced to death for crimes against humanity by an Iraqi court after a year-long trial over the killings of 148 people from the town of Dujail in 1982 and was subsequently executed by hanging on December 30, 2006.[20] In addition to the incidents in Dujail, Hussein was also implicated in the use of chemical weapons by the Iraqi government against

---

[18] Lieberman (2009).

[19] BBC News: 1983: Harrods bomb blast kills six. http://news.bbc.co.uk/onthisday/hi/dates/stories/december/17/newsid_2538000/2538147.stm.

[20] BBC News: Saddam's Life and Times. http://news.bbc.co.uk/2/shared/spl/hi/middle_east/03/v3_iraq_timeline/html/trial_of_saddam.stm.

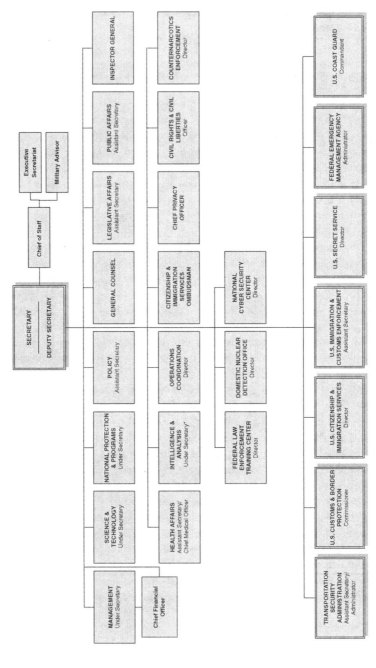

Fig. 10.1 Department of Homeland Security organization chart

the Kurds in Northern Iraq, in a military campaign that led to the death of 50,000–100,000 Iraqi Kurds.

> Saddam Hussein is the first world leader in modern times to have brutally used chemical weapons against his own people. His goals were to systematically terrorize and exterminate the Kurdish population in northern Iraq, to silence his critics, and to test the effectiveness of his chemical and biological weapons. Hussein launched chemical attacks against 40 Kurdish villages and thousands of innocent civilians in 1987–88, using them as testing grounds. The worst of these attacks devastated the city of Halabja on March 16, 1988.[21]

The exclusion of government or military targets, who may engage in oppressive tactics against civilian populations, provides for a definition more likely to be accepted by the international community. The democracy enjoyed by a number of Western governments, such as the United States, was the result of an armed rebellion. The exclusion of acts committed by nonstate actors against a government is consistent with the ideals promoted in the founding of the United States and other Western democratic nations. In addition, the exclusion of acts committed by nonstate actors against a government is consistent with the aforementioned issue brought up by many Arab countries during the early UN discussions on terrorism in the 1970s, in their desire to exclude people that struggle to liberate themselves from oppression and exploitation that use force from being labeled as terrorists. The controversy regarding terrorism in the modern age extends beyond academic or legal definitions.

A 1999 FBI report on terrorism defines domestic and international terrorism differently: differentiating domestic terrorism as acts that occur within the United States or its territories without foreign direction, intended to coerce the government or civilian population in furtherance of ideological goals. The main difference between the definitions is the qualification that international incidents are acts that either occur outside the US or in US territories under foreign influence or direction.[22]

A recent study by Smith et al. (2006), which uses the data from the ATS, examines ancillary and preparatory crimes committed by individuals preceding a terrorist attack. The goal of the study was twofold, to determine: "(1) [if] sufficient open source data exists to examine the temporal and spatial relationships that exist in terrorist group planning, and (2) if such data do exist, can patterns of routinized preparatory conduct be identified."[23] The findings, which show that many individuals planning an act of terrorism both reside and plan operations in relatively close proximity to the target location, provide insight into the potential intervention that may be utilized to address the phenomenon of terrorism.

> If preparatory behaviors can serve as pre-incident indicators to local law enforcement agencies, it is important to know the relationship between where these acts occur and the location

---

[21] Saddam's Chemical Weapons Campaign: Halabja, March 16, 1988. http://www.state.gov/r/pa/i/rls/18714.htm.

[22] FBI (1999, p. ii).

[23] Smith et al. (2006, p. 2).

of the residence of the terrorist and the target location. Once again, approximately one-half of the terrorists lived within a thirty mile radius of where they committed their planning activities. The same pattern persists when examining the relationship between the location of preparatory behaviors and the target location... For local law enforcement, knowledge that most terrorists "act locally" can be an important mindset as investigative agencies seek to prevent terrorism or apprehend the perpetrators of these acts. These local patterns may be used by agencies to more efficiently patrol known, high risk target areas and gather intelligence on suspected activities within a specific range from potential targets.[24]

The Smith et al. (2006) study found a bimodal spatial distribution among the 60 cases analyzed, in which approximately half the terrorist actors resided, planned, and prepared for the terrorist attack in relatively close proximity to the intended target. For those local actors, the potential for intervention by local law enforcement provides a contrasting view to the popular belief that terrorism is random and can happen anywhere. Although this study was exploratory, it provides insight into possible policy implications of the locality of these events. In addition to the implications provided by Smith et al. (2006), which include local law enforcement knowledge relating to more effective patrol of high-risk targets,[25] there is also the impact on the limitations to law enforcement, such as the inability to identify nonovert acts of conspiracies, such as meetings and phone calls.[26] However, the utilization of community policing may serve to increase the potential for law enforcement to become aware of these nonovert acts, through communication and cooperation with local communities.

In a recent study, Smith, Cothren, Roberts, and Damphousse (2008) examined antecedent conduct of terrorist group members for 118 environmental and 55 international incidents occurring in the United States in an attempt to identify patterns of conduct that might lead to intervention prior to the commission of actual terrorist incidents, which suggested that these patterns varied by type of terrorist group. The primary goal of this study was to add geospatial and temporal data to the earlier pilot study of preincident indicators of terrorist incidents, which had indicated that patterns of conduct could be identified. The findings from this study supported earlier studies, in that slightly over half of both international and environmental terrorists lived within 30 miles of the target in the days immediately preceding the terrorist incident, over 60% of the antecedent behaviors committed by both international and environmental terrorists occurred within 30 miles of the eventual target, and there was a bimodal distribution regarding the relationship between the terrorists' place of residence and the target location.

However, the temporal patterns for the international and environmental terrorists differed, as the planning process of environmental terrorists was relatively short and spontaneous (approximately 85% of their preparatory conduct occurred within 6 days of the incident) in contrast to the international terrorists (planning activities usually began 4–6 months prior to the incident). International terrorists engaged in a significantly larger number of preparatory activities per incident than environmental

---

[24] Ibid., pp. 72–73).
[25] Ibid., pp. 14–15).
[26] Ibid, p. 8.

terrorists, committing nearly three times as many known antecedent activities per incident as environmental terrorists. Smith et al. (2008) propose that this may have been due to the tendency to have a greater number of persons involved in international incidents, the size and scope of the planned incident, or the longer planning cycle for international terrorists (an average of 92 days between first planning and attack). For environmental terrorist incidents, there were a relatively low number of preparatory crimes and days involved in the planning sequence (an average of 15 days between first planning and attack), regardless of the number of persons involved. This may significantly impact law enforcement response, especially at the local level, as the type of actor may have a significant impact on the time available to engage in proactive police work in order to prevent a terrorist attack.[27]

10.3 Law Enforcement

The constitutional structure of the US government limits centralized power, guards states' rights, and preserves local municipal control over local law enforcement.[28] The United States has four primary distinctions among its law enforcement agencies: federal, state, local, and tribal. According to the Bureau of Justice Assistance (2002, 2005a, 2005b), there were over 800,000 full-time sworn law enforcement officers in the United States. Nearly 732,000 (87.5%) of these law enforcement officers are state and local officers, compared with a little over 100,000 (12.5%) federal law enforcement officers. Within local law enforcement, the size of the various agencies ranges from very small, with a handful of full-time sworn officers, to very large, with the largest municipal law enforcement agency in the world, the NYPD, with approximately 36,000 full-time sworn officers. Many of the smaller local agencies rely on state law enforcement agencies to supplement their efforts on major investigations, such as homicides, kidnappings, and serial offenses, as the smaller agencies do not have facilities necessary to conduct more advanced forensic investigations. Table 10.2 below depicts the different types of US law enforcement agencies, the

Table 10.2 Law enforcement statistics: http://www.ojp.usdoj.gov/bjs/lawenf.htm

Type of agency	Number of agencies	Number of full-time sworn officers
Local police	12,766	446,974
Sheriff	3067	175,018
Primary state	49	58,190
Special jurisdiction	1481	49,398
Constable/marshall	513	2323
State and local	17,876	731,903
Federal		104,884
Total		836,787

---

[27] Smith et al. (2008, pp. 79–82).
[28] Walker (2008) in Haberfeld and Cerrah (2008, p. 325).

number of agencies for each type of agency, and the total number of full-time sworn officers for each type of agency.[29]

10.3.1 Department of Homeland Security (DHS)

The Department of Homeland Security (DHS) was formed as a result of the Homeland Security Act of 2002.[30] While the mission of DHS is to lead the unified national effort to secure the country and preserve our freedoms, the primary mission is to prevent terrorist attacks within the United States, reduce the vulnerability of the United States to terrorism, minimize the damage, and assist in recovery from terrorist attacks in the United States.[31] DHS includes the Transportation Security Administration, Customs and Border Protection, Citizen and Immigration Services, Customs Enforcement, Secret Service, Federal Emergency Management, and Coast Guard, depicted in Fig10.1.[32]

10.3.2 Federal Bureau of Investigation (FBI)

The Federal Bureau of Investigation (FBI) was established in 1908 by Attorney General Charles Bonaparte during the Presidency of Theodore Roosevelt.[33] The mission statement of the FBI is to "protect and defend the United States against terrorist and foreign intelligence threats, to uphold and enforce the criminal laws of the United States, and to provide leadership and criminal justice services to federal, state, municipal, and international agencies and partners."[34]

1. Protect the United States from terrorist attack
2. Protect the United States against foreign intelligence operations and espionage
3. Protect the United States against cyber-based attacks and high-technology crimes
4. Combat public corruption at all levels
5. Protect civil rights
6. Combat transnational/national criminal organizations and enterprises
7. Combat major white-collar crime
8. Combat significant violent crime
9. Support federal, state, local, and international partners
10. Upgrade technology to successfully perform the FBI's mission (Fig. 10.2)

---

[29]US Department of Justice, Office of Justice Programs, Bureau of Justice Statistics. Law Enforcement Statistics: http://www.ojp.usdoj.gov/bjs/lawenf.htm.

[30]http://www.dhs.gov/xlibrary/assets/hr_5005_enr.pdf.

[31]http://www.dhs.gov/index.shtm.

[32]http://www.dhs.gov/xlibrary/assets/DHS_OrgChart.pdf.

[33]http://www.fbi.gov/libref/historic/history/origins.htm.

[34]http://www.fbi.gov/.

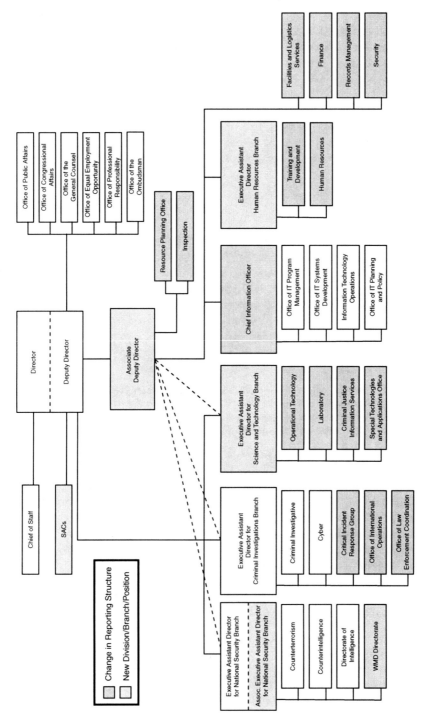

Fig. 10.2   Federal Bureau of Investigation organization chart

In 1980, the FBI created its first Joint Terrorism Task Force (JTTF) in New York City. The JTTFs are small cells of highly trained, locally based, investigators, analysts, linguists, special weapons and tactics (SWAT) experts, and other specialists from dozens of US law enforcement and intelligence agencies. Subsequent to the 9/11 attacks, the FBI extensively expanded the number of JTTFs throughout the United States, from 35 to over 100. In addition, the number of individuals assigned to the JTTFs has increased fourfold, from about a 1000 prior to 9/11 to over 4000. The FBI maintains a Terrorist Screening Center (TSC) and a consolidated Terrorist Watchlist, which is a single database of identifying information about those known or reasonably suspected of being involved in terrorist activity.[35]

10.4 Field Research

In order to address the phenomenon of terrorism in the twenty-first century, we must think globally and act locally.[36] The state of preparedness of United States (US) local law enforcement agencies in their proactive efforts to counter terrorism is shrouded in the dark.[37] For the US research, an act of terrorism is operationalized as the use of force by nonstate actors against a civilian population in an attempt to coerce a target audience to implement a political, economic, religious, or ideological change. This operationalization of terrorism is consistent with the recent FBI report, *Terrorism 2002–2005*, although the operationalization of terrorism excludes acts committed by state actors, also known as state terrorism.

> There is no single, universally accepted, definition of terrorism. Terrorism is defined in the Code of Federal Regulations as "the unlawful use of force and violence against persons or property to intimidate or coerce a government, the civilian population, or any segment thereof, in furtherance of political or social objectives (28 C.F.R. Section 0.85).[38]

Due to the dearth of research in the area of mobilization of local communities in intelligence gathering and other proactive tools to counter terrorist activities, the overwhelming majority of US local law enforcement's response to the phenomenon of terrorism remains unknown. The goal of this exploratory study is to assess the feasibility of implementation of some of the most basic tenets of the community-oriented policing philosophy in mobilization of the communities by local law enforcement agencies in their effort and strive to become proactive in the fight against local and global terrorist threat. Through utilization of focus groups in the Northeast region of the United States, the author measures and assesses the attitudes and perspectives of local law enforcement and nonlaw enforcement toward the possibility of engagement of the local community in a proactive effort to counter terrorism.

---

[35] http://www.fbi.gov/terrorinfo/counterrorism/tsc.htm.

[36] Haberfeld, King & Lieberman (2008).

[37] Lum, Haberfeld, Fachner & Lieberman (2009); Silke (1996, 2001, 2004).

[38] US DOJ: *Terrorism 2002–2005*. http://www.fbi.gov/publications/terror/terrorism2002_2005.pdf.

Cohen and Felson (1979) proposed a Routine Activities theory (RAT), which combines elements of deterrence and rational choice, to explain criminality. The three main categories that contribute to criminal activity include motivated offenders, suitable targets of criminal victimization, and capable guardians of persons or property. The probability of crime occurring increases when there is a presence of motivated offenders, a suitable target is available, and there is an absence or a paucity of capable guardians. Based on the definition of terrorism provided earlier, terrorism will also be a violation of existing law. Terrorism, under the proposed definition, is crime; therefore one could apply Routine Activities to the phenomenon. Cohen and Felson (1979) argue that changes in social patterns of routine activity affect crime rates by influencing the incidence of predatory crime, which are typically associated with rape, robbery, and burglary.

RAT focuses on predatory crime, or as they describe it – *direct-contact predatory violations*, which involve physical contact between at least one offender and at least one person or object targeted by the offender.[39] Although terrorism targets society as a whole, RAT can be applied to a terrorist act, which, as previously operationalized, involves the use of force by nonstate actors against a civilian population. The target may not be specifically selected, nor may there be direct contact typical of the crimes normally associated with RAT, but there will be direct contact between the offender and the target, such as through an explosive device detonated by the offender that impacts the target. Although there may not always be the physical direct contact, there will be a direct relationship between the offender and the target, albeit through another medium.

Cooperation and communication between the police and the community will provide an extension of the capable guardianship provided by police. The community can have a significant impact on the intelligence-gathering capabilities of local police agencies, both positively and negatively. Therefore, strategies that increase cooperation and communication between law enforcement and the public can be useful in detecting, deterring, and preventing future acts of terrorism. In addition, the level of community awareness and preparedness, which can be influenced through community policing, can impact the perception by an offender of the suitability of the target.[40] A community that successfully implements community policing strategies has the potential to decrease the probability that it will be targeted for a terrorist attack and may, in addition, decrease the prevalence of crime overall. Utilizing RAT as a model, community policing will provide both general deterrence, regarding all crime, and specific deterrence, regarding terrorism.

Bittner (1990) wrote extensively regarding the police, discussing the various functions of police in an urban environment, such as traffic control, peacekeeping, and crime control. The role of the police varies based on economic, geographic, and political factors. According to Bittner, the function of police could be best summed up with "something-that-ought-not-to-be-happening-and-about-

---

[39]Cohen and Felson (1979).
[40]Goldstein (1990).

which-someone-had-better-do-something-now!"[41] While this phrase may seem vague, it may be the most appropriate description of the role of police in modern society. Although the public associates policing with arresting criminals, research shows that most police spend only a small fraction of their time with this aspect of police work. However, the police are a unique profession in that their role is differentiated from all other nonmilitary professions through their authority to use coercive force.

Klockars (1985) provides the following definition of police: "Police are institutions or individuals given the general right to use coercive force by the state within the state's domestic territory."[42] The ability to legitimately use coercive force against citizens in a domestic setting is the factor that separates the profession from all others. Klockars refers to Bittner's "something-that-ought-not-to-be-happening-and-about-which-someone-had-better-do-something-now!" phrase, proposing that although the police have an obligation to do something, he does not mean an arrest, citing studies conducted in Boston, Washington D.C. and Chicago as examples supporting that a typical workday of an officer does not involve an arrest.

What is community policing? In order to apply the tenets of community policing, the first step is to identify what these tenets are. The concept of community policing is almost as amorphous as the concept of terrorism. Community policing can encompass any form of policing that involves a partnership between the community and the police, in which there is trust and communication that extends in both directions. Community policing in the United States has been implemented by municipalities to varying degrees over the past three decades, enhanced through P.L. 103-322 (1994),[43] which was also known as the 1994 Omnibus Crime Bill, which provided $8.8 billion for Community-Oriented Policing Services (COPS) programs. Although the bill provided funding to hire and train police officers for deployment in community-oriented policing, there is limited oversight to the implementation of such programs.

Community policing has been implemented to varying degrees in jurisdictions across the United States. The Community Patrol Officer Program (CPOP) began in New York City in 1984 as a pilot program in the 72nd Precinct, Sunset Park – Brooklyn, and was administered by the Vera Institute of Justice. The goal of the program, which consisted of 10 patrol officers supervised by one sergeant, was to provide a community-oriented, problem-solving policing program without restructuring patrol services. The officers were given a 10-day training program designed to provide them with the skills to allow each CPOP officer to be a planner, community organizer, and information link. The success of the program led to citywide

---

[41] Bittner (1990, p. 249).

[42] Klockars (1985, p. 12).

[43] "To amend the Omnibus Crime Control and Safe Streets Act of 1968 to allow grants to increase police presence, to expand and improve cooperative efforts between law enforcement agencies and members of the community to address crime and disorder problems, and otherwise to enhance public safety." http://thomas.loc.gov/cgi-bin/bdquery/z?d103:HR03355:%7CTOM:/bss/d103query.html%7C.

expansion and community-oriented policing was adopted, to varying degrees, by almost every major local law enforcement agency in the United States.[44]

Concepts and critiques of the professional model, as well as the findings and results from a series of police-focused experiments, compose the foundations of community policing. The concept of community policing is often traced back to Sir Robert Peel, the chief architect of the 1829 Metropolitan Police Act[45] that provided Nine Principles of Policing[46] (see Appendix), which included advocating for a strong relationship between the police and the public. The term community policing was not widely used until 150 years after Peel wrote his Principles of Policing. During the 1970s and early 1980s, community policing strategies were being developed and employed in an attempt to improve policing and establish a more effective and appropriate approach of policing.[47] Although there is no universal definition of community policing, Haberfeld (2002) provides 12 points that will be examined as a foundation for COP. The following are the 12 points of the Community-Oriented Policing and problem-solving philosophy illustrated by Haberfeld (2002):

1. Reassesses who is responsible for public safety and redefines the roles and relationships between the police and the community
2. Requires shared ownership, decision making, and accountability as well as sustained commitment from both the police and the community
3. Establishes new police expectations of and measurement standards for police effectiveness
4. Increases understanding and trust between police and community members
5. Supports community initiative by supplying community members with necessary information and skills, reinforcing their courage and strength, and ensuring them the influence to affect policies and share accountability for outcomes
6. Requires constant flexibility to respond to all emerging issues
7. Requires an ongoing commitment to develop long-term and proactive strategies and programs to address the underlying conditions that cause community problems
8. Requires knowledge of available community resources and how to access and mobilize them and the ability to develop new resources within the community
9. Requires buy-in of the top management of the police and other local government agencies as well as a sustained personal commitment from all levels of management and other key personnel
10. Decentralizes police services/operations/management, relaxes the traditional chain of command, and encourages innovation and creative problem solving
11. Shifts the focus of police work from responding to individual incidents to addressing problems identified by the community as well as by the police
12. Requires commitment to developing new skills through training[48]

---

[44] Haberfeld (2002, p. 159).

[45] JSTOR: *1829 Metropolitan Police* Act. http://www.jstor.org/.

[46] Reith (1948).

[47] Skogan (2004).

[48] Haberfeld (2002, pp. 160–161).

Is community policing the answer to the phenomenon of terrorism? One of the first issues that must be addressed is whether local law enforcement agencies are the appropriate agencies to respond to the threat of terrorism. Recent events in the United States, such as the September 11th and Murrah Building attacks, have shown that in the event of a terrorist attack, local agencies, including police, fire and other rescue personnel, will be the first responders.

> While it is true that the federal government is increasing its efforts in the area of terrorism prevention and response, a large degree of the responsibility for responding to threats of terrorism rests at the local level. Experience now tells us that the first responders to any incident will most assuredly be local police, fire and rescue personnel. Therefore, law enforcement officials must now strategically rethink public security procedures and practices in order to maximize the full potential of their resources.[49]

The Office of Community-Oriented Policing Services (COPS) supports the concept of local law enforcement involvement in counterterrorism strategies. In addition to law enforcement efforts to improve data and intelligence collection, increase the capacity to utilize technology, communicate with other public safety agencies, and prepare for and respond to incidents, the focus on prevention must be a primary concern. "A successful response to terrorism involves an array of activities, many of which are reliant on human intelligence gathering activities and productive partnerships between local law enforcement and other agencies."[50] Although the above-described components are important to intelligence gathering, the author contends that there is no greater source of information than the community at large.

> [U]ntil we learn to police in ways that build trusting relationships with those communities where criminals or terrorists can more easily live lives insulated from observation – no amount of additional funding or legal authority, consistent with living in a free society, will increase the capacity of our police forces to gather the crime and terror related information we desperately need.[51]

Community-Oriented Policing (COP) has been viewed as a positive development since its inception, in which politicians, citizens, police officials, and the media promote its function and use. However, many researchers and academics often question the effectiveness and impact of the COP strategy. Criticisms, such as the lack of a universal definition and the difficulty associated with testing, are frequently referenced. COP, by its very nature, must vary in its application in order to effectively respond to the needs and conditions specific to the individual community; therefore operationalization of community policing and empirical analyses of the effectiveness of its implementation across communities are problematic.

Although the effectiveness of applying COP to counter terrorism has not been empirically tested, there are two factors that may provide answers to its potential as a tool for local law enforcement. First, the way in which COP is defined may range among agencies, as well as the researcher or academic gathering the information and

---

[49]Chapman et al. (2002, p. 1).
[50]Chapman et al. (2002, p. 1).
[51]Lyons (2002, p. 530).

conducting the evaluations. It is important that the definition of COP is clearly oper-ationalized in order to test whether its application is effective. Second, the expected results also require operationalization in order to consider the utilization of COP as effective. If a decrease in terrorism indicates COP as an effective method for the prevention and regulation of terrorism, the extent of the decrease expected to occur should be determined. If effectiveness is viewed as obtaining information or intel-ligence that results in the apprehension of terrorists and the prevention of terrorist attacks from occurring, then the frequency of such occurrences should be defined.

In democratic nations, the balance between security and civil rights is challenged by the phenomenon of terrorism, in that the government is required to respond. However, an excessive response may lead to increased support among the passive supporters of groups and organizations that engage in extreme violence against civilian populations. The police agencies, both local and national, are required to respond, maintaining legitimacy by following governmental policies and the rule of law. There is always the fear that law enforcement agents will take it upon them-selves to "fight fire with fire" violating the laws they seek to uphold, which will ultimately delegitimize the agency and provide the terrorists with fertile ground for recruitment and fundraising. It is only through an appropriate legitimate response by law enforcement that the agency will prevent the passive supporters, which tend to be significantly greater in number than the active supporters, from becoming active members in the terrorist organization.

Numerous recent articles have discussed the responsibility of local law enforce-ment or community policing in relation to the threat of terrorism.[52] Based on the findings of Smith et al. (2006), an extended use of community policing to address the phenomenon of terrorism may have a significant impact by helping to gather intelligence and identify individuals planning an attack. In order to be successful in conducting a terrorist attack, individuals planning an attack must keep their plans from being identified by law enforcement. A significant percentage of individuals planning a terrorist attack both reside and engage in preparatory acts in relatively close proximity to the location of the intended target. COP can potentially have a great impact by providing this information to the public, not so that they will be afraid, but so that they would be empowered and know that, as individuals in the community, they have the ability to protect themselves and their community from the threat of terrorism.

While many communities are hesitant to provide information to police about crimes in their neighborhood, for a variety of reasons, including the fear of retribution. It is far less likely that a community member will hesitate providing information about an individual planning a terrorist attack, after becoming informed that studies[53] have shown that a significant percentage of individuals planning a terrorist attack both reside and engage in preparatory acts in relatively close

---

[52]Docobo (2005), Donnermeyer (2002), Henry (2002), Murray (2005), Pelfrey (2005), Scheider and Chapman (2003), and Sloan (2002).

[53]Smith et al. (2003, 2006). Smith (2008); Innes (2006).

proximity to the location of the intended target, which potentially puts the member of the community at risk.

While it is true that the federal government is increasing its efforts in the area of terrorism prevention and response, a large degree of the responsibility for responding to threats of terrorism rests at the local level. Experience now tells us that the first responders to any incident will most assuredly be local police, fire and rescue personnel. Therefore, all local law enforcement officials must now strategically rethink public security procedures and practices in order to maximize the full potential of their resources.

In the United States, taking into account the economic crises that began in 2008, the issue of allocating resources toward programs such as community policing may be perceived as problematic. However, the implementation of community policing may serve to address the needs of both the agency and the community. Bittner (1990) discusses the obstacles to the advancement of new programs, such as community policing, when faced with the resource limitations due to agency needs in other areas, such as crime control, traffic, and training. However, community policing has the potential to have far-reaching effects that can address many of the other areas of concern for an agency. The difficulty in measuring the success of a community-oriented policing strategy also limits the attractiveness of its implementation. It is often impossible to parse out the impact of such a program in relation to all the other efforts of an agency, in addition to the impact of external factors, such as economic conditions and other programs and agencies that are designed to address problems in a community.

Although the term community policing in the United States has only been popular in the past few decades, the concept of community policing has its roots in the earliest forms of modern policing, such as the Metropolitan police, which was formed as a result of the Metropolitan police Act of 1829. According to Bittner (1990), the Metropolitan Police were "a civil force seeking to attain the objectives of peace, order, and crime control in cooperation with the people" (p. 295). The duty to protect the rights, service the needs, and earn the trust of the population was imported from England to police departments in the United States, such as the establishment of the municipal police in New York in 1844.

Municipal police agencies derive their authority both from the state and from the people in the community that they serve; therefore police cannot function efficiently without the support from both. According to Bittner (1990), in the 1950s many European countries and in the United States, police departments began public relations campaigns to portray themselves more positively to the communities they served. This was during a time when political propaganda and commercial advertising became professionalized and used sophisticated and technical methods, in part due to the technological advances in media utilizing television. This was also at a time in the United States, during the Civil Rights Era, when the police were viewed by a significant portion of the public as corrupt and brutal. Confidence in the local law enforcement agency is integral to the functioning of the agency. Communities that do not have confidence in the police are less likely to provide information to law enforcement, without which police are less likely to be able to address the conditions in the community they serve. The public will be less likely to report criminal activity to an agency perceived as illegitimate, whether due to corruption, brutality, or incompetence.

Training is an important component that will impact the success of community policing. The officers policing an area must have some basic understanding of the culture and norms of the residents and others that are a part of the community, such as individuals that own or are employed at local commercial or industrial establishments. Proper planning and preparation are integral to preventing poor performance. Rimmer (2008) posits that "effective and continual training of police and law enforcement officers in cultural awareness is critical to the delivery of community policing."[54] Most of the western world, especially among densely populated metropolitan areas, has a diverse mixture of culture, ethnicity, and religion; therefore police need to be appropriately trained and representative of the communities they serve. In addition to the level of proper training and representativeness of the police, the other aspect of community policing that must be addressed is the extent of the involvement of the community.

Existing literature does not provide an examination of the perspectives of the police and the communities they serve the threat of terrorism and the potential impact of communication between the police and the community. The recent findings by Smith et al. (2008, 2006) provide evidence that much of the planning that precedes a terrorist attack occurs locally. Therefore, members of a community as well as local police have the potential to significantly impact terrorism through intelligence gathering and identification of potential actors and the preparatory acts that are likely to occur prior to an attack.

The communities in which the research was conducted varied in terms of the racial, socioeconomic, and geographic composition. The research was conducted at five locations over three states in the Northeast region of the United States, including communities in New York, New Jersey, and Connecticut. None of the communities were more than about an hour and a half (with normal traffic) drive from New York City. In the participating communities examined, the number of full-time law enforcement agents varied from approximately 50 officers for the smallest department to over 500 for the largest department, with the three other departments ranging from the 80s through the low 100s. As per the confidentiality agreement between the researcher and the participating law enforcement agencies, the names of the communities and their law enforcement agencies are withheld.

There were a total of 52 participants in this study, with 22 community participants and 30 local law enforcement participants. The community member focus groups ranged in participants from a low of four to a high of eight. The local law enforcement focus groups ranged in participants from a low of four to a high of seven. The length of the focus groups ranged from a low of approximately 50 min to a high of approximately 1 h and 45 min. Among the nine focus groups conducted, the composition of each group varied from focus groups that were racially

---

[54]Rimmer (2008, p. 39).

homogenous (one focus group consisted of all White male participants from 39 to 59 years old with an average age of about 47, while another consisted of all Black participants – with only one woman) to heterogenous (a few focus groups had participants of varied racial self-identification, sex, and socioeconomic status). For a relatively small population, the participants represented a fair range of diversity.

This research was exploratory and therefore not intended to provide generalizable results, rather the research was intended to provide a foundation for future research by providing data that support the use of community policing as a model for proactive counterterrorism across the United States. The study was limited by many factors, including the time and resources available to the researcher during this project. The relatively low number of participants ($N = 52$) limits the statistical analyses that can be conducted on the data collected.

For one of the five locations, the researcher was unable to obtain participation from a corresponding community group. Over the course of 2 months, the researcher attempted to schedule a community focus group, but was unsuccessful, despite contacting public officials and individuals associated with community groups. Due to time limitations, the researcher decided to proceed with analyses with four community groups, as there was not vast variation among the four other community focus groups conducted. This missing community focus group may negatively impact the validity of the findings.

During one of the law enforcement focus groups, the recording device malfunctioned, recording approximately 15 min of the hour and a half focus group. This prevented the researcher from being able to compare the transcript created by a research assistant at the time of the focus group with the audio recording of the focus group. The researcher made some minor changes to the transcript for which the audio was not available, but based on the accuracy of the transcript provided by the research assistant, when compared with the 15 min recorded, the researcher is confident that the substance of the final abridged transcript is a fair and accurate representation of the focus group.

The findings from this study are not generalizable to the target population, urban and suburban communities in the United States, as there are significant differences among communities and the local law enforcement agencies that serve them, due to issues such as location (geography and topography), economy, and population (diversity and density) of the community. There are numerous variables that will impact the interaction between the local law enforcement agencies and communities which may either promote or hinder the partnership between the police and the community. Included in these variables is the diversity of the agency, the socioeconomic status of the community, the resources available to the community, geographic considerations, such as the number of police officers covering a geographic area, and pre-existing or historical issues between the police and the community.

As with any survey instrument, some of the participants may have misunderstood, misinterpreted, or misread the directions. Some of the language or phrasing of statements provided in the questionairres and surveys may have been confusing to the participants. Throughout the nine focus groups conducted, there were a minimum of two occurrences in which there appeared to have been, based on the dialog with the specific individual in the focus group, an incident in which the participant filled out the survey using the opposite response from the Likert-type scale instructions that were printed on the top of each survey. Despite the fact that the researcher emphasized the order of the possible responses prior to providing the participants with the survey instruments at the end of the focus group, some of the participants may have unintentionally provided answers that were contrary to their perspectives.

The concept of distance is not consistent among all regions in the United States. While the distances discussed in the Smith et al. (2006) study may have significance, the application of the concept of locality to those distances may differ based on geographic features and population density. In a rural section of the United States, the distance of 50 miles may be perceived as a small distance, while the same distance in an urban center may be perceived as a very large distance. The operationalization of distance may need to vary across the types of areas examined in order to provide results that are more applicable to the target population.

This research, which utilized both quantitative and qualitative measures, represents an innovative study, which has not been attempted before. This study, through the utilization of focus groups, has the potential to uncover a wealth of information not yet considered by terrorism researchers. The variables among the communities and the local law enforcement agencies, which were in three different states, also enhance the generalizability of the findings. Replication of this study would be relatively simple, both with communities and law enforcement agencies around the country. Furthermore, study provides an innovative tool in the community-oriented policing repertoire and assessment tool about the state of proactive policing at the local level.

The policy implications of this study are significant in their application to counterterrorism and law enforcement in general. This research provides insight that may assist police trainers, educators, and academics in efforts to design training that will adapt current training related to community-oriented policing to address the phenomenon of terrorism. In addition, this research may enhance the development of training modules or and policy/procedures regarding in-service or academy training in the area of community mobilization and intelligence gathering. Properly trained police will be able to facilitate community involvement, providing, as per Routine Activities, an extension of the capable guardian and diminishing the suitability of local targets.

The relationship between local police and the community can have a significant impact on the ability of police to gather intelligence and identify individuals involved in the planning of or preparatory acts that precede an act of terrorism. The Smith et al. (2006) study provides evidence that approximately half of these individuals both reside and conduct planning and preparation for an act of terrorism in relatively close proximity to the target location. With community cooperation, as per the Cohen and Felson (1979) Routine Activities theory, the community becomes an extension of the capable guardians, which can result in a decrease in acts of terrorism. Community policing provides a foundation for a comprehensive proactive response to the threat of terrorism. In addition, greater communication, trust, and partnership between the community and local law enforcement agency will likely serve to impact all criminal activity, including, but not limited to, acts of terrorism.

This research has found evidence of overwhelming support, both by the communities and local law enforcement agencies examined, for the implementation of community policing in an effort to provide a proactive approach to counterterrorism. Among the 10 hypotheses, the research found support for a majority. Among the first eight hypotheses, the greatest support was for the hypothesis most closely linked to the application of community policing in proactive counterterrorism; Research Hypothesis #8, which stated that "an effective method to gather intelligence about local terrorist activity is through communication with members of the community." This is the basis for the application of RAT as a theoretical model, providing an extension of the capable guardianship necessary to deter or detect crime and, in this case, terrorism.

Due to the size of the sample, the demographic variables collected from the questionnaires were not able to provide any significant tendencies, although these variables, which include age, racial self-identification, socioeconomic status, and education, provide for interesting future research possibilities. During the research, there was some anecdotal evidence of differences based on these demographic factors, especially among race and socioeconomic status, which was not altogether unexpected. Future research further examining the impact of these demographic variables on the perspectives of both community and law enforcement may provide guidance in enacting policies designed to both foster community policing and address the phenomenon of terrorism.

The support for community policing as a tool for local law enforcement to counter terrorism provides a foundation for future research, which may be able to find more generalizable results, which could have significant policy implications. In part due to the shift in the leadership of the United States, there is great potential to address the phenomenon of terrorism so as to reduce the future prevalence of acts of terrorism. With the increasing lethality of terrorist attacks in recent years, against targets both in the United States and on foreign lands, there is reason to believe that if this issue is not addressed, the next major attack could be comparable to, or more devastating than, the attacks of 9/11.

References

Barghothi, J. (1996). International terrorism in historical perspective. In C. B. Fields & R. H. Moore Jr. (Eds.) *Comparative criminal justice: traditional and non-traditional systems of law and control* (pp. 83–96). Prospect Heights, IL: Wavelength Press, Inc.

Bittner, E. (1990). *Aspects of police work*. Boston, MA: Northeaster University Press.

Bureau of Justice Assistance (2002). *State and local anti-terrorism training program*. Washington, DC: US Department of Justice.

Bureau of Justice Assistance (2005a). *Intelligence-led policing: The new intelligence architecture*. Washington, DC: US Department of Justice.

Bureau of Justice Assistance (2005b). *National criminal intelligence sharing plan*. Washington, DC: US Department of Justice, Bureau of Justice Assistance.

Chapman, R., Baker, S., Bezdikan, V., Cammarata, P., Cohen, D., Leach, N., Schapiro, A., Scheider, M., & Varana, R. (2002). *Local law enforceent response to terrorism: Lessons in prevention and preparedness.* Community Oriented Policing Services, US Department of Justice. Police Executive Research Forum: Washington, DC. Retrieved April 1, 2008 from http://www.cops.usdoj.gov/.

Cohen, L.E., & Felson, M. (1979). Social Change and Crime Rate Trends: A Routine Activities Approach. *American Sociological Review, 44*, 588–608.

Crenshaw, M. (1995). Thoughts on relating terrorism to historical contexts. In M. Crenshaw (Ed.) *Terrorism in context* (pp. 3–24). University Park, PA: The Pennsylvania State University Press.

Crenshaw, M. (2005). Political explanations. In *Addressing the causes of terrorism: The club de Madrid series on democracy and terrorism (Volume 1)* (pp. 13–18). Retreived December 3, 2008, from http://media.clubmadrid.org/docs/CdM-Series-on-Terrorism-Vol-1.pdf

DeSa, T.M., & McCarthy, K.E. (2009). The solo crusader: Theodore Kaczynski and Timothy McVeigh. In M.R. Haberfeld & A. von Hassel (2009). *A new understanding of terrorism: Case studies, trajectories, and lessons learned* (pp. 37–58). New York, NY: Springer.

DHS (2009, April 7). *Rightwing extremism: Current economic and political climate fueling resurgence in radicalization in radicalization and recruitment.* DHS Office of Intelligence and Analysis. Retrieved May 1, 2009, from http://www.fas.org/irp/eprint/rightwing.pdf

Docobo, J. M. (2005). Community policing as the primary prevention strategy for homeland security at the local law enforcement level. *Homeland Security Affairs, 1*(1), *Article 4.* Retrieved June 2nd, 2008 from http://www.hsaj.org/pages/volume1/issue1/pdfs/1.1.4.pdf

Donnermeyer, J. F. (2002). Local preparedness for terrorism: A view from law enforcement. *Police Practice and Research, 3*(4), 347–360.

FBI (1999). Terrorism in the United States. *Counterterrorism threat assessment and warning unit, counterterrorism division.* Retrieved December 5th, 2007 from http://www.fbi.gov/publications/terror/terror99.pdf

Goldstein, H. (1990). *Problem-oriented policing.* New York: McGraw-Hill.

Haberfeld, M. R. (2002). *Critical issues in police training.* Upper Saddle River, NJ: Prentice Hall.

Haberfeld, M. R., & Cerrah, I. (2008). *Comparative policing.* Los Angeles, CA: Sage Publications.

Haberfeld, M., King, J., & Lieberman, C. (n.d.). *Terrorism within a comparative international context: The counter-terrorism response and preparedness.* NIJ Grant #2004-DB-BX-1010.

Henry, V. E. (2002). The need for a coordinated and strategic local police approach to terrorism: A practitioner's perspective. *Police Practice and Research, 3*(4), 319–336.

Hewitt, C. (2003). *Understanding terrorism in America: From the Klan to Al Qaeda.* New York, NY: Routledge.

Hoffman, B. (1998). *Inside terrorism.* New York, NY: Columbia University Press.

Innes, M. (2006, May). Policing uncertainty: Countering terror through community intelligence and democratic policing. *The ANNALS of the American Academy of Political and Social Science, 605*(1), 222–241.

International Criminal Court (1998). *Rome statute of the international criminal court.* The Hague, Netherlands: Public Information and Documentation Section of the ICC. Retrieved June 2nd, 2008 from http://untreaty.un.org/cod/icc/statute/english/rome_statute(e).pdf

Klockars, C.B. (1985). *The idea of police.* Beverly Hills, CA: Sage.

LaFree, G., Dugan, L., Fogg, H. V., & Scott, J. (2006). *Building a global terrorism database.* US Department of Justice.

Lieberman, C. A. (2009). Community policing & counter terrorism: Community policing philosophy as a tool for local law enforcement to counter terrorist activities.

Lum, C., Haberfeld, M., Fachner, G., & Lieberman, C. (2009). Police strategies to counter terrorism: What we know and what we need to know. In D. Weisburd, T. Feucht, I. Hakimi, L. Mock, & S. Perry (Eds.), *To protect and to serve: Police and policing in an age of terrorism.* New York, NY: Springer.

Lum, C., Kennedy, L. W., & Sherley, A. J. (2006). The effectiveness of counter-terrorism strategies: A Campbell systematic review. Retrieved June 2nd, 2008 from http://db.c2admin.org/doc-pdf/Lum_Terrorism_Review.pdf

Lyons, W. (2002). Partnerships, information and public safety: Community policing in a time of terror. Policing: *An International Journal of Police Strategies and Management, 25*(3), 530–542.

McGarrell, E. F., Freilich, J. D., & Chermak, S. (2007). Intelligence-led policing as a framework for responding to terrorism. *Journal of Contemporary Criminal Justice, 23*(2), 142–158.

Murray, J. (2005). Policing terrorism: A threat to community policing or just a shift in priorities? *Police Practice and Research, 6*(4), 347–361.

National Commission on Terrorist Attacks Upon the United States (2002). *The 9/11 commission report.* New York, NY: W. W. Norton & Company, Inc.

National Intelligence Estimate (2007, July). *The terrorist threat to US homeland.* National Intelligence Estimate. Retrieved June 9th, 2008 from http://www.dni.gov/press_releases/20070717_release.pdf

Pelfrey, W. V. (2005). The cycle of preparedness: Establishing a framework to prepare for terrorist threats. *Journal of Homeland Security and Emergency Management, 2*(1).

Pillar, P. R. (2001). *Terrorism and U.S. foreign policy.* Washington, DC: Brookings Institution Press.

Reith, C. (1948). *A short history of the British police.* London, UK: Oxford University Press.

Rimmer, C. (2008). Communities Defeat Terrorism: Building trust between police and local communities. *Fulbright Commission.*

Scheider, M. C., & Chapman, R. (2003, April). Community policing and terrorism. *Homeland Security Institute.* Retrieved May 10th, 2008 from http://www.homelandsecurity.org/journal/articles/Scheider-Chapman.html

Schmid, A. P. (2004). Frameworks for conceptualizing terrorism. *Terrorism and Political Violence, 16*(2), 197–221.

Schmid, A. P., & Jongman, A. J. (2005). *Political terrorism: A new guide to actors, authors, concepts, data bases, theories, & literature.* New Brunswick, NJ: Transaction Publishers.

Shane, J. (2009). September 11, 2001 Attacks against the United States and the law enforcement response. In M. R. Haberfeld & A. von Hassel (2009). *A new understanding of terrorism: Case studies, trajectories, and lessons learned* (pp. 99–142). New York, NY: Springer.

Silke, A. (1996). Terrorism and the blind men's elephant. *Terrorism and Political Violence, 8*(3), 12–28.

Silke, A. (2001). The devil you know: Continuing problems with research on terrorism. *Terrorism and Political Violence, 13*(4), 1–14.

Silke, A. (2004). *Research on terrorism: Trends, achievements and failures.* London: Frank Cass.

Skogan, W. G. (2004). *Community policing: Can it work?* Belmont, CA: Thompson Wordsworth.

Sloan, S. (2002). Meeting the terrorist threat: The localization of counter terrorism intelligence. *Police Practice and Research, 3*(4), 337–345.

Smith, B. (2008). A look at terrorist behavior: How they prepare, where they strike. *National Institute of Justice, 260,* 2–5. Retrieved February 2nd, 2009 from http://www.ncjrs.gov/pdffiles1/nij/222899.pdf

Smith, B. L., Cothren, J, Roberts, P., & Damphousse, K. R. (2008). Geospatial Analysis of terrorist activities: The identification of spatial and temporal patterns of preparatory behavior of international and environmental terrorists. *US Department of Justice.* NIJ Grant 2005-IJ-CX-0200. Retrieved July 15th, 2008 from http://www.ncjrs.gov/pdffiles1/nij/grants/222909.pdf

Smith, B. L., Damphousse, K. R., & Roberts, P. (2006). Pre-incident indicators of terrorist incidents: The identification of geographic and temporal patterns of preparatory conduct. *US Department of Justice.* NIJ Award Number 2003-DT-CX-0003. Retrieved December 10th, 2007 from http://www.ncjrs.gov/pdffiles1/nij/grants/214217.pdf

US Senate (2007). *Dirty bomb vulnerabilities.* Washington, DC: Permanent Subcommittee on Investigations Staff Report. Retrieved September 16th, 2008 from http://hsgac.senate.gov/public/_files/REPORTDIRTYBOMBVULNERABILIITESFinal1007.pdf

Chapter 11
Best Practices – Lessons We Learned

11.1 Intelligence File

One of the most important "lessons to be learned" that we were exposed to during our research was the need to invest more time and resources in proper intelligence gathering and, within the context of this activity, the most important part is the creation of the Intelligence File. This chapter is based on the information we received from the police agencies we visited and conducted our research at and, in addition, on personal experience of one of the authors who was involved during her law enforcement career in creating and maintaining Intel files.

There are a number of general themes that need to be discussed prior to the recommendations about the creation and maintenance of the Intelligence files, and they have much to do with the gathering and processing of the information. It can be safely assumed that the western governments' ability to collect intelligence had long exceeded their capacity to analyze it. The massive amounts of information collected by various law enforcement agencies cannot be realistically processed in any effective and expeditious manner. Information collected from human sources, wiretaps, electronic surveillance, satellites, etc., surpasses the ability of any law enforcement agency to perform any type of up-to-date analysis that could assist operational forces of law enforcement counterterrorist response.

In addition, in a number of countries that struggle with a foreign threat, the need for skillful linguists exceeds their availability. For example, in United States, in July 2000, the National Commission on Terrorism (the Bremer Commission) recognized that a shortage of trained linguists undercuts US security and stated that "All U.S. government agencies face a drastic shortage of linguists to translate raw data into useful information. This shortage has a direct impact on counter-terrorism effort."

In addition, there are also the pitfalls of bogus intelligence that require additional skills on the part of law enforcement officers to deal with, analyze, and not overreact to. There are no silver bullets or one piece of information that, when analyzed properly, will provide enough information for the authorities to prevent the next terrorist attack. Multiple, seemingly unrelated pieces of intelligence must be pieced together for the scenarios to be revealed. It is the job of investigators and analysts to put these disparate parts of the picture together. The biggest and the most important asset that

M.R. Haberfeld et al., *Terrorism Within Comparative International Context*,
DOI 10.1007/978-0-387-88861-3_11, © Springer Science+Business Media, LLC 2009

these investigators and analysts must create and cultivate is the Intelligence File. However, as with any other important asset there are major considerations that need to be evaluated with regard to the form and format of this file. The first consideration is related to the decision of maintaining the file in a paper or electronic format. Therefore, this chapter will start with the following concerns regarding the positive and negative arguments for both paper and electronic intelligence files:

Paper or Computer: Pros and Cons

• Security considerations
• Access – portability
• Sharing capabilities – interoperability
• Technical problems
• Archiving
• Tampering

11.1.1 Security Considerations

There are always major security considerations when one is trying to collect and protect sensitive information – these can be summarized in the following concerns:

Security

• Open access
• Need to know basis
• Misplacement
• Access verification
• Disaster vulnerability
• Replication options

Access and portability of the files are the second concern that needs to be addressed and encompasses the following issues:

Access – Portability
- Volume – size
- Links
- Applications
- Stand alone

No information is good enough without the ability to share it with the relevant investigators, units, and other agencies. However, here we still come across obstacles that need to be addressed and fall under the following categories:

Sharing Capabilities – Interoperability
- Matching systems
- Security considerations
- Man-made disasters
- Natural disasters

Technical problems are the reality of life that every computer user faces more frequently than desired. These problems center on the following issues:

Technical Problems
- Power loss
- Interoperability in place but not utilized
- Interoperability in place locally but no internationally (Interpol, Europol)
- Technical problems overseas due to man-made or natural disasters

---

One of the biggest concerns in creating and maintaining viable files for long-term periods is the problem of archiving. It is sometimes beyond resolution and a lot of useful information gets shredded because of lack of space to maintain the paper files; therefore the electronic versions become a tempting alternative. However, despite the appeal, an agency needs to consider the following matters prior to making any decision with regard to getting rid of the paper version in favor of the electronic one:

Archiving
- Space
- Access
- Security
- Liability
- Links

The last issue of concern is tampering. No matter how good the security measure put in place by the agency to protect the content of the Intelligence File, any file, be it paper or electronic, is vulnerable. Based on the type of information stored and the working environment of a given agency, consideration needs to be given to the following matters:

Tampering
- Intentional
  - Hackers
  - Crackers
  - Conventional thieves
- Unintentional
  - Insider
  - Outsider

Once the decision how to maintain and protect the file is reached the task of creating, one needs to be addressed. The following recommendations are based on the personal experience of one of the authors as well as on the field notes taken in law enforcement agencies in the countries visited by the researchers.

Creating an Intel File
Information included or to be gathered:
- Name(s)
  - including all aliases (AKA)
- Date of birth (DOB)
  - including all fake DOB's
- Nationality
  - including all citizenships real & forged nationalities
- Physical descriptions
  - including past, present, disguised, and projections

Affiliations: Past, Current & Projected

- Professional Associations
- Personal Associations
  - Ideological
  - Religious
- Peripheral Associations
- Family members
  - Formal (blood & marriage)
  - Informal

Other Sources of Intelligence

- Informants
- Surveillance
- Wire-tapes
- Reports
- Finances
- Photographs
- Fingerprints
- Criminal record
- DNA samples
- Hand-writing samples
- Contact addresses
- Educational background
- Skills & Expertise
- Hobbies

Sources of Intelligence

- Travel patterns
  - past, present, and projected
- Media related information
  - Websites
  - Books, newspapers & magazines
  - TV appearances
- Any and all other information available regarding the suspect

Create Links (A)

- Duplicate all information available from other files regarding the suspect

- Create duplicates of all the information that makes references to other suspects and create new files if necessary

- Create a linkage system that will refer the investigator to the other/relevant files

Create a Back-Up System

- Electronic system
- Paper system
- For both the electronic and the paper systems, store an additional copy of intelligence files in another location

Create a Security Access System

- Security access on need to know basis
- Different levels of security clearance
  - for both local and international access
- Design an accountability system
  - identification/signature system
- Design a secure handling of the information system

Create Links (B)

- Identify other sources of information within your organization that should be consulted, periodically, for updating

  - i.e. Organized Crime Bureau, Narcotics

- Identify a list of organizations, web sites, and other entities that should be contacted periodically for updating and other relevant assistance

  - i.e. specific offices within DHS, Interpol, Europol

Develop Personal Relationships

- With relevant personnel in your organization
- With the relevant personnel in other organizations at a local, state, federal, and international level
- With CIs – past, current, potential

It is beyond the scope of this chapter to address all the potential problems that can and will occur during the creation and maintenance of the Intelligence File; however, the information provided herein can serve as a template for consideration for those who already do, or might in the future, engage in this so viable activity that was one of the most important lessons we learned during our research project.

11.2 Investigative Techniques and Intelligence Gathering

After the decision is made how to create and maintain the Intelligence File, one of the very important sources of information will come from investigative process of the suspected terrorists and intelligence gathering from alternative sources. The following recommendations are based on personal experience of the authors (Haberfeld et al. 2007a, 2007b) and the Dyson (2005) text *Terrorism: Investigator's Handbook:*

Intelligence Gathering through Interviewing: Typology

- Suspects
  - Command/Leadership
  - Active Cadre
- Supporters
  - Active
  - Passive
- Witnesses

Interviewing Suspects

- Evaluate the suspect
  - Criminal
  - Crazy
  - Crusader
- Pick a techniques based on the evaluation
- Reassess evaluation after initial interview
  - If correct – continue
  - If incorrect – change interview technique and consider changing the investigator/interviewer

Recommended Techniques for Interviewing Criminal-Type Suspect

- Routine or conventional
  - Who, what, when, where, why & how
- Confrontational
  - Challenge or threaten
- Good cop – Bad cop
  - Develop trust
- Obnoxious
  - offensive manners & presence

Recommended Techniques for Interviewing Crusader-Type Suspect

- Open ended questions
  - Get the suspect talking
- The perfect dummy
  - Reiterate the statements of the suspect
- Best friends
  - "We are both human"

Recommended Techniques for Interviewing Crusader-Type Suspect

- "Just the facts"
  - Get into a pattern of quick & concise responses
- Best friends
  - "I understand your cause…"
  - "Tell me more…"

Interviewing Potential Informants

- Assess/evaluate the degree of affiliation
  - Active or passive supporter; Witness
- Choose technique based on evaluation
- Reassess after initial interview
  - If correct – continue
  - If incorrect – change interview technique and consider changing the interviewer

Interviewing Informants

- Inside target
  - Occupies a position within the group
- Periphery target
  - Associates with the group
- Outside target
  - Little or no relationship to the group
    - Lukewarm – some natural relationship
    - Cold start – no relationship

Informant Motivations

- Financial
- Working off "a beef"
- Blackmail
- Would-be spy
- Patriotism
- Do-gooder
- Soldier of fortune
- Fear
- Problem solver
- Town crier
- Need for excitement
- Need to feel important
- Need for attention
- Need for association with status
- Advisor
- Revenge
- Prior relationship with contact officer
- "Other people are doing it"

Vetting the Informant

- Signs of hesitance
- Comparing notes to external information
- Bringing another officer to debrief
- Asking other informants
- Checking records of other agencies
- Polygraph
- Signing the report

Reliability & Validity of Informant

Check the information provided
by the informant with other sources:

- Other agencies

- Internet – websites

- Research findings & theories

- Past history or Modus Operandi of the
  group or actor(s)

Alternative Intelligence Gathering

- Scanning the local environment
  - Including surveillance
- Scanning the communication patterns of
  the suspected groups through the media
  - Television, radio, the internet & periodicals
- Review the relevant literature
- Specifically follow up the trends in money
  laundering schemes

Alternative Intelligence Gathering

Follow up on issues around the world:

- Economic and social climate
- General trends in organized crime
- Political developments
- Patterns of terrorist activities

References

Dyson, W. E. (2005). *Terrorism: The investigator's handbook*. Cincinnati, OH: Anderson
    Publishing.
Haberfeld, M. R., von Hassell, A., & Lieberman, C. (2007a). *Recruiting and handling a confi-
    dential informant: Police service of Northern Ireland*. PowerPoint presentation for John Jay
    College of Criminal Justice (CRJ 819).
Haberfeld, M. R., von Hassell, A., & Lieberman, C. (2007b). *Investigative techniques*. PowerPoint
    presentation for John Jay College of Criminal Justice (CRJ 819).

Chapter 12
Best Practices – Lessons to be Learned

As mentioned in the introductory part of the book, the primary goal behind this research project was to create effective training modules to enable local law enforcement agencies, in the cross-comparative environment, to address terrorism-related incidents, and to not just react but prevent and de-escalate resentment from community or support from community toward homegrown terrorist organizations and individuals.

In the focus groups and interviews, the researchers attempted to operationalize homegrown terrorism as incidents and events that were, are, or will be perpetrated by various organizations, be it structured and well-known groups, or individuals associated with larger organization, or anybody who operates within the borders of a country, who resides there for a significant enough period of time to forge personal and professional relationships with the local populations.

The idea behind this operationalization was not to limit the concept of "homegrown" to people born in the country or naturalized citizens, but to include people who make a given country their home based on employment and social ties; even if they are peripheral to community, they would still identify themselves as stakeholder in a place where they have their primary residence, employment, place of operation, etc. In today's multicultural environment, "homegrown" cannot be defined by place of birth or even a citizenship in a given country. Even though terrorists and suspected terrorists may be foreign citizens, their prolonged presence in a given country (such as in the case of Theo van Gogh murder in Holland) would fall under the category of "homegrown" terrorism, as presented by the research team to the subjects of the interviews and focus groups.

The notion of "homegrown" terrorism is as problematic as the concept of Community-Oriented Policing (COP). It encompasses a multitude of factors and translates directly to the complexity of identification, minimization, and elimination by local law enforcement agencies, which, by default, are skewed toward orientation that is focused on legal, long-term residents, rather than transients or illegal aliens, about whom the local law enforcement has much less available intelligence to begin with and, furthermore, has much less possibility to interact with, under the COP model.

Historically and traditionally, local law enforcement agencies tend to stay away and avoid intense interactions with minority groups for reasons that are partially political, operational, and xenophobic. The scarce interactions that existed in the past were more of a token like, symbolic in nature, and bow toward the minorities than a real, fully developed interactions. This, unfortunately, appears to be the case nowadays as well, regardless of the country visited by the team.

Looking at the local community of legal residents vis-à-vis local law enforcement, there is no doubt that the local legal residents are situated better to identify the potential threat that is either in its inception, or evolving, or ready to explode; the community is in a much better position than local law enforcement. However, the biggest impediment to making use of this position is the lack of understanding on the part of the community of what is in fact evolving in front of their eyes, in terms of actually identifying the threat, in each various stages.

The local law enforcement, on the other hand, is much better positioned to identify the threat than any more sophisticated group within the community, and this is precisely at this junction that the authors propose to identify some sort of bridging steps or missing links that can be filled based on the mutual cooperation between the community and local law enforcement. The local law enforcement can provide the community with the tools to be much more aware of their surroundings, which will enable the community to feed back information to the police.

How does this concept differ from traditional the COP approach, which emphasizes such cooperation? It differs in drastic manner, while traditional COP approach focuses on traditional crimes, majority of which are recognizable and identifiable on the part of the community; street crimes of various natures do not require much clarification by local law enforcement to the community they police. Typical predatory crimes and vice crimes, like rape, robbery, assault, murder, and burglary are easily recognizable by most of the members of the community that is victimized by their occurrence. While community members may be able to identify traditional crime, recognizing terrorist preparatory acts requires more training, education, and information from police with regard to the phenomenon of terrorism, and the specific intelligence law enforcement requires in order to be proactive in counterterrorism.

Terrorist-related preparatory and ancillary acts are much more subtle than the crimes we are accustomed to on a daily basis. There is, of course, the never-ending debate around the concept of terrorist versus freedom fighter, which exacerbates the problem of cooperation. In addition, the modus operandi of homegrown terrorists is much more subtle and invisible than the modus operandi of traditional criminals, the level of sophistication might not necessarily be much higher than in other traditional crimes, but the spherical behavior is different.[1] What the researchers are looking at, in terms of indoctrination in the community, are patterns of behavior that are not well defined by local law enforcement as well, but by introducing some of the basic concepts from the existing literature to the law enforcement community (like Hacker's typologies of terrorists), the police can be placed in a much better position in identifying the profiles of the local homegrown terrorists, and convey these profiles for the consumption of the public or the local community. If the local police receive the proper counter terrorist training (based on the outline of the modules

---

[1] Haberfeld (2009); Haberfeld & von Hassel (2009).

identified by the researchers at the end of this chapter), they will be receiving the adequate knowledge to pass it down to the local community.

One cannot, of course, ignore the fact that by advocating for such a training that would be passed from the local police force to the public during various community meetings, there is a danger that might lead to mobilization of one neighbor against another; however, looking at the history of policing, and going back to England, prior to the Medieval times, the concept of avocational policing was the first concept of effective law enforcement for local communities that involved, among other things, community members identifying illegal or criminal behaviors of those who lived among them. Only when policing became increasingly political, which included primarily the collection of taxes for "the Crown," the move from avocational to vocational policing became the flavor of quite a few centuries continuing to the modern times.

Hence, going back to how policing originally developed or evolved, when small communities policed their own, through avocational mode and the Tything, what these researchers advocate claims to be a valid modality of policing of what appears to be a local homegrown terrorism. The local community is therefore charged, in a manner of speaking, with identifying the threat, but also with proactive behavior, that can potentially reverse the original threat. An example of such target group would be found in one of the focus groups in Spain. A local Muslim student, born and raised in Madrid and the third-generation to live in Spain, complained, in an adamant manner, about feelings of alienation within the community his family, including parents and grandparents, has resided in for more than a century.

In a way, this community-oriented avocational type of policing of the homegrown threat is also a call to remove some of the burden placed on the shoulders of law enforcement over the past 15 centuries, to not just protect the community, but also to try to minimize and eliminate the criminality within, which essentially is truly much more of a problem that needs to be tackled by the community itself and the larger government, and not primarily the local law enforcement. According to Pickering, McCullough, and Wright-Neville (2008), the Belonging Model of counterterrorism policing, as well as the Social Cohesion Model of counterterrorism policing, enhances the positive cultural work of police and the quality of interaction between the police and the diverse communities' forums. Such interactions contribute further to the development of more democratic forms of policing.

Part of the perceptions and attitudes that shape or contribute to our biases are directly related to stated and written opinions expressed by our rulers, politicians, and religious leaders. Addressing individual perceptions and attitudes toward the "others" at a community level can be shaped and modified based on presentation of new information. The key to the effectiveness of this "re-education" lies in – or can be found in – the medium through which this new information is introduced. This is why the team paid a special attention to the interviews with the media people, be it journalists, television directors, or movie producers, as they have a tremendous impact on the way attitudes toward terrorism and terrorists are shaped. The role of the local law enforcement, albeit not an enviable one, would therefore be to try to counter the stereotypes introduced and reintroduced by the various media outlets, religious leaders, and some agenda-driven politicians. Since policing is, by its very nature, a very political institution, this charge might be proven to be beyond difficult; however, with proper and nonthreatening training it can be achieved.

As the British historian Charles Reith (1975) alluded to, the greatest empires in the history of mankind collapsed due to the lack of effective local law enforcement that would separate the government or ruler from the community. The law enforcement's role is to maintain the status quo, no matter what culture or period in the history – effective police play a critical role in maintaining the status quo that allows cultures to flourish, rather than disappear or disintegrate; police are or, one might argue, could be the force that prevent society from entering a state of Anomie.

This research was an exploratory venture, attempting to identify the necessary components for the creation of effective law enforcement training that would be beneficial for the local police and at the same time fully accepted and supported by the community they serve. The recommendation for the creation of the useful and relevant training modules is based on the recognition that the current influence factors within the society that filer down the concepts about terrorism and terrorist are derived, beyond the governmental officials, from the religious leaders and the media to the community and should truly start with the community, and transferred through the local police forces to the government decision makers for the proper allocation of resources for the fight against the "enemy within."

12.1 Outline of a C-T Training Module

The following training modules were created and modified over the past 6 years by the following professors for the graduate course titled: "Counter-terrorism policies for Law Enforcement," which was originally created by Dr. Haberfeld and Dr. Louden for the NYPD Police Certificate Program at John Jay College of Criminal Justice. The modules represent a customized version created for the NYPD students; however, it is strongly recommended, pending situational and localized revisions, to all law enforcement agencies tackling the problem of terrorism and counter-terrorist response.

Dr. Maria (Maki) Haberfeld
Dr. Robert Louden
Prof. Agostino von Hassell
Dr. Lior Gideon
Dr. Charles Lieberman
Course Title: Counterterrorism Polices for Law Enforcement

Week 1: Introduction
         Defining Terrorism
         Relevance of Counterterrorism to NYPD
Week 2: The History and Evolution of Terrorism
         Simonsen & Spindlove – Chapters 1, 2, and 3

Haberfeld & Cerrah – Chapter 1
Brief History of Terrorism
State & Religious Sponsored Terrorism
The Fear of Fear Itself

Week 3: Terrorism around the World – An Overview of the Threat [Part I]
Simonsen & Spindlove – Chapters 4, 5, 9, and 10
Haberfeld & Cerrrah – Chapters 11 and 6
British Isles and Western Europe
Central and Eastern Europe
Southern and Southeast Asia
The Pacific Rim

Week 4: Terrorism around the World - An Overview of the Threat [Part II]
Simonsen & Spindlove – Chapters 11 and 12
Haberfeld & Cerrrah – Chapters 3 and 4
Latin America
North America
The Caribbean

Week 5: Terrorism around the World – An Overview of the Threat [Part III]
Simonsen & Spindlove – Chapters 6, 7, and 8
Lewis – Chapters 8 and 9
Haberfeld & Cerrrah – Chapters 5 and 9
North Africa
Central Africa
Southern Africa
The Persian Gulf
The Middle East

Week 6: The Counter Terrorism Response – Overview of Techniques [Part I]
Simonsen & Spindlove – Chapter 13 pp. 299–309
Haberfeld & Cerrrah – Chapter 8
The Roles of Counterterrorism
Hijackings
Intelligence Gathering
Counterterrorism Units
Antinarcotics: Using Existing Tools

Week 7: The Counterterrorism Response – Overview of Responses around the World [Part IIa]
Simonsen & Spindlove – Chapter 13 pp. 309–315
Haberfeld & Cerrrah – Chapter 10
Great Britain
France
Germany
Israel

Week 8: The Counterterrorism Response – Overview of Responses of US Agencies [Part IIb]
Haberfeld & Cerrrah – Chapters 12 and 13

Local
State
Federal
Joint Cooperation within the United States
International Cooperation
Week 9: Investigative Techniques and Legal Implications Part I
Haberfeld & Cerrrah – Chapter 14
Interviewing
Records Checks
Confidential Informants ("CI")
Undercover Operations
Assessing an Individual Understanding
The Use of "Offsite" Locations
Week 10: Handling a Terrorist Attack – Types of Attacks [Part Ia]
Handouts TBA
Bombs and Bomb Threats
Hijackings
Hostages
Physical Structures
Written Policies and Procedures
Week 11: Handling a Terrorist Attack – Bioterrorism [Part Ib]
Handouts TBA
Types of Substances
Proactive Response
Reactive Response
Written Policies and Procedures
Week 12: Handling a Terrorist Attack – Contingency Planning [Part II]
Handout TBA
Communication Process
Victims
Securing the Crime Scene
Written Policies and Procedures
Week 13: Handling a Terrorist Attack [Part III]
Handouts TBA
Concepts of Stress
Stress Managements Strategies
Postincident Debriefing
Managing Stress within the Internal and the Overlapping Communities
Week 14: Putting It All Together – Terrorism in the Twenty-first Century
Simonsen & Spindlove – Chapter 4
Haberfeld & Cerrrah – Chapter 14
A Larger Scale Phenomenon
Cyberterrorism
Identifying the Threats
Projections for the Future

Week 15: Final Examination and Course Evaluation
Although this training module was created for a college environment, the topics included can be easily customized for a training academy delivery in any law enforcement environment, and it is recommended that they would be adjusted for local relevance.

12.2 Required Texts

Haberfeld, M. R. (2009). Today's terrorism - introduction and analysis: The have nots versus the haves. In M. R. Haberfeld & A. von Hassel (Eds.) *A new understanding of terrorism: Case studies, trajectories, and lessons learned* (pp. 1–8). New York, NY: Springer.

Haberfeld, M. R., & von Hassel, A. (2009). Proper proactive training to terrorist presence and operations in friendly urban environments. In M. R. Haberfeld & A. von Hassel (Eds.) *A new understanding of terrorism: Case studies, trajectories, and lessons learned* (pp. 9–22). New York, NY: Springer.

Haberfeld, M. R., & Cerrah, I. (eds.). (2007). *Comparative policing: The struggle for democratization*. Thousand Oaks, CA: Sage Publishing.

Pickering, S., McCullough, J., & Wright-Neville, D. (2008). *Counter-terrorism policing: Community, cohesion & security*. New York, NY: Springer Science + Business Media, LLC.

Reith, C. (1948). *A short history of the British police*. London, UK: Oxford University Press.

Simonsen, C. E. & Spindlove, J. R. (2006). *Terrorism today: The past, the players, the future* (3rd ed.). Upper Saddle River, NJ: Prentice Hall.

Supplementary: Handouts depending on developments.

Appendix A
IRB-Approved Consent Form

John Jay College   Principal Investigators: Haberfeld, Grant & King

Consent Form

This study will help us to better understand the relationship between terrorism and community support. Please remember that you are *not* required to participate in this research study. It is voluntary and you may choose to quit participating if you begin to feel upset or uncomfortable.

The information provided by you will help the research team gain a better understanding of the problem but will not be disseminated in any way that will directly identify you as a respondent. Your answers will be always kept strictly anonymous. Your identity will be strictly confidential and kept as such by the research team.

Please read the attached information sheet before completing this form and consenting to participate in our study.

_____   I have read and understood the above information about the study.

_____   I have volunteered to participate in this project.

_____   I have been informed of the basic procedures of the study by the researchers, and by reading the information sheet (of which I have been given a copy for my records).

_____   I understand that by agreeing to participate in this study, I will be asked to complete some questionnaires and review my file.

_____   I understand that I may choose to quit my participation at any time with no penalty.

_____   I understand that any information that I give out for the purpose of this study will be kept confidential.

Thank you for agreeing to participate in this study.

Printed Name of Participant: _____

Signature of Participant: _____

Date: _____

Printed Name of Researcher: _____

Signature of researcher: _____

Date: _____

M.R. Haberfeld et al., *Terrorism Within Comparative International Context,*   167
DOI 10.1007/978-0-387-88861-3, © Springer Science+Business Media, LLC 2009

Appendix B
IRB Review Form

IRB Review Form

1. Objectives of the study

The principal objective of this study is to set up a template for Counter terrorist training by Police Departments in the United States. However, we believe that many of the lessons learned may well be adapted to international police forces and could be adapted as a baseline for their training curriculums.

2. Methodology

The NIJ project was funded to examine counterterrorism training and practices in law enforcement agencies internationally. Initially identified were the countries of Spain, Ireland, United Kingdom, Turkey, and Lebanon. As such, the research team will be visiting the respective countries to meet with law enforcement, security officials and various members of the community to assess the current state of affairs and training needs. At each identified locations, each of the agencies and community groups will be asked to meet with the research team for discussions of the questions at hand. A snowball method of identification will also be used, to the extent that on-site meetings identify other relevant individuals with whom the team should meet.

3. Explanation of the research plans for the upcoming year

Due the late release of funds by NIJ, January 2005, and the constraints of travel during the Academic year, three sites were initially scheduled. We have traveled to Ireland, Spain, and the United Kingdom. The initial plan was to be in the United Kingdom during July 2005. However, due to the Tube bombings of July 7 and 21, these plans were cancelled and have recently, October 15, been completed. Additionally, due to the arrest of several senior police officials, concerning the assignation of former Prime Minister Rafik Hariri, that we were in contact with for our visit to Lebanon and the political situation in Lebanon and Syria, we have asked NIJ to drop Lebanon from the proposal and are in negotiations with NIJ for substitution of this country.

During the coming year, we plan to revise some of these sites for follow-up questions and more in-depth analysis as well as the initial visit to NIJ-agreed country.

Index

Breinigsville, PA USA
29 December 2009

229626BV00005B/8/P